DASH Diet Cookbook for Beginners

**500 Healthy Low-Sodium Recipes
to Lose Weight and Lower Blood Pressure.
21-Day Meal Plan Included**

Elisabeth Garcia– 2021 Edition

© 2021- All Rights Reserved

© Copyright 2021 - All rights reserved.

The content contained within this book may not be reproduced, duplicated, or transmitted without direct written permission from the author or the publisher.

Under no circumstances will any blame or legal responsibility be held against the publisher, or author, for any damages, reparation, or monetary loss due to the information contained within this book, either directly or indirectly.

Legal Notice:

This book is copyright protected. It is only for personal use. You cannot amend, distribute, sell, use, quote, or paraphrase any part, or the content within this book, without the consent of the author or publisher.

Disclaimer Notice:

Please note the information contained within this document is for educational and entertainment purposes only. All effort has been executed to present accurate, up-to-date, reliable, complete information. No warranties of any kind are declared or implied. Readers acknowledge that the author is not engaged in the rendering of legal, financial, medical, or professional advice. The content within this book has been derived from various sources. Please consult a licensed professional before attempting any techniques outlined in this book.

By reading this document, the reader agrees that under no circumstances is the author responsible for any losses, direct or indirect, that are incurred as a result of the use of the information contained within this document, including, but not limited to, errors, omissions, or inaccuracies.

All the images/pictures contained within this book have been regularly provided by:

Sthutterstock.com

Canva.com

All the images/pictures contained within this book belong to the respective owners.

CONTENTS

PART ONE – DASH DIET

What Does DASH Mean? - 6
What Are the Benefits? - 7
What to Eat and What to Avoid - 8
Q & A - 11
Top 10 Tips for DASH Diet Success - 13

PART TWO – RECIPES

Breakfast - 15
Soups and Chowders - 26
Salads - 39
Plant-Based Mains - 52
Poultry - 63
Beef, Pork, and Lamb - 75
Fish and Seafood - 83
Side Dishes - 93
Dishes with Sauces - 103
Snacks - 108
Desserts - 118

PART THREE – 21 DAY MEAL PLAN

Caloric Intake on The DASH Diet - 127
Daily Servings Table - 128
21-Day Meal Plan - 129

INGREDIENT INDEX - 135
CONVERSION MEASURES - 138

RECIPE INDEX

BREAKFAST 14
   1. Apple and Spice Oatmeal 15
   2. Apple Oats 15
   3. Apple-Cinnamon Baked Oatmeal 15
   4. Apples and Cinnamon Oatmeal 15
   5. At-Home Cappuccino 15
   6. Banana Almond Yogurt 16
   7. Banana Cookies 16
   8. Banana Steel Oats 16
   9. Banana-Berry Smoothie 16
  10. Barley Porridge 16
  11. Basil and Tomato Baked Eggs 17
  12. Berries Deluxe Oatmeal 17
  13. Blueberry Breakfast Quinoa 17
  14. Blueberry Muffins 17
  15. Blueberry Pancakes 17
  16. Blueberry-Maple Oatmeal 18
  17. Chocolate Smoothie 18
  18. Coconut Crepes 18
  19. Crunchy Flax Almond Crackers 18
  20. Egg Burrito 18
  21. Egg Muffins 19
  22. Energy Oatmeal 19
  23. English Muffin with Berries 19
  24. Fruit and Yogurt Breakfast Salad 19
  25. Fruity Green Smoothie 19
  26. Fruity Yogurt Parfait 20
  27. Gingered Green Tea 20
  28. Granola 20
  29. Greek-Style Breakfast Scramble 20
  30. Healthy French Toast 20
  31. Healthy Low-Fat Granola 21
  32. Healthy Start Yogurt Bowls 21
  33. Hearty Pineapple Oatmeal 21
  34. Kale and Apple Smoothie 21
  35. Lean Country-Style Sausage 21
  36. Lemon-Zucchini Muffins 22
  37. Mango Lassi 22
  38. Mediterranean Scramble 22
  39. Open-Faced Breakfast Sandwich 22
  40. Papaya and Coconut Shake 23
  41. Peanut Butter Oats 23
  42. Peach and Berry Pancake 23
  43. Protein Bowl 23
  44. Scones with Nuts and Fruits 23
  45. Scrambled Pesto Eggs 23
  46. Spiced Pumpkin Pancakes 24
  47. Swiss Chard Omelet 24
  48. Tartine with Cream Cheese 24
  49. Toast with Almond Butter 24
  50. Veggie Omelet 24
  51. Veggie Scramble 25
  52. Warm Quinoa with Berries 25
  53. Whole Grain Pancakes 25

SOUPS AND CHOWDERS 26
  54. Beans Soup 26
  55. Beef Soup 26
  56. Beef Stew with Veggies 26
  57. Carrot Soup 26
  58. Chickpea and Tomato Soup 27
  59. Cod and Corn Chowder 27
  60. Creamy Asparagus Soup 27
  61. Cream of Wild Rice Hot Dish 28
  62. Curried Cream Tomato Soup 28
  63. Curried Lentil Soup 28
  64. Easy Kale and White Bean Soup 28
  65. Easy Vegetable Stock 29
  66. Fire-Roasted Corn Soup 29
  67. Gazpacho with Chickpeas 29
  68. Greek Lemon-Drop Soup 29
  69. Green Beans Soup 30
  70. Green Bean and Tomato Soup 30
  71. Green Detox Soup 30
  72. Grilled Tomatoes Soup 30
  73. Hearty Beef and Vegetable Soup 30
  74. Hearty Ginger Soup 31
  75. Home-Style Turkey Soup 31
  76. Ingenious Eggplant Soup 31
  77. Lentil and Sausage Soup 32
  78. Lentil Soup 32
  79. Low Sodium Vegetable Soup 32
  80. Minestrone Soup 32
  81. Mixed Greens Soup 33
  82. Mushroom Barley Soup 33
  83. Potato Leek Soup 33
  84. Potato-Fennel Soup 33
  85. Pumpkin Cream Soup 34
  86. Pumpkin Soup 34
  87. Quibebe Soup 34
  88. Roasted Squash Soup 34
  89. Sausage Minestrone with Kale 35
  90. Steamy Salmon Chowder 35
  91. Summer Berry Soup 35
  92. Sweet Black-Eyed Pea Soup 36
  93. Turkey Bean Soup 36
  94. Turkey Soup 36
  95. Vegetable Garbanzo Bean Stew 36
  96. Vegetarian Chilli 37
  97. White Chicken Chilli 37
  98. Wild Rice Mushroom Soup 37
  99. Zesty Tomato Soup 37
 100. Zucchini Noodles Soup 38

SALADS 39
 101. Ambrosia Toasted Almonds 39
 102. Apple Blue Cheese Salad 39
 103. Apple Lettuce Salad 39
 104. Apple Salad with Figs 39
 105. Apple-Fennel Slaw 39
 106. Arugula Peach Almond Salad 40
 107. Asian Vegetable Salad 40
 108. Baby Beet and Orange Salad 40
 109. Bean Salad with Vinaigrette 40
 110. Beet Walnut Salad 41
 111. Blue Cheese Spinach Salad 41
 112. Braised Celery Root 41
 113. Butternut Squash Apple Salad 41
 114. Chicken Salad with Pineapple 42
 115. Chopped Greek Salad 42
 116. Classic Chicken Salad 42
 117. Corn Salad 42
 118. Couscous Salad 43
 119. Cucumber Pineapple Salad 43
 120. Dilled Pasta Salad 43
 121. Dilled Shrimp Salad 44
 122. English Cucumber Salad 44
 123. Fattoush 44
 124. French Green Lentil Salad 44
 125. Grilled Chicken Salad 45

1

126. Lentil and Goat Cheese Salad 45
127. Lentil Salad with Mango 45
128. Mango Tango Salad 46
129. Mixed Bean Salad 46
130. Pasta Salad with Vegetables 46
131. Pickled Onion Salad 46
132. Potato Salad 47
133. Quick Bean and Tuna Salad 47
134. Rice and Beans Salad 47
135. Roasted Beet Salad 47
136. Salad Greens with Pears 48
137. Salad Greens with Squash 48
138. Salmon and Peaches Salad 48
139. Shrimp and Black Bean Salad 48
140. Spiced Melon Salad 49
141. Spinach Berry Salad 49
142. Steak and Berry Salad 49
143. Sweet Persimmon Salad 49
144. Tabbouleh Salad 49
145. Tarragon Chicken Salad 50
146. Thai Cobb Salad 50
147. Tossed Greens with Pasta 50
148. Watermelon Shrimp Salad 50
149. Yellow Pear Salad 51

PLANT-BASED MAINS 52
150. Aromatic Spaghetti 52
151. Baked Falafel 52
152. Baked Tempeh 52
153. Bean Hummus 52
154. Bow Ties and Beans 52
155. Briam 53
156. Broccoli Balls 53
157. Carrot Cakes 53
158. Cauliflower Steaks 53
159. Cauliflower Tots 53
160. Chana Masala 53
161. Chickpea Curry 54
162. Chile Rellenos 54
163. Chunky Tomatoes 54
164. Corn Patties 54
165. Dill Zucchini Patties 54
166. Eggplant Croquettes 55
167. Garbanzo Stir Fry 55
168. Garden Stuffed Squash 55
169. Garlic Shells 55
170. Glazed Eggplant Rings 55
171. Hasselback Eggplant 56
172. Honey Sweet Potato Bake 56
173. Korma 56
174. Lentil Curry 56
175. Lentil Quiche 56
176. Loaded Potato Skins 56
177. Mac Stuffed Sweet Potatoes 57
178. Marinated Tofu 57
179. Marinated Tofu Skewers 57
180. Minty Chickpea Tabbouleh 57
181. Mushroom Cakes 57
182. Mushroom Florentine 58
183. Mushroom Stroganoff 58
184. Paella 58
185. Pakoras 58
186. Portobello Florentine 58
187. Quinoa Bowl 59
188. Quinoa Burger 59
189. Seitan Patties 59
190. Spinach Casserole 59
191. Stuffed Portobello 59
192. Sweet Brussel Sprouts 60
193. Sweet Potato Balls 60

194. Taco Casserole 60
195. Tempeh Reuben 60
196. Tofu Parmigiana 60
197. Tofu Stir Fry 60
198. Tofu Stroganoff 61
199. Tofu Tikka Masala 61
200. Tofu Turkey 61
201. Turmeric Cauliflower Florets 61
202. Vegan Chili 61
203. Vegan Meatballs 62
204. Vegan Meatloaf 62
205. Vegan Shepherd Pie 62
206. Vegetarian Kebabs 62
207. Vegetarian Lasagna 62
208. Vegetarian Sloppy Joes 63
209. White Beans Stew 63
210. Zucchanoush 63
211. Zucchini Grinders 63
212. Zucchini Soufflé 63

POULTRY 64
213. Artichoke Spinach Chicken 64
214. Avocado and Chicken Mix 64
215. Baked Chicken and Apples 64
216. Baked Chicken and Wild Rice 64
217. Balsamic Roast Chicken 64
218. Balsamic Turkey Peach Mix 65
219. Barbecue Chicken Pizza 65
220. Buffalo Chicken Salad Wrap 65
221. Chicken and Asparagus Mix 65
222. Chicken and Asparagus Penne 66
223. Chicken and Celery Mix 66
224. Chicken and Chili Zucchini 66
225. Chicken and Dill Green Beans 66
226. Chicken and Mustard Sauce 67
227. Chicken and Olives Pan 67
228. Chicken and Veggies 67
229. Chicken Brats 67
230. Chicken Burritos 68
231. Chicken Cutlets with Fruit 68
232. Chicken Quesadillas 68
233. Chicken Salad with Pineapple 68
234. Chicken Sliders 69
235. Chicken with Mustard Greens 69
236. Chicken with Paprika Scallions 69
237. Chicken with Red Onion Mix 69
238. Chipotle Chicken 69
239. Cinnamon Roasted Chicken 70
240. Coconut Chicken and Spinach 70
241. Garlic Turkey and Mushrooms 70
242. Honey Crusted Chicken 70
243. Hot Turkey and Rice 71
244. Italian Chicken and Vegetable 71
245. Lemon or Lime Glaze 71
246. Lemony Leek and Chicken 71
247. Lime Turkey with Potatoes 71
248. Orange Chicken 72
249. Orange-Rosemary Chicken 72
250. Oregano Turkey Mix 72
251. Paella with Chicken 72
252. Pasta with Grilled Chicken 73
253. Turkey and Artichokes Mix 73
254. Turkey and Bok Choy 73
255. Turkey and Broccoli Crepe 73
256. Turkey and Creamy Broccoli 74
257. Turkey Stove Casserole 74
258. Turkey Wrap 74

BEEF, PORK, AND LAMB 75
261. Beef Brisket 75
259. Asian Pork Tenderloin 75

260. Beef and Vegetable Stew	75
262. Beef Fajitas with Peppers	76
263. Beef Ragù with Broccoli Ziti	76
264. Beef Stroganoff	76
265. Beef Tacos	77
266. Chili Lamb	77
267. Cumin Lamb Mix	77
268. Curried Pork Tenderloin	77
269. Fennel Lamb and Mushrooms	78
270. Garlic Pork Mix	78
271. Grilled Pork Fajitas	78
272. Lamb Chops with Kale	78
273. Lamb Stir Fry	78
274. Meatloaf	79
275. Mint Meatballs Spinach Sauté	79
276. Nutmeg Pork Black Beans	79
277. Paprika Pork with Carrots	79
278. Pork Chops with Black Currant	79
279. Pork Medallions with Herbes	80
280. Pork Tenderloin with Apples	80
281. Pork Tenderloin & Blue Cheese	80
282. Pork Tenderloin with Fennel	81
283. Pork Tenderloin with Orange	81
284. Pork with Avocados	81
285. Rosemary Pork Chops	81
286. Shepherd's Pie	82
287. Sirloin	82

FISH AND SEAFOOD 83

288. Allspice Shrimps	83
289. Aromatic Salmon with Fennel	83
290. Baked Cod	83
291. Basil Halibut	83
292. Braised Seabass	83
293. Broccoli and Cod Mash	83
294. Celery Crab Salad	84
295. Clams Stew	84
296. Cod in Orange Juice	84
297. Cod in Tomatoes	84
298. Cod in Yogurt Sauce	84
299. Cod Relish	84
300. Cod with Grapefruit	84
301. Cold Crab Mix	85
302. Crispy Mediterranean Tilapia	85
303. Crusted Salmon Horseradish	85
304. Cucumber and Seafood Bowl	85
305. Curry Snapper	86
306. Dill Steamed Salmon	86
307. Fish Salsa	86
308. Fish Spread	86
309. Five-Spices Sole	86
310. Greek Style Salmon	86
311. Green Onion Salmon	87
312. Grilled Tilapia	87
313. Grouper with Tomato Sauce	87
314. Halibut with Radish Slices	87
315. Herbed Sole	87
316. Horseradish Cod	87
317. Juicy Scallops	88
318. Lemon Swordfish	88
319. Lemon Zest Seabass	88
320. Lime Calamari	88
321. Limes and Shrimps Skewers	88
322. Mint Cod	88
323. Mustard Arctic Char	89
324. Mustard Tuna Salad	89
325. Onion Tilapia	89
326. Paprika Tilapia	89
327. Paprika Tuna	89
328. Parsley Trout	89
329. Rosemary Salmon	89
330. Salmon and Corn Salad	90
331. Salmon in Capers	90
332. Salmon with Basil and Garlic	90
333. Salmon with Grated Beets	90
334. Scallop Salad	90
335. Shallot Tuna	90
336. Shrimp Putanesca	90
337. Spanish Style Mussels	91
338. Spiced Scallops	91
339. Spicy Ginger Seabass	91
340. Spicy Shrimps	91
341. Spinach Halibut	91
342. Tilapia Veracruz	91
343. Tomato Halibut Fillets	91
344. Tuna and Pineapple Kebob	92
345. Tuna Stuffed Zucchini Boats	92
346. Turmeric Pate	92
347. Vinegar Trout	92
348. Yogurt Shrimps	92

SIDE DISHES 93

351. Baby Minted Carrots	93
352. Black Bean Cakes	93
349. Acorn Squash with Apples	93
350. Asparagus with Hazelnut	93
353. Braised Kale	94
354. Broccoli, Garlic and Lemon	94
355. Brown Rice Pilaf	94
356. Brussels Sprouts with Shallots	94
357. Buttermilk Mashed Potatoes	94
358. Cauliflower Mashed Potatoes	95
359. Celery Root and Apple Puree	95
360. Chinese-Style Asparagus	95
361. Cilantro Brown Rice	95
362. Corn Pudding	95
363. Couscous with Cranberries	96
364. Creamed Swiss Chard	96
365. Creole-Style Black-Eyed Peas	96
366. Curried Cauliflower	96
367. Fresh Fruit Kebabs	97
368. Garlic Mashed Potatoes	97
369. Glazed Root Vegetables	97
370. Honey Sage Carrots	97
371. Kasha with Spring Vegetables	97
372. Low-Fat Creamed Spinach	98
373. Marinated Eggplant	98
374. Parmesan Roasted Cauliflower	98
375. Pesto-Stuffed Tomatoes	98
376. Polenta with Mushrooms	99
377. Quick-Sautéed Cucumbers	99
378. Roasted Asparagus	99
379. Roasted Asparagus & Orange	99
380. Roasted Brussels Sprouts	99
381. Roasted Green Beans	100
382. Roasted Potatoes	100
383. Roasted Winter Squash	100
384. Sauteed Zucchini Coins	100
385. Seared Endive	100
386. Shrimp Ceviche	101
387. Smashed "Fried" Potatoes	101
388. Spicy Red Cabbage	101
389. Sweet Carrots	101
390. Tangy Green Beans	102
391. Thyme Roasted Beets	102
392. Lentil Ragout	102

DISHES WITH SAUCES 103

393. Asian-Style Lettuce Wraps	103
394. Chicken and Garlic Sauce	103
395. Chicken and Ginger Sauce	103

396. Chicken and Mustard Sauce 103
397. Chicken Fajitas 104
398. Chipotle Aioli Dip 104
399. Cod and White Sauce 104
400. Dash Apple Sauce French Toast 104
401. Grapes with Sour Cream 105
402. Grilled Chicken Skewers 105
403. Grilled Salmon with Lemon 105
404. Meatballs and Coconut Sauce 105
405. Pork Chops Mushroom Sauce 106
406. Pork Chops with Mushroom 106
407. Pork with Cilantro Sauce 106
408. Shrimp with Lemon Sauce 106
409. Spiced Applesauce 106
410. Tzatziki Greek Yogurt Sauce 107
411. Vegetarian Spaghetti Sauce 107
412. Whole-Wheat Spaghetti Ragu 107

SNACKS 108
416. Black Bean Cakes 108
417. Braised Celery Root 108
413. Arugula and Salami 108
414. Asian Asparagus Dish 108
415. Black-Eyed Pea Dip 108
418. Braised Kale 109
419. Broccoli with Lemon 109
420. Brown Rice Pilaf 109
421. Buffalo Chicken Dip 109
422. Caramelized Onion Dip 109
423. Cheese Log with Apple Slices 110
424. Corn Pudding 110
425. Cornbread with Southern Twist 110
426. Crab Stuffed Mushrooms 110
427. Crunchy Garbanzo Bean 111
428. Deviled Eggs Guac Style 111
429. Fish Tacos 111
430. Forbidden Rice with Mangoes 111
431. Grilled Shrimp with Lime 111
432. Guacamole with Pomegranate 112
433. Honey Orange Sauce 112
434. Hummus Dip 112
435. Hummus with Carrot 112
436. Hummus with Cucumber Slices 112
437. Lemon Rice 113
438. Mashed Cauliflower 113
439. Mediterranean Hummus Dip 113
440. Nilla, Pecan, and Pretzel Mix 113
441. Pita Chips 113
442. Potato Casserole 114
443. Pumpkin Walnut Cookie 114
444. Ricotta Bruschetta 114
445. Roasted Bananas and Potatoes 114
446. Roasted Tomato Bruschetta 114
447. Root Veggies with Glaze 115
448. Shrimp with Spicy Cocktail 115

449. Sour Cream Carrot Sticks 115
450. Spiced Carrot Raisin Bread 115
451. Spring Rolls 115
452. Sunflower, Dill 'n Garlic Dip 116
453. Sweet and Spicy Snack Mix 116
454. Tasty Turkey Burgers 116
455. Tasty Zucchini 116
456. Tea Cookies Flavored 117
457. Trail Mix 117
458. Tuna Kabobs 117

DESSERTS 118
459. Apples with Dip 118
460. Apricot and Almond Crisp 118
461. Baked Apples Stuffed 118
462. Banana Bread 118
463. Berries Marinated 118
464. Black and Blueberry Yogurt 119
465. Broiled Plums 119
466. Chocolate Pudding 119
467. Cookies and Cream Shake 119
468. Creamy Fruit Dessert 119
469. Fig Bars 120
470. Fruit and Nut Bar 120
471. Fruit Compote a la Mode 120
472. Fruitcake 120
473. Grapes with Sour Cream 121
474. Lemon Cheesecake 121
475. Lemon Pudding Cakes 121
476. Mixed Berry Pie 121
477. Mixed Berry Coffeecake 121
478. Mixed Fruit Smoothie 122
479. Orange Dream Smoothie 122
480. Peach Crumble 122
481. Peach Floats 122
482. Pineapple Pops 123
483. Poached Pears 123
484. Poached Pears with Yogurt 123
485. Pumpkin Cream Cheese Dip 123
486. Pumpkin Pie 123
487. Rainbow Ice Pops 124
488. Red, White and Blue Parfait 124
489. Seasonal Fruit Palette 124
490. Soft Chocolate Cake 124
491. Strawberries and Cream 124
492. Strawberries Crepes 125
493. Sweet Potato and Squash Pie 125
494. Tofu Chocolate Pudding 125
495. Two-Ingredients Ice Cream 125
496. Vanilla Poached Peaches 125
497. Watermelon-Cranberry 126
498. White Chocolate Pie 126
499. Whole-Grain Banana Bread 126
500. Yogurt Berry Burst Popsicles 126

INTRODUCTION

It can feel like diets drain you of all your energy and make eating a chore rather than a pleasure of life. With the DASH diet, thousands of recipes can be made because it focuses on controlled portions and smart ingredients, rather than restrictions of food. We believe everything is fine in moderation and apply this to our diet plan. No more grumbling bellies, the DASH diet is made so you can eat whenever you need without guilt.

This isn't a fad diet, it's a lifestyle change. No added supplements or pills to trick you into thinking you're losing weight. With the DASH diet, wellness and good food is at the core. If you struggle with high blood pressure, obesity, or type two diabetes, this diet will be not only a diet but a life saver.

This book contains 500 DASH foolproof recipes that are healthy, varied in flavor and origin, delicious, and completely safe for your diet. Before jumping straight into recipes, we will discuss the benefits of the DASH diet, foods you should eat on the diet and foods you should avoid, and also a Q&A session that will answer all your left- over questions.

WHAT DOES DASH MEAN?

The acronym DASH means Dietary Approaches to Stop Hypertension. The DASH diet isn't a fad diet, but rather a lifelong approach to healthy eating. The goal of this diet is to change your eating habits to reduce high blood pressure that can cause fatal diseases and disorders. The DASH diet isn't a quick fix for weight loss, but rather a diet that can be managed and kept up with throughout a lifetime. You'll see that my recipes use a variety of ingredients, so sacrificing taste for health is not a problem.

The DASH diet treats and prevents high blood pressure by reducing the sodium in your diet and increasing foods with nutrients proven to lower blood pressure, such as potassium, magnesium, and calcium. It doesn't just reduce high blood pressure but also lowers your risk for osteoporosis, heart disease, and strokes. The DASH diet consists of meals heavy in vegetables, fruits, and whole-grain food. Along with these main food groups, the diet also adds in modest amounts of low-fat dairy, fish, poultry, and nuts.

WHAT ARE THE BENEFITS

We now know what the DASH diet is and some of the benefits that make this diet worthy to adapt into your life, but let's look a little deeper.

PREVENTION AND TREATMENT OF HIGH BLOOD PRESSURE

Thousands of Americans are on blood pressure regulating medication that can be avoided with a healthy diet change. The DASH diet gives you that change in a manageable way. With lower blood pressure, the chances of catching diseases like heart disease, strokes, kidney disease, and heart attacks are greatly reduced. The NIH has stated that "if people with high blood pressure followed the DASH diet precisely, this could prevent around 400,000 deaths from cardiovascular disease over 10 years." The DASH diet can make a significant improvement in the health and safety of our entire population.

HELP TREAT AND PREVENT METABOLIC SYNDROME

The DASH diet reduces levels of blood pressure, blood sugar, triglycerides, bad cholesterol, and insulin resistance. This is a dream come true for those struggling with metabolic syndrome, obesity, and type 2 diabetes. In only a few weeks, you'll see changes through your blood pressure points and systolic pressure for those with metabolic syndrome. Not only this, but the DASH diet can also reduce the risk for Colorectal cancer. This diet is proven to be a lifesaving solution to numerous health problems people struggle with every day.

LOSING WEIGHT

Losing weight doesn't have to be your goal when starting the DASH diet. However, the diet can come with weight loss benefits, if that's what you're looking for. Since the diet already excludes common foods that lead to weight gain, such as sugar and red meat, you may naturally find yourself losing weight when starting the diet. If you'd like to healthily increase this weight loss, lower the number of poultry and fish in your plan and up the number of vegetables. Also, despite being taught that 3 meals a day are the golden rule, many meals a day actually allows your metabolism to work smarter, not harder, to help you shed those extra pounds.

BETTER IMMUNE SYSTEM

The DASH diet incorporates foods that are high in antioxidants. These food groups help your body produce protection for your cells against free radicals. While antioxidants can help prevent cancer, heart disease, and other fatal diseases, they can also help boost your immune system and keep you safe. This is especially important during this time as flu season approaches and Covid-19 is still out there.

WHAT TO EAT AND WHAT TO AVOID

Now let's talk about what foods you can eat on the diet and what should be avoided. We will also look at portion sizes for healthy DASH diet meals throughout the day. Remember, the DASH diet is a lifelong change, so don't constrict your diet, only change it
.

GOOD FOODS TO EAT

Grains are essential in the DASH diet. This can include pasta, rice, cereal, and bread. Grains are the main servings of your diet, meaning you should consume around 6-8. This varies depending on the person, but for an average 2,000 calorie diet, this is a suitable number of servings. One serving can come in the form of a slice of whole wheat bread, half a cup of cooked pasta or rice, or one ounce of dry cereal.

Vegetables: for the average 2,000 calorie diet, 4-5 servings of vegetables should be eaten throughout the day. Fiber and vitamin-rich vegetables are great for the DASH diet. Make sure your plate is as colorful as can be by combining different colored vegetables on your plate. Make sure to also include leafy greens for a nice dose of iron and protein in your diet. Half a cup of cooked or raw vegetables amounts to one serving, while an entire cup of leafy greens means one serving.

Fruits come next and should be eaten at the same amount as vegetables. This means you're eating 4-5 servings of delicious fruit. Fruits are important to the DASH diet because they are high in fiber, potassium, magnesium, and other vital vitamins and minerals. A wide variety of fruits can be eaten and to up the amount of fiber you eat, don't peel the skin off some of your favorite fruits, such as apples. The skin is packed with fiber nutrients.

Nuts, seeds, and legumes should be also consumed on par with fruits and vegetables. Strive to have 4-5 servings a day of these super-packed nutritional foods. They provide protein, potassium, magnesium, fiber, phytochemicals, and other nutrients. Various beans, seeds, and nuts can be added to your diet to achieve these serving goals.

Low-fat or fat-free dairy products should make up only 2-3 servings of your daily nutritional intake. This can include milk, cheese, or yogurt. When buying these items, we stress the fact that they should be low or fat-free. Dairy is placed in the DASH diet for a boost in calcium, protein, and vitamin D, not for a boost in calories and fat.

Poultry and fish are allowed on the DASH diet, with a maximum of 6 one-ounce servings a day. However, you should try to aim to eat mainly vegetables and replace what would be meat in your food with vegetables. If you do choose to eat meat, avoid seasoning with salt and remove the skin before eating. When eating fish, go for fish that are high in omega-3 fatty acids. This can be fish like salmon as they are great for heart health,

BAD FOODS TO EAT

Sweets are not a staple of the DASH diet. It's recommended to have sweets 5 servings or fewer a week. Again, the DASH diet is not about restricting yourself from foods you crave but instead eating them in moderation. This is why the DASH diet allows you to have these "cheat" foods at small moderations throughout the week.

Alcohol has been proven to raise blood pressure. It's recommended that for women, no more than one drink a day should be consumed, and for men, no more than two per day. The best bet is to quit alcohol completely, but we understand that a drink now and then is fine. If you find yourself drinking a little more than you should each night, try keeping alcohol outside of the house. This way you can drink it on a night out, but the easy access from the fridge is removed.

Red meat should be avoided or eaten very rarely with the DASH diet. Red meat is high in fat and sodium content, which are both bad for your DASH diet. If you're craving meat, stick with poultry or lean pork.

Full-fat dairy products like heavy whipping cream or 2% milk should be avoided. This ups the servings of fat you're having in a day and in order to stay on the DASH diet you need to make your servings conscientiously count.

Beware of beverages. Many beverages, like soda, are made with high amounts of sugar and artificial sweeteners. Avoid drinking these and getting your sugar servings from filling foods instead. Eat your calories rather than drink them.

Fast food should be avoided because it is often high in sodium because of the processing of the food. This includes chips, pizza, and other unhealthy snacks. They can also hide secret sugars put in to make the food taste better, but the healthy nutrients decline.

Q & A

By now you should have a well-rounded idea of what the DASH diet entails. You know the servings and types of food you should be eating, the foods to avoid, and how the DASH diet can benefit you. However, in case you have any longing questions, here are some answers and tips you can keep in mind as you start your journey to better health.

HOW DIFFICULT IS IT TO STICK TO THE DASH DIET?

The DASH diet isn't like other diets that you'll fall off of because of fatigue from restricting foods. Since the DASH diet allows for the consumption of a variety of foods, you won't get bored from sticking to a traditionally strict and restrictive program. This is what makes the DASH diet a lifelong change for lifelong health, rather than a quick fix to weight loss. With growing numbers of obesity in the world. The DASH diet is a way to curb these numbers without sacrificing your desired foods to eat. This is why the diet allows for 5 servings of sugar a week because we know those cravings will eventually come around, and moderate consumption is the only way to curb them.

WHERE CAN I BUY FOOD FOR MY DASH DIET? DO I NEED TO PURCHASE ANY SUPPLEMENTS OR PILLS TO ACCOMPANY THE DIET?

Why the DASH diet is great is because it's accessible. You can buy all the ingredients for any recipe you want to make, under DASH guidelines, from the grocery store, farmers market, health store, or anywhere else you choose to buy your food from. There is no added supplements or gatekeeping in terms of ingredients you'd have to buy online. This diet involves only you, a new grocery list, and a trip to the market.

DO YOU NEED TO EXERCISE ON THE DASH DIET?

You do not need to exercise to see the health benefits of the DASH diet. However, exercise along with the diet can boost your health to the next level. Cardio along with strength training can allow you to burn more calories, lose weight, and reach your health goals sooner. Exercise doesn't have to be big, either. You can start as simply as walking for 30 minutes a day.

MY BLOOD PRESSURE IS GOOD, SHOULD I FOLLOW THE DASH DIET?

The DASH diet is formed to reduce blood pressure in those with high blood pressure. If you already have good blood pressure, this diet may not be right for you. Concepts of the DASH diet, like eating more vegetables and avoiding red meat can serve to help anyone. The diet ultimately focuses on healthy eating, which is a good lesson for people, high blood pressure or not. However, a more personalized diet that's targeted to your needs will fit those with good blood pressure better. Check with your doctor or physicians about other options for lifelong healthy eating diet plans that are suited for

WHEN WILL I SEE THE RESULTS?

Many people following the DASH diet see results in lower blood pressure and weight in just two weeks. This depends on factors like your sex, starting weight, age, and more. However, the results do come fairly quickly with this diet and continue to benefit you throughout your time on the diet.

WHAT CAN I DRINK ON THIS DIET?

Water is always the go-to option for any diet, and this is no exception. Water hydrates while not adding extra calories or sugar to the diet. Watch that you're not consuming your calories in the form of drinks by drinking too much soda or alcohol while on the diet.

HOW LONG IS THE DIET?

This diet is designed to be a lifelong change for people that join it. The diet allows for occasional "cheat days" so you don't feel like you're completely missing out on the unhealthy foods you had before the diet. The DASH diet isn't a quick fix, but rather a sustainable journey.

TOP 10 TIPS FOR DASH DIET SUCCESS

MAKE A LIST BEFORE GOING TO THE STORE.
Often, we don't plan before going to the grocery store. This can result in buying more food than you needed and getting distracted by non-healthy foods that aren't right for the DASH diet. Find healthy and delicious DASH diet recipes beforehand and write down all the ingredients you need. You won't be tempted by the other food in the grocery store because your mind will be set on the delicious meals you've already thought of that are in agreement with the DASH diet rules.

EAT BEFORE GOING SHOPPING.
Similar to the last tip, never shop hungry. When you're hungry you have a wandering eye that will want to eat more than what's on your list. Also, when you're hungry you may gravitate towards snacks and processed foods for a quick fix to your hunger. Processed foods are a big no for the DASH diet since they're often high in sodium, so avoid the temptations by not shopping when you're hungry.

CUT BACK ON MEAT.
This can be a fast or gradual process, depending on how big of a meat eater you are. Much of the sodium we try to avoid comes from meat. You don't have to cut out all meat from the jump but reduce your intake. If you eat meat every day, try eating only 6 days a week. The same can be applied to meals, if you eat meat at every meal, take it down to at only 2 meals. You can even just reduce the serving size of meat that you eat at each meal.

COOK WEAR IS IMPORTANT TO CONSIDER.
Certain tools in the kitchen will be more beneficial to the DASH diet than others. Here are three items that you should have in your kitchen. The first is a nonstick pan. This eliminated the need to coat the pan in oil or butter. Since oils and fats are low on the list of food groups you should be eating, it's best to cut down on these fats when you can. Next, a steamer. Steamers are great because all it adds to your DASH-approved vegetable is water. Healthy food, cooked to perfection. Lastly, a spice mill to grind up whole, natural spices so you avoid livening up your meals with salt.

KEEP DASH APPROVED FOOD AT HOME

Diets are all about avoiding temptation. When you keep junk food and sweets around next to your healthy options, you're more likely to pick the former. However, if you have the basic DASH food staples, like grains, vegetables, nuts, and fruit you're more likely to eat these out of convenience, rather than leave to go to the store and indulge in junk food. Out of sight, out of mind.

DON'T BE AFRAID TO ASK.

It can feel difficult to go out to eat and still maintain your diet. If you want to order something off the menu but are afraid that the salt content may be too high, ask the waiter to ask the chef.

DRINK ONLY WATER.

This is a hard feat for some and an easy one for others. If you're a big soda or juice fan, this tip is for you. Even when buying juice, you may think it'll be fine because it's a serving of your fruit intake for the day. This may be true, however, there may also be so many added sugars to the drink that the one fruit serving was ultimately canceled out by the influx of sugar in the juice.

RINSE OFF CANNED FOODS.

Canned vegetables are a quick way to buy vegetables, prepare them, and have them last. They're perfectly okay to eat under the DASH diet. However, the juice in the can carries a lot of excess salt. Get rid of most of this excess by simply rinsing your vegetables off with water before you eat them.

ASK FOR THE LUNCH PORTION.

It's important with the DASH diet to keep your calories at the respected amount. Often at restaurants, a large portion is given and when it's on your plate, your mind feels obligated to eat it.

FRUIT FOR DESSERT.

If you're craving something sweet to finish off your meal, turn to fruit. If regular fruit doesn't satisfy you, there are tons of recipes here on how to turn an average dish of fruit into a yummy dessert and still maintain the health that the fruit on its own originally had.

BREAKFAST

1. Apple and Spice Oatmeal

INGREDIENTS (Servings: 1)

1 sweet apple, such as Gala, peeled, cored, and cut into ½-inch dice
⅔ cup water
⅓ cup old-fashioned (rolled) oats
1 pinch of ground cinnamon
1 pinch of freshly grated nutmeg
A few grains of kosher salt
½ cup fat-free milk, for serving

DIRECTIONS (Ready in about: 15 min)
In a small saucepan, mix the water, apple, oatmeal, nutmeg, cinnamon, and salt. Bring to a boil over medium heat, reduce heat to low, and cover. Cook over low heat until oats are tender, about 4 minutes. Microwave: In a 1-liter microwave-safe bowl, combine the apple, water, oatmeal, cinnamon, nutmeg, and salt. You should cover it and microwave on high power until oats are tender, about 4 minutes. Uncover carefully, mix and let stand 1 minute. Transfer the oatmeal to a bowl, pour in the milk, and serve.
Per serving: Kcal 190, Sodium 1 mg, Protein 5 g, Carbs 39 g, Fat 2.5 g

2. Apple Oats

INGREDIENTS (Servings: 4)

2 apples, cored, peeled, and cubed
1 cup gluten-free oats
1½ cups of water
1½ cups of almond milk
Cooking spray
2 tbsp. swerve
2 tbsp. almond butter
½ tsp. cinnamon powder
1 tbsp. flax seed, ground

DIRECTIONS (Ready in about: 7 h 10 min)
With cooking spray, grease a slow cooker and toss the oat with the water and other ingredients inside. Stir a little and simmer for 7 hours. Divide into bowls and serve for breakfast.
Per serving: Kcal 140, Sodium 44 mg, Protein 5 g, Carbs 28.5 g, Fat 4 g

3. Apple-Cinnamon Baked Oatmeal

INGREDIENTS (Servings: 2)

2 cups steel-cut oats
8 cups of water
1 tsp. cinnamon
½ tsp. allspice
½ tsp. nutmeg
¼ cup brown sugar
1 tsp. vanilla extract
2 apples, diced
1 cup raisins
½ cup unsalted, roasted walnuts, chopped

DIRECTIONS (Ready in about: 50 min)
Spray the cooker with non-stick cooking spray. Add all the ingredients to the cooker except the nuts. Mix well to combine. Put the cooker on low heat for 30 minutes. Serve garnished with chopped walnuts.
Per serving: Kcal 312, Sodium 4 mg, Protein 9 g, Carbs 60 g, Fat 7.5 g

4. Apples and Cinnamon Oatmeal

INGREDIENTS (Servings: 2)

1½ cups unsweetened plain almond milk
1 cup old-fashioned oats
¼ tsp. ground cinnamon
1 large, unpeeled apple, cubed
2 tbsp. toasted walnut pieces

DIRECTIONS (Ready in about: 20 min)
Bring the milk to warm over medium heat and add the oatmeal and apple. Beat until almost all the liquid is absorbed, about 4 minutes. Add the cinnamon. Pour the oat mixture into two bowls and garnish with walnuts.
Per serving: Kcal 377, Sodium 77 mg, Protein 13 g, Carbs 73 g, Fat 16 g

5. At-Home Cappuccino

INGREDIENTS (Servings: 2)

1 cup low-fat (1%) or fat-free milk
3 tbsp. ground espresso beans

DIRECTIONS (Ready in about: 10 min)
Heat the milk in a medium-hot saucepan until steamed. (Or microwave over high heat for about 1 minute.) Meanwhile, add cold water to the bottom of the coffee pot until the steam has evacuated. Add the coffee beans to the basket and screw them on. Bring to a boil over high heat and cook until coffee stops splashing from the vertical flow under the lid. Remove from the heat. Transfer the hot milk into a blender and mix until frothy. Divide the coffee between two cups. Pour in an equal amount of milk from the blender to cover the coffee, then pour in the remaining milk. Serve hot.
Per serving: Kcal 135, Sodium 112 mg, Protein 10 g, Carbs 17 g, Fat 2 g

6. Banana Almond Yogurt

INGREDIENTS (Servings: 1)

1 tbsp. raw, crunchy, unsalted almond butter	¼ cup uncooked old-fashioned oats
¾ cup low-fat plain Greek yogurt	½ large banana, sliced
	⅛ tsp. ground cinnamon

DIRECTIONS (Ready in about: 5 min)
Use the microwave to soften the almond for 15 seconds. Transfer the yogurt into a medium bowl and whisk in the almond butter, oatmeal, and banana. Sprinkle with cinnamon.
Per serving: Kcal 337, Sodium 65 mg, Protein 25 g, Carbs 48 g, Fat 12 g

7. Banana Cookies

INGREDIENTS (Servings: 12)

1 cup almond butter	2 cups gluten-free oats
¼ cup stevia	1 tsp. cinnamon powder
1 tsp. vanilla extract	1 cup almonds, chopped
2 bananas, peeled and mashed	½ cup raisins

DIRECTIONS (Ready in about: 25 min)
Use the microwave to soften the almond for 15 seconds. Transfer the yogurt into a medium bowl and whisk in the almond butter, oatmeal, and banana. Sprinkle with cinnamon.
Per serving: Kcal 280, Sodium 20 mg, Protein 8 g, Carbs 29 g, Fat 16 g

8. Banana Steel Oats

INGREDIENTS (Servings: 3)

1 small banana	½ cup rolled oats
1 cup almond milk	1 tbsp. honey
¼ tsp. cinnamon, ground	

DIRECTIONS (Ready in about: 25 min)
Take a saucepan and add half the banana, mix the almond milk, ground cinnamon. Season with the sunflower seeds. Stir until the banana is well mashed, bring the mixture to a boil, and add the oats. Simmer for 5-7 minutes and reduce the heat to medium-low until the oatmeal is tender. Cut the remaining half of the banana into cubes and place it on the oats.
Per serving: Kcal 358, Sodium 48 mg, Protein 7 g, Carbs 76 g, Fat 6 g

9. Banana-Berry Smoothie

INGREDIENTS (Servings: 1)

½ ripe banana, preferably frozen	½ cup plain low-fat yogurt
½ cup fresh or frozen blueberries	¼ tsp. vanilla extract
½ cup low-fat (1/%) milk	1 tbsp. amber agave nectar (optional)

DIRECTIONS (Ready in about: 10 min)
Peel and cut the banana into pieces. Combine all ingredients, including sweetener (if using), in a blender until smooth. Transfer into a tall glass and serve immediately.
Per serving: Kcal 180, Sodium 95 mg, Protein 8 g, Carbs 33 g, Fat 2 g

10. Barley Porridge

INGREDIENTS (Servings: 4)

1 cup barley	2 cups of water
1 cup of wheat berries	Toppings, such as hazelnuts, honey, berry, etc.
2 cups unsweetened almond milk	

DIRECTIONS (Ready in about: 30 min)
Take a portable saucepan and put it on medium-high heat. Add barley, almond milk, wheat berries, water, and bring to a boil. Reduce the heat and allow it to simmer for 25 minutes. Divide into bowls and garnish with desired toppings. Serve and enjoy!
Per serving: Kcal 295, Sodium 10 mg, Protein 6 g, Carbs 56 g, Fat 8 g

11. Basil and Tomato Baked Eggs

INGREDIENTS (Servings: 2)

½ garlic clove, minced
½ cup canned tomatoes
¼ cup fresh basil leaves, roughly chopped
¼ tsp. chili powder
½ tbsp. olive oil
2 whole eggs
Pepper to taste

DIRECTIONS (Ready in about: 25 min)

Preheat the oven to 375°F. Take a small baking dish and grease it with olive oil. Add the garlic, basil, tomatoes, chili, olive oil to a plate and mix. Break the eggs into a plate, leaving a space in between. Sprinkle the entire plate with sunflower seeds and pepper. Place in the oven and bake for 12 minutes until the eggs have solidified, and the tomatoes are foamy. Serve with the basil on top. Enjoy!

Per serving: Kcal 235, Sodium 126 mg, Protein 14 g, Carbs 7 g, Fat 16 g

12. Berries Deluxe Oatmeal

INGREDIENTS (Servings: 2)

1½ cups unsweetened plain almond milk
⅛ tsp. vanilla extract
1 cup old-fashioned oats
2 tbsp. toasted pecans
¾ cup mix of blueberries, blackberries, and coarsely chopped strawberries

DIRECTIONS (Ready in about: 20 min)

Heat the vanilla and almond milk in a saucepan over medium heat. The moment the mixture starts to simmer, add the oatmeal and stir for about 4 minutes, or until most of the liquid is absorbed. Add the berries. Pour the mixture into two bowls and garnish with a toasted pecan.

Per serving: Kcal 261, Sodium 115 mg, Protein 7 g, Carbs 63 g, Fat 10 g

13. Blueberry Breakfast Quinoa

INGREDIENTS (Servings: 4)

2 cups low-fat/nonfat milk
1 cup quinoa, uncooked
¼ cup honey
½ tsp. cinnamon
¼ cup chopped almonds, pecans, or walnuts
½ cup fresh blueberries

DIRECTIONS (Ready in about: 40 min)

In a portable saucepan, bring the milk to a boil. Add the quinoa and bring to a boil. Cover, reduce heat and cook until most of the liquid is absorbed about 12 to 15 minutes. Keep away from heat. Add the rest of the ingredients to the quinoa, cover, and let it stand for another 10 minutes before serving. For a finer consistency, add more milk.

Per serving: Kcal 320, Sodium 70 mg, Protein 12 g, Carbs 59 g, Fat 5 g

14. Blueberry Muffins

INGREDIENTS (Servings: 12)

2 bananas, peeled and mashed
1 cup almond milk
1 tsp. vanilla extract
¼ cup pure maple syrup
1 tsp. apple cider vinegar
¼ cup coconut oil, melted
2 cups almond flour
4 tbsp. coconut sugar
2 tsp. cinnamon powder
2 tsp. baking powder
2 cups blueberries
½ tsp. baking soda
½ cup walnuts, chopped

DIRECTIONS (Ready in about: 35 min)

In a bowl, combine the bananas with the almond milk, vanilla, and other ingredients and mix well. Divide the dough into 12 muffin cups and bake at 350 degrees F for 25 minutes. Serve the muffins for breakfast.

Per serving: Kcal 180, Sodium 322 mg, Protein 4 g, Carbs 31 g, Fat 5 g

15. Blueberry Pancakes

INGREDIENTS (Servings: 12)

2 eggs, whisked
4 tbsp. almond milk
1 cup full-fat yogurt
3 tbsp. coconut butter, melted
½ tsp. vanilla extract
1½ cups almond flour
2 tbsp. stevia
1 cup blueberries
1 tbsp. avocado oil

DIRECTIONS (Ready in about: 17 min)

In a bowl, combine the eggs with the almond milk and the other ingredients except for the oil and mix well. Warm a pan with oil over medium heat, add ¼ cup of the batter, spread into the pan, cook 4 minutes, turn, cook another 3 minutes and transfer to a plate. Repeat with the rest of the batter and serve the pancakes for breakfast.

Per serving: Kcal 64, Sodium 152 mg, Protein 2 g, Carbs 5 g, Fat 4 g

16. Blueberry-Maple Oatmeal

INGREDIENTS (Servings: 1)

½ cup rolled oats
½ cup water or nonfat milk
⅛ tsp. of sea salt
1 tbsp. chia seeds (optional)
1-2 tsp. maple syrup
2 cups fresh blueberries

DIRECTIONS (Ready in about: 30 min)

In a bowl or jar, combine oats, water or milk, and salt. Cover and place in refrigerator overnight. Before serving, top with chia seeds, maple syrup, and blueberries.

Per serving: Kcal 260, Sodium 160 mg, Protein 9 g, Carbs 49, Fat 3 g

17. Chocolate Smoothie

INGREDIENTS (Servings: 2)

1 ripe banana, frozen at least overnight
⅔ cup low-fat (1%) milk
⅔ cup plain low-fat yogurt
4 ice cubes
2 tbsp. chunky peanut butter
2 tbsp. unsweetened cocoa powder
1 tbsp. amber agave nectar (optional)

DIRECTIONS (Ready in about: 5 min)

Peel and cut the banana into pieces. In a blender, combine the banana with the milk, yogurt, peanut butter, cocoa powder, sweetener (if using), and ice cubes. Pour into two tall glasses and serve immediately.

Per serving: Kcal 250, Sodium 134 mg, Protein 13 g, Carbs 31 g, Fat 11 g

18. Coconut Crepes

INGREDIENTS (Servings: 12)

2 tbsp. coconut oil, melted
1 tsp. cinnamon powder
2 tsp. stevia
1 cup almond flour
1 tbsp. flaxseed, ground
2 cups of coconut milk

DIRECTIONS (Ready in about: 16 min)

In a bowl, combine the flour with the flax seeds, milk, half the oil, cinnamon, and stevia, and mix well. Heat a pan with the remaining oil over medium heat, add ¼ cup pancake batter, spread into the pan, cook 2-3 minutes per side and transfer to a plate. Repeat with the rest of the pancake batter and serve them for breakfast.

Per serving: Kcal 71, Sodium 50 mg, Protein 1 g, Carbs 8 g, Fat 3 g

19. Crunchy Flax Almond Crackers

INGREDIENTS (Servings: 20)

½ cup ground flaxseeds
½ cup almond flour
1 tbsp. coconut flour
2 tbsp. hemp hearts
¼ tsp. sunflower seeds
1 egg white
2 tbsp. unsalted almond butter, melted

DIRECTIONS (Ready in about: 75 min)

Preheat the oven to 300°F. Line a baking sheet with parchment paper, set aside. Add the flax seeds, almonds, coconut flour, hemp seeds, seeds in a bowl and mix. Add the egg white and melted almond butter, stir until combined. Transfer the dough to a sheet of baking paper and cover it with another sheet of paper. Wrap the dough. Cut the cookies and bake for 60 minutes. Let them cool and enjoy!

Per serving: Kcal 98, Sodium 76 mg, Protein 2 g, Carbs 1 g, Fat 6 g

20. Egg Burrito

INGREDIENTS (Servings: 1)

Cracked black pepper
1 whole wheat tortilla
¼ cup of rinsed and drained canned black beans
1 tbsp. chopped fresh cilantro
¼ cup chopped tomato
1 tbsp. low-sodium salsa
1 tbsp. olive oil
2 tbsp. chopped white onion
1 clove garlic, minced
2 eggs whites
1 whole egg
1 cup spinach
⅛ cup shredded low-fat cheddar cheese

DIRECTIONS (Ready in about: 35 min)

Heat the oil in a skillet over medium heat. Include the garlic and onion and cook for about 30 sec. Meanwhile, beat the whites and the whole egg. Add the eggs, spinach, cheese, and pepper. Cook until the eggs are no longer running (2-3 min). Remove the pan from the fire. Heat the tortilla in a flat skillet over medium heat. Put the beans in a saucepan and bring to a boil. Place the hot tortilla on a plate and pour the beans in the center of the tortilla, in line. Add the vegetable and egg mixture and garnish with cilantro, tomato, and salsa. Fold it into a burrito and enjoy!

Per serving: Kcal 460, Sodium 709 mg, Protein 28 g, Carbs 39 g, Fat 24 g

21. Egg Muffins

INGREDIENTS (Servings: 6)

4 cups chopped spinach
½ cup chopped green bell pepper
½ cup chopped red bell pepper
4 tbsp. chopped green onion, white ends discarded
Pinch of paprika
14 egg whites
3 whole eggs
⅛ tsp. chile pepper flakes
¼ tsp. dried oregano
2 tbsp. finely chopped fresh parsley
⅛ tsp. cracked black pepper

DIRECTIONS (Ready in about: 55 min)

Preheat the oven to 375°F. Mix all the vegetables in a large bowl, mixing evenly. In another large bowl, whisk together the egg whites, whole eggs, red pepper flakes, oregano, parsley, pepper, and paprika. Drizzle a muffin pan with olive oil, making sure to spray the sides evenly. Pour the vegetables into each muffin halfway through cooking. Pour about ⅓ cup of the egg mixture into each muffin pan, slowly so as not to stir the vegetables. Place the muffin pan on the middle oven rack and bake 25 to 30 minutes or until the eggs are no longer runny in the center. Remove from the oven immediately to prevent the eggs from overcooking or drying out. Serve hot.

Per serving: Kcal 93, Sodium 182 mg, Protein 14 g, Carbs 4 g, Fat 3 g

22. Energy Oatmeal

INGREDIENTS (Servings: 1)

¼ cup water
¼ cup low-fat milk
½ cup old-fashioned oats
4 egg whites, beaten
⅛ tsp. ground cinnamon
⅛ tsp. ground ginger
¼ cup blueberries

DIRECTIONS (Ready in about: 35 min)

In a small saucepan, heat the water and milk over medium heat. Add the oat, constantly stirring for about 4 minutes or until most of the liquid is absorbed. Gradually add the beaten egg whites, stirring constantly. Cook for another 5 minutes or until the eggs are no longer runny. Mix the cinnamon and ginger with the oat mixture and pour the mixture into a bowl. Garnish with berries. Serve.

Per serving: Kcal 270, Sodium 250 mg, Protein 23 g, Carbs 60 g, Fat 4 g

23. English Muffin with Berries

INGREDIENTS (Servings: 11)

100% whole wheat English muffin, halved
1 tbsp. low-fat cream cheese
4 strawberries, thinly sliced
½ cup blueberries, mashed

DIRECTIONS (Ready in about: 25 min)

Toast the English muffin halves. Distribute cream cheese evenly over each toasted half and garnish with fruit.

Per serving: Kcal 231, Sodium 271 mg, Protein 8 g, Carbs 43 g, Fat 4 g

24. Fruit and Yogurt Breakfast Salad

INGREDIENTS (Servings: 6)

2 cups water
¼ tsp. salt
¾ cup Quick-cooking brown rice
¾ cup bulgur
1 large apple, cored, chopped
1 large pear, cored, chopped
1 orange, peeled and cut into sections
1 cup dried cranberries
8 oz. low fat (or non-fat) Greek yogurt, plain

DIRECTIONS (Ready in about: 25 min)

Heat water in a large pot. Add salt, rice, and bulgur to boiling water. Lower heat to low. Cover, and simmer for 10 minutes. Remove from heat. Transfer grains to a large bowl and keep in the refrigerator until chilled. Remove chilled grains from the refrigerator. Add apple, pear, orange, and dried cranberries. Fold in the yogurt and mix until grains and fruit are well mixed. Serve.

Per serving: Kcal 189, Sodium 117 mg, Protein 5 g, Carbs 38 g, Fat 1.5 g

25. Fruity Green Smoothie

INGREDIENTS (Servings: 8)

2 cups fresh spinach leaves
1 medium banana, peeled
7-8 strawberries, trimmed
½ cup of orange juice
1 cup crushed ice

DIRECTIONS (Ready in about: 10 min)

In a blender, bring all of the ingredients together and blend until smooth. Serve in a tall glass.

Per serving: Kcal 235, Sodium 64 mg, Protein 5 g, Carbs 56 g, Fat 1.5 g

26. Fruity Yogurt Parfait

INGREDIENTS (Servings: 1)

1 cup low-fat plain Greek yogurt
¼ cup blueberries
¼ cup cubed strawberries
¼ cup cubed kiwifruit
1 tsp. ground flaxseeds or flaxseed meal
½ cup low-calorie granola

DIRECTIONS (Ready in about: 15 min)
Pour half the yogurt into a small glass bowl or parfait plate. Garnish with a thin layer of blueberries, strawberries, kiwi fruit, flaxseed, and granola. Put the remaining yogurt and add the remaining fruit, flax seeds, and granola.
Per serving: Kcal 388, Sodium 99 mg, Protein 30 g, Carbs 41 g, Fat 21 g

27. Gingered Green Tea

INGREDIENTS (Servings: 1)

¼ cup water
¼ cup low-fat milk
½ cup old-fashioned oats
4 egg whites, beaten
⅛ tsp. ground cinnamon
⅛ tsp. ground ginger
¼ cup blueberries

DIRECTIONS (Ready in about: 35 min)
Put the ginger in a saucepan and mash the slices with the handle of a wooden spoon. Add water and bring to a boil over high heat. Add the tea bag to a cup. Pour the hot water with the ginger. Let steep for 2 to 3 minutes. With a spoon, remove the ginger and the teabag. Drink hot.
Per serving: Kcal 2, Sodium 5 mg, Protein 0 g, Carbs 1 g, Fat 12 g

28. Granola

INGREDIENTS (Servings: 10)

¼ cup packed light brown sugar
2 tbsp. water
1 tbsp. vegetable oil
1 tsp. ground cinnamon
½ cup fat-free milk, for serving
1 tsp. maple flavoring or vanilla extract
4 cups old-fashioned (rolled) oats
1 cup dark raisins
½ cup chopped dates

DIRECTIONS (Ready in about: 45 min)
Preheat the oven to 300°F. In a medium bowl, combine the water, brown sugar, oil, cinnamon, and maple flavoring until the sugar has dissolved. Add the oat and toss until lightly coated. Distribute evenly on a large, rimmed baking sheet. Cook, stirring occasionally and bringing the toasted edges to the center of the granola until the oats are evenly crisp about 40 minutes. Take it out of the oven and add the raisins and dates. Let it cool totally. Store in a sealed shut holder for as long as about fourteen days.
Per serving: Kcal 205, Sodium 54 mg, Protein 7 g, Carbs 41 g, Fat 2.5 g

29. Greek-Style Breakfast Scramble

INGREDIENTS (Servings: 1)

Non-stick cooking spray
1 cup fresh spinach, chopped
½ cup mushrooms, chopped
¼ onion, chopped
1 whole egg and 2 egg whites
2 tbsp. feta cheese
Freshly ground black pepper, to taste

DIRECTIONS (Ready in about: 15 min)
Heat a non-stick skillet over medium heat. Spray with cooking spray and add spinach, mushrooms, and onion. Sauté for 2-3 minutes until the onions are translucent and the spinach is softened. Meanwhile, beat the egg and whites in a bowl. Add the feta cheese and pepper. Pour the egg mixture over the vegetables. Cook eggs, stirring with a spatula, for 3-4 minutes or until cooked through and serve hot.
Per serving: Kcal 150, Sodium 440 mg, Protein 17 g, Carbs 6 g, Fat 7 g

30. Healthy French Toast

INGREDIENTS (Servings: 4)

4 egg whites
1 whole egg
1 cup unsweetened almond milk
½ tsp. ground cinnamon
1 tsp. vanilla extract
¼ tsp. ground nutmeg
½ tsp. powdered stevia
8 slices whole-grain bread (½-1 inch thick)

DIRECTIONS (Ready in about: 15 min)
Combine the egg whites, whole egg, almond milk, cinnamon, vanilla, nutmeg, and stevia in a shallow bowl. Plunge each slice of bread in the mixture for about 1 minute per side so that the bread absorbs the liquid and aromas. Heat a grill pan until very hot and coat it with olive oil. Place each soaked slice of bread on the griddle and bake for about 3 minutes per side, or until golden brown and crisp. Serve immediately.
Per serving: Kcal 305, Sodium 438 mg, Protein 15 g, Carbs 49 g, Fat 7 g

31. Healthy Low-Fat Granola

INGREDIENTS (Servings: 8)

4 cups old-fashioned oats	¼ sliced almonds
¼ cup flax seed	⅓ cup maple syrup
¼ cup wheat germ	¼ cup apple juice
¼ cup coconut flakes	1 tsp. cinnamon
¼ cup pumpkin or sunflower seeds	1 tsp. vanilla
	¼ tsp. salt

DIRECTIONS (Ready in about: 45 min)
Preheat the oven to 325°F. Combine all the ingredients in an enormous bowl. Mix well to cover all the ingredients. Line rimmed cookie sheet with parchment paper. Distribute the mixture evenly on the baking sheet. Bake for 30 to 35 minutes, stirring once until lightly browned.
Per serving: Kcal 180, Sodium 85 mg, Protein 5 g, Carbs 30.5 g, Fat 5 g

32. Healthy Start Yogurt Bowls

INGREDIENTS (Servings: 2)

2 cups plain low-fat (or non-fat) Greek yogurt	½ cup granola with nuts and seeds
1 cup fresh or frozen berries	1 tsp. honey or maple syrup

DIRECTIONS (Ready in about: 25 min)
Divide the yogurt into 2 shallow bowls. Arrange half of the berries on the left side of each bowl. Add half of the granola to the right side of each bowl. Drizzle ½ tsp. of honey or syrup over each bowl and serve.
Per serving: Kcal 300, Sodium 185 mg, Protein 15 g, Carbs 42 g, Fat 7 g

33. Hearty Pineapple Oatmeal

INGREDIENTS (Servings: 5)

Non-stick cooking spray	1 whole egg and 2 egg whites
1 cup fresh spinach, chopped	2 tbsp. feta cheese
½ cup mushrooms, chopped	Freshly ground black pepper, to taste
¼ onion, chopped	

DIRECTIONS (Ready in about: 5 h 10 min)
Heat a non-stick skillet over medium heat. Spray with cooking spray and add spinach, mushrooms, and onion. Sauté for 2-3 minutes until the onions are translucent and the spinach is softened. Meanwhile, beat the egg and whites in a bowl. Add the feta cheese and pepper. Pour the egg mixture over the vegetables. Cook eggs, stirring with a spatula, for 3-4 minutes or until cooked through and serve hot.
Per serving: Kcal 180, Sodium 229 mg, Protein 5 g, Carbs 31 g, Fat 5 g

34. Kale and Apple Smoothie

INGREDIENTS (Servings: 1)

1 cup stemmed and loosely packed kale leaves, well washed	⅓ cup apple cider
	2 tbsp. sunflower seeds
	6 ice cubes
½ sweet apple, cored and coarsely chopped	8 fresh mint leaves

DIRECTIONS (Ready in about: 10 min)
Stir all the ingredients together in a blender until smooth. Transfer into a tall glass and serve immediately.
Per serving: Kcal 171, Sodium 31 mg, Protein 5 g, Carbs 19 g, Fat 10 g

35. Lean Country-Style Sausage

INGREDIENTS (Servings: 6)

½ pound lean ground pork loin	1 tsp. dry mustard
	1 tsp. onion powder
½ pound lean ground turkey breast	1 tsp. sage
	1 tsp. ground black pepper
½ tsp. red pepper flakes (optional)	1 tsp. sugar

DIRECTIONS (Ready in about: 15 min)
In an enormous bowl, combine all the ingredients. Form 12 meatballs with the mixture. Spray a large nonstick skillet with cooking spray and place over medium heat. Add the meatballs and cover. Cook until golden brown and juices run clear, about 5 minutes per side. If using a thermometer, cook until internal temperature reaches 165°F. Transfer to a serving plate and serve immediately.
Per serving: Kcal 109, Sodium 52 mg, Protein 15 g, Carbs 1 g, Fat 4 g

36. Lemon-Zucchini Muffins

INGREDIENTS (Servings: 12)

2 cups all-purpose flour	1 cup shredded zucchini
½ cup sugar	¾ cup nonfat milk
1 tbsp. baking powder	2 tbsp. olive oil
¼ tsp. salt	2 tbsp. lemon juice
¼ tsp. cinnamon	1 egg
¼ tsp. nutmeg	Non-stick cooking spray

DIRECTIONS (Ready in about: 35 min)
Preheat oven to 400°F. Prepares muffin pan by lightly spraying with cooking spray or by lining muffin cups. In a portable bowl, combine the flour, sugar, baking powder, salt, cinnamon, and nutmeg. In another bowl, combine zucchini, milk, oil, lemon juice, and egg. Mix well. Add the zucchini mixture to the flour mixture and stir until combined. Don't mix too much. Pour batter into prepared muffin cups. Cook for 20 minutes or until the mixture turns golden brown.
Per serving: Kcal 145, Sodium 63 mg, Protein 3 g, Carbs 25 g, Fat 4 g

37. Mango Lassi

INGREDIENTS (Servings: 1)

1 ripe mango, pitted, peeled, and coarsely chopped	½ cup fat-free milk
	½ cup plain nonfat yogurt
Pinch of ground cardamom (optional)	3 ice cubes

DIRECTIONS (Ready in about: 10 min)
In a blender, combine the mango, yogurt, milk, and ice cubes until smooth. Pour into a tall glass. Sprinkle with cardamom, if necessary. Serve immediately.

Per serving: Kcal 235, Sodium 148 mg, Protein 13 g, Carbs 47 g, Fat 1 g

38. Mediterranean Scramble

INGREDIENTS (Servings: 1)

2 tbsp. olive oil	2 eggs whites
⅛ cup chopped red onion	1 whole egg
1 medium clove garlic, minced	⅛ tsp. dried oregano
	⅛ tsp. black pepper
¼ cup rinsed and drained, chopped canned artichoke hearts	⅛ cup low-fat feta cheese
	¼ cup sliced red bell pepper

DIRECTIONS (Ready in about: 15 min)
Warm a small non-stick pan over medium heat. Add the oil to the hot pan, and when the oil is hot, add the onion and garlic. Cook for 1 minute before adding the pepper strips and artichoke hearts. Sauté vegetables for another 3 minutes or until onion is translucent and pepper is tender. In a small bowl, beat the whites and egg until stiff and season with oregano and black pepper. Pour in the eggs and mix them with a spatula. Cook, 3 to 4 minutes or until the eggs are no longer runny. Remove from heat, top with feta cheese and cover until the feta cheese begins to melt. Serve immediately.
Per serving: Kcal 424, Sodium 572 mg, Protein 21 g, Carbs 5 g, Fat 37 g

39. Open-Faced Breakfast Sandwich

INGREDIENTS (Servings: 1)

1½ tsp. olive oil	1 slice 100% whole wheat bread
2 egg whites, beaten	
½ cup spinach	2 thick tomato slices
Black pepper, to taste	1 thin slice of low-fat cheddar cheese
1 tsp. brown mustard	

DIRECTIONS (Ready in about: 25 min)
Heat up the oven to 400°F. Heat up a small non-stick skillet over medium heat. Include the oil in the hot pan and when the oil is hot, add the egg whites. Beat the eggs while cooking, then add the spinach and season with pepper to taste. Spread mustard on the bread, add the tomato and scrambled eggs, and garnish with the cheese. Heat in the oven up until the cheese is melted about 2 minutes.
Per serving: Kcal 286, Sodium 516 mg, Protein 20 g, Carbs 27 g, Fat 12 g

40. Papaya and Coconut Shake

INGREDIENTS (Servings: 2)
1 ripe papaya, seeded, peeled, and cut into 1-inch chunks
1 cup plain low-fat yogurt
1 cup coconut water (not coconut milk)
2 tbsp. wheat germ
½ tsp. zero-calorie sweetener (optional)

DIRECTIONS (Ready in about: 10 min)
Combine all ingredients, including sweetener (if using), in a blender. Pour into two tall glasses and serve.
Per serving: Kcal 158, Sodium 40 mg, Protein 8 g, Carbs 26 g, Fat 3 g

41. Peanut Butter Oats

INGREDIENTS (Servings: 4)
1 tbsp. chia seeds
½ cup almond milk
2 tbsp. peanut butter
1 tbsp. stevia
½ cup gluten-free oats
2 tbsp. raspberries

DIRECTIONS (Ready in about: 6 h 10 min)
In a glass jar, combine the oat with the chia seeds and other ingredients except for the raspberries, mix a little, cover and refrigerate for 6 hours. Garnish with raspberries and serve them.
Per serving: Kcal 454, Sodium 102 mg, Protein 14.5 g, Carbs 51 g, Fat 24 g

42. Peach and Berry Pancake

INGREDIENTS (Servings: 4)
½ cup all-purpose flour
¼ cup vanilla yogurt
⅛ tsp. salt
1 tbsp. butter
½ cup fat-free milk
3 eggs (lightly beaten)
½ cup fresh raspberries
2 medium peaches (peeled and sliced)
½ tsp. sugar

DIRECTIONS (Ready in about: 40 min)
Put the raspberries, peaches, and sugar in a bowl. Gently toss to coat. Put milk, eggs, and salt in a bowl. Whisk until combined. Gradually add flour as you whisk. Place butter in a pie plate and melt in a preheated oven at 400°F for 3 minutes. Remove from the oven and spread melted butter all over. Add the batter and bake for 22 minutes or until browned and puffed. Top with yogurt and mixed fruits.
Per serving: Kcal 199, Sodium 149 mg, Protein 8 g, Carbs 38 g, Fat 3 g

43. Protein Bowl

INGREDIENTS (Servings: 1)
¾ cup low-fat cottage cheese
½ banana, thinly sliced
1 tbsp. almond butter
¼ cup uncooked old-fashioned oats

DIRECTIONS (Ready in about: 10 min)
Mix the ingredients in a little bowl together and enjoy!
Per serving: Kcal 424, Sodium 572 mg, Protein 21 g, Carbs 5 g, Fat 37 g

44. Scones with Nuts and Fruits

INGREDIENTS (Servings: 1)
½ tsp. baking soda
2 cups almond flour
¼ cup cranberries, dried
¼ cup apricots, chopped
¼ cup sunflower seeds
¼ cup sesame seeds
1 egg, whisked
¼ cup walnuts, chopped
2 tbsp. stevia

DIRECTIONS (Ready in about: 25 min)
In a bowl, combine the flour with the baking soda, blueberries, and other ingredients and mix well. Form a square dough, spread it out on a floured work surface, and cut it into 16 squares. On a baking sheet filled with parchment paper, placed the squares and bake the buns at 350°F for 12 minutes. Serve the scones for breakfast.
Per serving: Kcal 238, Sodium 161 mg, Protein 9 g, Carbs 8.5 g, Fat 19 g

45. Scrambled Pesto Eggs

INGREDIENTS (Servings: 2)
2 large whole eggs
½ tbsp. almond butter
1 tbsp. creamed coconut milk
Sunflower seeds and pepper as needed
½ tbsp. pesto

DIRECTIONS (Ready in about: 10 min)
Take a bowl and crack open your eggs. Season with a pinch of sunflower seeds and pepper. Pour the eggs into a pan. Add the almond butter and turn on the heat. Cook over low heat and gently add the pesto. Once the eggs are cooked and scrambled, remove them from the heat. Pour in the coconut cream and mix well. Turn on the heat and cook on LOW for a while until it has a creamy texture. Serve and enjoy!

46. Spiced Pumpkin Pancakes

INGREDIENTS (Servings: 10)

2 cups whole wheat flour
2 tsp. baking powder
1 tsp. baking soda
1 tsp. cinnamon
½ tsp. ground nutmeg
½ tsp. ground ginger
¼ cup brown sugar
1 egg yolk
1 cup canned pumpkin
2 tbsp. coconut oil
2 cups skim milk
2 egg whites

DIRECTIONS (Ready in about: 25 min)
Combine the baking powder, flour, baking soda, cinnamon, nutmeg, and ginger in a bowl. In another bowl, combine brown sugar, egg yolk, pumpkin, and coconut oil. Add the milk. Pour the milk mixture into the bowl with the dry ingredients and mix until combined. Don't mix too much. Beat egg whites in a bowl until frothy. Add the whites to the pancake batter. Warm a non-stick griddle or huge skillet over medium-high heat. Spray with non-stick cooking spray. When the griddle becomes hot, pour ¼ cup of batter onto the pan. Cook until boiling, flip, and cook until lightly browned.
Per serving: Kcal 150, Sodium 360 mg, Protein 6.5 g, Carbs 32 g, Fat 2 g

47. Swiss Chard Omelet

INGREDIENTS (Servings: 2)

2 eggs, lightly beaten
2 cups Swiss chard, sliced
1 tbsp. almond butter
½ tsp. sunflower seeds
Fresh pepper

DIRECTIONS (Ready in about: 10 min)
Take a non-stick skillet and put it on medium-low heat. Once the almond butter has melted, add the Swiss chard and cook for 2 minutes. Pour the eggs into the pan and gently add them to the chard. Season with garlic and pepper sunflower seeds. Cook for 2 minutes. Serve and enjoy!
Per serving: Kcal 260, Sodium 250 mg, Protein 14 g, Carbs 4 g, Fat 21 g

48. Tartine with Cream Cheese

INGREDIENTS (Servings: 1)

1 slice whole-grain bread
2 tbsp. spreadable fat-free cream cheese
2 large strawberries, hulled and sliced
1 tsp. honey (optional)

DIRECTIONS (Ready in about: 15 min)
Toast the bread in a toaster. Spread with cream cheese and garnish with strawberries. Season with honey, if needed.
Per serving: Kcal 167, Sodium 370 mg, Protein 9 g, Carbs 27 g, Fat 12 g

49. Toast with Almond Butter

INGREDIENTS (Servings: 1)

2 slices 100% whole wheat bread
2 tbsp. almond butter
1 small banana, sliced
⅛ tsp. ground cinnamon

DIRECTIONS (Ready in about: 10 min)
Toast and spread each slice of the bread with almond butter. Place the banana slices on top and sprinkle with cinnamon.
Per serving: Kcal 484, Sodium 421 mg, Protein 19 g, Carbs 56 g, Fat 21 g

50. Veggie Omelet

INGREDIENTS (Servings: 1)

1 tbsp. olive oil
¼ cup coarsely chopped broccoli
2 tbsp. chopped red onion
1 clove garlic, minced
¼ cup chopped zucchini
2 egg whites
1 whole egg
⅛ cup shredded low-fat cheddar cheese
⅛ tsp. sea salt
⅛ tsp. cracked black pepper

DIRECTIONS (Ready in about: 15 min)
Heat a medium non-stick skillet over medium heat and add the oil once the pan is hot. When the oil is hot, add the broccoli and cook for a minute before adding the onion, garlic, and zucchini. Fry for 3-4 minutes. In a small bowl, beat the whites and the whole egg and season with salt and pepper. Reduce the heat and add the beaten eggs to the pan with the vegetables, making sure to tilt the pan so that the eggs evenly coat the vegetables. After 30 seconds, turn off the heat, turn the tortilla over, and spread the cheese on half of the tortilla. Overlay the other half over the cheese and cover the pan with a lid. Cook, 1 to 2 minutes or until cheese is melted. Serve immediately.
Per serving: Kcal 279, Sodium 580 mg, Protein 22 g, Carbs 6 g, Fat 20 g

51. Veggie Scramble

INGREDIENTS (Servings: 4)

1 cup mixed greens (such as collard greens, mustard greens, and kale)
¼ cup chopped red onion
¼ cup chopped red bell pepper
½ cup chopped broccoli
2 tbsp. extra virgin olive oil
2 tbsp. water
1 large clove garlic, minced
3 whole eggs
3 egg whites
⅛ tsp. sea salt
Pinch of black pepper

DIRECTIONS (Ready in about: 15 min)

Rinse the vegetables and pat them dry, cut off the thick part of the stems, and cut the leaves into 1-inch pieces. Chop the onion, pepper, and broccoli into small, even-sized pieces. Heat a large non-stick skillet over medium-high heat and add the oil once the pan is hot. Add the vegetables once the oil is hot and sauté for about 3 minutes or until the vegetables start to wilt. Pour water into the pan, cover the pan with a lid, and steam for 2-3 minutes. Remove the lid, add the broccoli, bell pepper, onion, and garlic. Meanwhile, beat the eggs, whites, salt, and pepper in a medium bowl. Once the onion is translucent, add the beaten egg mixture. Stir to break up and distribute the eggs evenly. Cook until the eggs are no longer liquid but a little damp, turn off the heat and serve immediately.

Per serving: Kcal 145, Sodium 179 mg, Protein 9 g, Carbs 4 g, Fat 11 g

52. Warm Quinoa with Berries

INGREDIENTS (Servings: 2)

1 cup uncooked quinoa
1 cup unsweetened coconut milk
1 cup of water
½ cup blackberries
2 tbsp. toasted chopped pecans
2 tsp. honey, optional

DIRECTIONS (Ready in about: 35 min)

Rinse the quinoa. In a covered pot, bring the quinoa, coconut milk, and water to a boil over high heat. Reduce the heat and cook for 10 to 15 minutes or until the liquid is absorbed. The cooked quinoa should be slightly al dente; it's ready when most of the grains have uncoiled, and you can see the unwound germ. Let the quinoa sit in the covered pot for about 5 minutes. Stir gently with a fork and pour into two bowls, then add the blackberries, nuts, and honey.

Per serving: Kcal 476, Sodium 94 mg, Protein 14 g, Carbs 70 g, Fat 17 g

53. Whole Grain Pancakes

INGREDIENTS (Servings: 4)

1 tsp. vanilla extract
1 small banana, mashed
2 cups unsweetened almond milk
¼ cup unsweetened applesauce
1¼ cups whole wheat flour
¼ cup old-fashioned oats
2 tsp. baking powder
¼ tsp. sea salt
½ tsp. ground cinnamon
3 tbsp. brown sugar
½ cup of toasted almonds (chopped) or walnuts

DIRECTIONS (Ready in about: 30 min)

In a medium bowl, combine the wet ingredients. In another larger bowl, combine the dry ingredients. Add the wet ingredients to the dry ingredients and mix well until smooth. Heat a roasting pan over medium heat, then coat with olive oil. Use a ladle to pour the batter over the pan and cook the pancakes for 2-3 minutes. Return them to a boil and continue cooking for about a minute. Remove from heat and stack on a covered plate until all pancakes are cooked through. Serve immediately.

Per serving: Kcal 301, Sodium 483 mg, Protein 9 g, Carbs 55 g, Fat 10 g

SOUPS AND CHOWDERS

54. Beans Soup

INGREDIENTS (Servings: 4)

½ onion, diced
⅓ cup green beans, soaked
½ sweet pepper, chopped
2 potatoes, chopped
1 tbsp. fresh cilantro, chopped
1 tsp. chili flakes
3 cups of water

DIRECTIONS (Ready in about: 45 min)

Put all the ingredients in the pot and close the lid. Cook the soup over medium heat for 40 minutes or until all ingredients are tender.

Per serving: Kcal 87, Sodium 13 mg, Protein 19 g, Carbs 0.5 g, Fat 0.5 g

55. Beef Soup

INGREDIENTS (Servings: 4)

1-pound beef sirloin, chopped
4 oz. leek, chopped
1 tbsp. margarine
1 tsp. chili powder
1 potato, chopped
3 cups of water

DIRECTIONS (Ready in about: 52 min)

Pour the margarine into the saucepan and melt. Add the chopped sirloin, chili powder, and leek. Cook the ingredients for 4 minutes (for 2 minutes per side). After that add the chopped potato and water. Close the cover. Cook the beef soup for 40 minutes over medium heat.

Per serving: Kcal 228, Sodium 128 mg, Protein 36 g, Carbs 12 g, Fat 10 g

56. Beef Stew with Veggies

INGREDIENTS (Servings: 4)

4 large white or red-skinned potatoes (peeled and chunked)
3 tbsp. all-purpose flour
18 small boing onions (cut into 2 crosswise)
⅓ cup fresh flat-leaf parsley (minced)
3 cups salt-free vegetable stock
4 large carrots (peeled and chunked)
½ cup red wine (optional)
2 tbsp. olive oil
1 bay leaf
1-pound boneless lean beef stew meat (visible fat trimmed, cubed)
½ fennel bulb (trimmed and thinly sliced)
3 large shallots (chopped)
3 portobello mushrooms (cleaned with a brush, chunked)
2 fresh thyme sprigs
¾ tsp. ground black pepper (divided)

DIRECTIONS (Ready in about: 50 min)

Dredge meat in flour. Heat oil in a pan over medium flame. Cook beef until all sides are browned. Transfer to a plate and set aside. Reduce the stove's heat to medium. Add shallots and fennel to the pan. Sauté for 8 minutes or until lightly golden. Stir in bay leaf, thyme sprigs, and ¼ tsp. of pepper. Cook for a minute. Add the cooked beef, wine, and vegetable stock. Bring to a boil. Cover the pan and turn the heat to low. Simmer for 45 minutes or until the meat is tender. Stir in mushrooms, onions, potatoes, and carrots. Simmer for 30 minutes. Remove bay leaf and thyme sprigs. Add the rest of the pepper and parsley. Transfer to a bowl and serve at once.

Per serving: Kcal 244, Sodium 185 mg, Protein 31 g, Carbs 37 g, Fat 11 g

57. Carrot Soup

INGREDIENTS (Servings: 6)

10 carrots, scraped and sliced
1½ tbsp. sugar
2 cups of water
¼ tsp. ground black pepper
3 tbsp. all-purpose (plain) flour
¼ tsp. ground nutmeg
2 tbsp. chopped fresh parsley
4 cups fat-free milk

DIRECTIONS (Ready in about: 65 min)

In an enormous saucepan, heat the carrots, sugar, and water. Cover the saucepan with the mixture and simmer until the carrots become tender approximately 20 minutes. Drain the carrots, reserving some of the liquid, and set them aside. In another saucepan over medium-high heat, combine the flour, pepper, nutmeg, and milk. Cook, constantly stirring, until the white sauce thickens. Add the cooked carrots and white sauce. Blend until smooth. Add the reserved liquid to the desired consistency. Pour into separate bowls and garnish each with 1 tsp. of parsley. Serve immediately.

Per serving: Kcal 124, Sodium 140 mg, Protein 7 g, Carbs 24 g

58. Chickpea and Tomato Soup

INGREDIENTS (Servings: 6)

¼ cup of fresh cilantro or parsley (chopped)
¼ tsp. hot pepper sauce
¼ cup red onion (chopped)
1 cup cherry tomatoes (quartered)
¼ cup lime juice
½ cup cucumber (seeded and chopped)
3 garlic cloves (minced)
6 cups unsalted vegetable juice
6 lime wedges
1 15 oz. can chickpeas (rinsed and drained)

DIRECTIONS (Ready in about: 40 min)

Put the lime juice, garlic, hot pepper sauce, cilantro, onion, cucumber, tomatoes, vegetable juice, and chickpeas in a bowl. Mix until combined. The bowl should be covered and chill in the fridge for at least an hour. Scoop in chilled individual bowls and top with a lime wedge before serving.

Per serving: Kcal 125, Sodium 156 mg, Protein 13 g, Carbs 51 g, Fat 4 g

59. Cod and Corn Chowder

INGREDIENTS (Servings: 6)

1 tsp. canola oil
2 reduced-sodium bacon strips, cut into 1-inch pieces
1 small yellow onion, chopped
2 celery ribs, cut into ½-inch dice
½ large red bell pepper, cored and cut into ½-inch dice
3 tbsp. all-purpose flour
3 cups Homemade Chicken Broth or canned low-sodium chicken broth 1½
2 cups low-fat (1%) milk
½ tsp. kosher salt
⅛ tsp. freshly ground black pepper
Pinch of dried thyme
2 cups fresh or thawed frozen corn kernels
Chopped fresh parsley
1 tsp. canola oil
2 reduced-sodium bacon strips, cut into 1-inch pieces
1 small yellow onion, chopped
2 celery ribs, cut into ½-inch dice
½ large red bell pepper, cored and cut into ½-inch dice
3 tbsp. all-purpose flour
3 cups Homemade Chicken Broth or canned low-sodium chicken broth 1½
2 cups low-fat (1%) milk
½ tsp. kosher salt
1-pound skinless cod fillets, cut into bite-sized pieces
1-pound skinless cod fillets, cut into bite-sized pieces
⅛ tsp. freshly ground black pepper
Pinch of dried thyme
2 cups fresh or thawed frozen corn kernels
Chopped fresh parsley

DIRECTIONS (Ready in about: 60 min)

Heat the oil in a big saucepan over medium heat. Cook the bacon, occasionally stirring, until golden, about 6 minutes. With a slotted spoon, transfer the bacon to paper towels to drain, leaving the fat in the pot. Add the onion, celery, and red pepper to the pot and cook over medium heat, occasionally stirring, until just tender, about 5 minutes. Sprinkle with flour and mix for 30 seconds. Combine the broth, milk, salt, pepper, and thyme and bring to a boil. Reduce heat to medium-low and simmer to combine flavors, about 15 minutes. Add the cod, bacon, and corn and cook until the cod is opaque about 5 minutes. Pour the ladle into the bowls, sprinkle with parsley, and serve hot.

Per serving: Kcal 215, Sodium 390 mg, Protein 21 g, Carbs 23 g, Fat 4 g

60. Creamy Asparagus Soup

INGREDIENTS (Servings: 6)

2 cups peeled and diced potatoes
½ pound fresh asparagus, cut into ¼-inch pieces
½ cup chopped onion
2 stalks celery, chopped
Black pepper, to taste
4 cups of water
2 tbsp. butter
½ cup whole-wheat (whole-meal) flour
1½ cups fat-free milk
Lemon zest, to taste

DIRECTIONS (Ready in about: 40 min)

In an enormous saucepan over high heat, combine the potatoes, asparagus, onions, celery, and water. Bring to a boil. Reduce heat, cover, and simmer until vegetables are tender for about 15 minutes. Add the butter. In a small bowl, combine the flour and milk. Slowly pour the mixture into the pot, stirring constantly. Boost the heat to medium-high and continue stirring until the soup thickens for about 5 minutes. Keep away from heat. Season with lemon zest and split black pepper to taste. Serve in hot bowls.

Per serving: Kcal 140, Sodium 76 mg, Protein 6 g, Carbs 22 g, Fat 4 g

61. Cream of Wild Rice Hot Dish

INGREDIENTS (Servings: 4)

1 cup diced celery
2 cloves garlic, minced
1 cup diced carrot
½ tbsp. canola oil
1½ cups diced yellow onion
1 tsp. fennel seeds, crushed
2 cups 1 percent milk
1 tbsp. minced parsley
2 cups low-sodium vegetable stock
1½ cups chopped kale
1 cup unsalted prepared white beans
1 tsp. ground black pepper
½ cup wild rice, cooked

DIRECTIONS (Ready in about: 50 min)

Warm the oil in a soup pot over medium flame. Add garlic, celery, carrot, and onion. Cook until browned while constantly stirring. Add spices, stock, parsley, and kale. Stir and bring to a boil. Put milk and beans in a food processor. Process until pureed. Transfer to a pot with soup. Add rice and simmer for half an hour.

Per serving: Kcal 236, Sodium 180 mg, Protein 25 g, Carbs 19 g, Fat 25 g

62. Curried Cream Tomato Soup

INGREDIENTS (Servings: 8)

2 tbsp. olive oil
1½ cups chopped onion
1 cup finely chopped celery
1 tsp. minced garlic
1 tbsp. curry powder, or to taste
3 cups canned tomatoes, drained
1 bay leaf
½ tsp. thyme
Black pepper, to taste
1 cup long-grain brown rice
6 cups low-sodium vegetable broth
1 cup fat-free milk
1½ cups apple cubes

DIRECTIONS (Ready in about: 55 min)

In an enormous saucepan, heat the oil over medium heat. Add the chopped onion, celery, and garlic. Sauté until tender, about 4 minutes. Add the curry powder and cook, stirring for about 1 minute. Add the tomatoes, bay leaf, thyme, black pepper, and rice. Stir constantly while bringing to a boil. Add the broth. Heat up to the point of boiling again and simmer for approximately 30 minutes. When the rice is tender, remove the bay leaf. Pour the soup into a food processor or blender and beat until smooth. Return the soup to the pot and add the milk and the apple cubes. Cook until heated through. Serve in individual hot bowls immediately.

Per serving: Kcal 205, Sodium 89 mg, Protein 8 g, Carbs 32.5 g, Fat 5 g

63. Curried Lentil Soup

INGREDIENTS (Servings: 6)

2 tbsp. olive oil
1 medium onion, diced
1 large carrot, diced
1 celery stalk, diced
2 tbsp. curry powder
6 cups vegetable broth
1½ cups dried lentils
½ tsp. salt
Freshly ground black pepper, to taste
1 can coconut milk
3 cloves garlic, minced

DIRECTIONS (Ready in about: 70 min)

In an enormous saucepan, heat oil over medium heat. Add onion, carrot, celery, and garlic and sauté, frequently stirring, until just tender, about 5 to 6 minutes. Add the curry powder and mix for another minute. Add the broth, lentils, salt, and pepper. Stir and bring to a boil over high heat. Cover, lower the heat, and cook until lentils are tender (35 to 40 minutes). Using an immersion blender, blend the soup to desired consistency. Mix the coconut milk. Reheat gently over medium-low heat until warm.

Per serving: Kcal 400, Sodium 302 mg, Protein 19 g, Carbs 39 g, Fat 20 g

64. Easy Kale and White Bean Soup

INGREDIENTS (Servings: 8)

2 tbsp. olive oil
1 medium onion, diced
2 medium carrots, diced
2 celery stalks, diced
3 garlic cloves, minced
½ tsp. red pepper flakes
1 tbsp. rosemary
6 cups chicken broth
2 cans (15 oz.) white beans with liquid
2 bay leaves
2 cups kale, chopped
Freshly ground black pepper, to taste
Parmesan cheese, grated, for serving

DIRECTIONS (Ready in about: 30 min)

In an enormous saucepan, heat olive oil over medium-high heat. Add the onions, carrots, celery, and garlic and cook, frequently stirring, for 3-4 min. until tender. Add the red pepper flakes, rosemary, chicken broth, beans, and bay leaves. Lower the heat and bring to a boil. Reduce the heat to low, add the cabbage and simmer for 15 min. Remove the bay leaves. Transfer two cups of the soup to a blender and beat until smooth. Return to the pan and mix. Season with ground black pepper and Parmesan cheese.

Per serving: Kcal 260, Sodium 420 mg, Protein 26 g, Carbs 70 g, Fat 6 g

65. Easy Vegetable Stock

INGREDIENTS (Servings: 6)

12 fresh white mushrooms, brushed clean and coarsely chopped
3 tsp. olive oil
1 large yellow onion, cut into 1-inch pieces
2 celery stalks with leaves, cut into 1-inch pieces
3 large carrots, cut into 1-inch pieces
6 cloves garlic, halved
6 fresh flat-leaf parsley sprigs
8 cups of water
4 fresh thyme sprigs
⅛ tsp. salt
1 bay leaf

DIRECTIONS (Ready in about: 50 min)

In an enormous saucepan, heat 2 tsp. of olive oil over medium-high heat. Add the mushrooms and sauté until just starting to brown 4-5 minutes. Shift the mushrooms to the side of the pan and add the remaining tsp. of oil, onion, carrots, celery, and garlic. Increase the heat and sauté, frequently stirring, until the vegetables are golden brown, about 10 minutes. Add the parsley, water, thyme, salt, and bay leaf. Bring to a boil, then lower the heat to medium-low and simmer, uncovered, for 25 to 30 minutes. Take it away from the heat and let cool slightly. Carefully strain the broth into a container through a colander or sieve lined with paper towels or gauze (muslin). Use immediately, cover, and refrigerate for up to 3 days or freeze in airtight containers for up to 3 months. Makes about 6 cups.

Per serving: Kcal 22, Sodium 94 mg, Protein 0 g, Carbs 1 g, Fat 7 g

66. Fire-Roasted Corn Soup

INGREDIENTS (Servings: 12)

4 cups corn kernels
1½ tbsp. olive oil
3 cups chopped onion
2 cups chopped carrots
2 cups chopped celery
2 tsp. chopped garlic
¼ cup all-purpose flour
1 tbsp. chopped parsley
1 tsp. cumin
6 cups vegetable stock
2 jalapeno peppers, minced
1½ cups half-and-half
1 tsp. salt
⅛ tsp. white pepper

DIRECTIONS (Ready in about: 85 min)

Heat oven to 500°F. Place the corn kernels on a baking sheet. Bake until they start to caramelize, about 8 minutes. In an enormous saucepan, heat oil over medium-high heat. Add the onion, carrots, celery, and garlic, stirring constantly. Cook until vegetables are tender, about 5 minutes. Reduce the heat and add corn, flour, and cumin. Stir until the flour is evenly dispersed. Add the vegetable broth and jalapeño peppers and simmer for about 30 minutes. Combine half and half, salt, pepper, and parsley. Remove from the heat and serve.

Per serving: Kcal 119, Sodium 184 mg, Protein 3 g, Carbs 17 g, Fat 0.5 g

67. Gazpacho with Chickpeas

INGREDIENTS (Servings: 6)

6 cups unsalted vegetable juice
1 can (15 oz.) chickpeas, rinsed and drained
1 cup (about 16) cherry tomatoes, quartered
¼ cup chopped red onion
½ cup chopped, seeded cucumber
¼ cup of chopped fresh cilantro or parsley
1-3 garlic cloves, minced
¼ tsp. hot pepper sauce
¼ cup lime juice
6 lime wedges

DIRECTIONS (Ready in about: 70 min)

In an enormous bowl, add the chickpeas, vegetable juice, tomatoes, cucumber, onion, cilantro, chili sauce, garlic, and lime juice and mix them very well. Cover and refrigerate until chilled or for at least 1 hour. To serve, pour the chilled soup into individual chilled bowls and garnish with a lemon wedge. Serve immediately.

Per serving: Kcal 125, Sodium 156 mg, Protein 7 g, Carbs 24 g, Fat 1 g

68. Greek Lemon-Drop Soup

INGREDIENTS (Servings: 6)

6 cups low-sodium chicken broth
3 chicken breast halves, skinless, cooked, and shredded
2 eggs
⅓ cup lemon juice
Lemon slices, for garnish
¾ cup long-grain rice

DIRECTIONS (Ready in about: 40 min)
In a large pot, bring the chicken broth and rice to a boil. Just reduce the heat, cover the pot and simmer for 15 minutes. Add the chicken and simmer for another 2-3 minutes. Keep away from heat. In a bowl, whisk together the eggs and lemon juice. Slowly add 1 cup of hot soup broth, stirring constantly. Add the hot egg mixture to the pot and stir to combine. Serve with a lemon wedge.
Per serving: Kcal 315, Sodium 180 mg, Protein 28 g, Carbs 36 g, Fat 7 g

69. Green Beans Soup

INGREDIENTS (Servings: 4)
- 2 garlic cloves, minced
- 2 tsp. olive oil
- 1-pound green beans trimmed and halved
- 2 tomatoes, cubed
- 1 yellow onion, chopped
- 1 tsp. sweet paprika
- 2 tbsp. parsley, chopped
- 1-quart low-sodium chicken stock

DIRECTIONS (Ready in about: 30 min)
Heat up a pot with the oil over medium-high heat, add the garlic and the onion, stir and sauté for 5 minutes. Add the green beans and the other ingredients except for the parsley, stir, bring to a simmer and cook for 20 minutes. Add the parsley, stir, divide the soup into bowls and serve.
Per serving: Kcal 87, Sodium 245 mg, Protein 4 g, Carbs 14 g, Fat 2.5 g

70. Green Bean and Tomato Soup

INGREDIENTS (Servings: 9)
- ½ tsp. salt
- ¼ tsp. pepper
- ¼ cup fresh basil (minced)
- 1 garlic clove (minced)
- 3 cups fresh tomatoes (diced)
- 1 cup chopped onion
- 1-pound fresh green beans (cut into smaller pieces)
- 2 tsp. butter
- 6 cups vegetable or chicken broth (reduced sodium)
- 1 cup chopped carrots

DIRECTIONS (Ready in about: 50 min)
Melt butter in a pan over medium flame. Add carrots and onion and cook for 5 minutes. Add garlic, beans, and broth. Bring to a boil. Lower the heat and cover the pan. Simmer for 20 minutes. Add salt, pepper, basil, and tomatoes. Cover the pan and simmer for 5 more minutes.

71. Green Detox Soup

INGREDIENTS (Servings: 2)
- 1 large zucchini, chopped
- 1 tsp. fresh mint, chopped
- ½ cup celery stalk, chopped
- 1 tsp. ground paprika
- 1 tbsp. olive oil
- 2 tbsp. lime juice
- 1 cup low-fat yogurt
- 1 onion, diced

DIRECTIONS (Ready in about: 22 min)
Heat the olive oil in the pan. Include the chopped onion and cook for 2 minutes. Mix it very well. Add the zucchini, mint, and celery stalk. Cook the vegetables for 10 minutes. Mix them from time to time. Then add the lemon juice and ground paprika. Mix the vegetables with the hand mixer and remove them from the heat. Add the yogurt and mix the soup well.
Per serving: Kcal 103, Sodium 64 mg, Protein 5 g, Carbs 11 g, Fat 5 g

72. Grilled Tomatoes Soup

INGREDIENTS (Servings: 4)
- 2-pounds tomatoes
- ½ cup shallot, chopped
- 1 tbsp. avocado oil
- ½ tsp. black pepper
- ¼ tsp. minced garlic
- 1 tbsp. dried basil
- 3 cups low-sodium chicken broth

DIRECTIONS (Ready in about: 30 min)
Cut the tomatoes in half and grill on the preheated 390°F grill for 1 minute per side. After that, transfer the roasted tomatoes to the blender and beat until smooth. Place the shallot and avocado oil in the pan and grill until golden brown. Add the mixed roasted tomatoes, ground black pepper, and minced garlic. Bring the soup to a boil and sprinkle with dried basil. Simmer the soup for another 2 minutes.
Per serving: Kcal 415, Sodium 204 mg, Protein 14 g, Carbs 8 g, Fat 39 g

73. Hearty Beef and Vegetable Soup

INGREDIENTS (Servings: 8)
- 1 tbsp. vegetable oil
- 1 large yellow onion, chopped (2 cups)
- 2 medium carrots, cut into ½-inch dice
- 1 bay leaf
- 1 tsp. kosher salt
- 1 (14.5 oz.) can no-salt-added canned diced tomatoes in juice, undrained
- ½ tsp. freshly ground black pepper
- ½ tsp. dried thyme

2 tbsp. chopped fresh parsley
2 big celery ribs, cut into ½-inch dice
2 medium parsnips, cut into ½-inch dice
1½ pounds ground sirloin
1-quart Homemade Beef Stock or canned low-sodium beef broth
2 cups water

DIRECTIONS (Ready in about: 60 min)
Heat the oil in a big saucepan over medium heat. Add the onion, carrots, celery, and parsnip and cook, occasionally stirring, until the onion is tender, about 5 minutes. Place the vegetables on the side of the pan. Place the meat on the empty side of the pot and cook, stirring occasionally and breaking up the meat with the side of a spoon, until the meat loses its raw appearance, about 5 minutes. Mix the meat and the vegetables. Mix the broth, water, tomatoes with their juice, parsley, salt, pepper, thyme, and bay leaf. Bring to a boil over high heat. Reduce the heat to medium-low and simmer until the vegetables are tender about 20 minutes. Discard the bay leaf. Pour into bowls and serve hot.

Per serving: Kcal 217, Sodium 395 mg, Protein 22 g, Carbs 17 g, Fat 7 g

74. Hearty Ginger Soup

INGREDIENTS (Servings: 4)
3 cups coconut almond milk
½ pound boneless chicken breast halves, cut into chunks
3 tbsp. fresh ginger root, minced
2 tbsp. fish sauce
¼ cup fresh lime juice
2 tbsp. green onions, sliced
1 tbsp. fresh cilantro, chopped
2 cups of water

DIRECTIONS (Ready in about: 10 min)
Take a saucepan and add the coconut and almond milk and water. Bring the mixture to a boil and add the chicken strips. Reduce the heat to medium and simmer for 3 minutes. Add the ginger, lemon juice, and fish sauce. Sprinkle with green onions and cilantro and serve.

Per serving: Kcal 415, Sodium 200 mg, Protein 14.5 g, Carbs 8 g, Fat 39 g

75. Home-Style Turkey Soup

INGREDIENTS (Servings: 10)

For the Broth:
4 cups water
8 cups low-sodium chicken broth
1 turkey carcass
3 large onions, 1 quart. and 3 chopped

For the Soup:
4 carrots, peeled and cut into thin strips
1 cup chopped celery
¼ tsp. dried thyme
¼ cup chopped fresh parsley
1 bay leaf
¼ cup uncooked pearl barley
½ tsp. ground black pepper
1 can (14 oz.) unsalted tomatoes
½ pound of leftover light turkey meat, cut into bite-size chunks
1 can (16 oz.) of white beans, rinsed and drained
1 onion, chopped

DIRECTIONS (Ready in about: 2 h 45 min)
In a large saucepan, combine the turkey carcass, water, broth, and onion cut into quarters. Bring to a boil over high heat. Reduce the warmth, cover, and simmer for 1 hour. Filter the mixture, removing the carcass and onion. Cool the liquid in the refrigerator, overnight if possible, and skim the fat from the surface of the broth. Return the liquid to the pot. Add the soup ingredients to the broth mixture. Heat up the mixture to the point of boiling and cook, covered, for about 1 hour. Pour into individual bowls and serve immediately.

Per serving: Kcal 178, Sodium 131 mg, Protein 15 g, Carbs 25 g, Fat 2 g

76. Ingenious Eggplant Soup

INGREDIENTS (Servings: 4)
1 large eggplant, washed and cubed
1 tomato, seeded and chopped
2 tbsp. parsley, chopped
½ cup parmesan cheese, crumbled
2 tbsp. extra virgin olive oil
2 tbsp. distilled white vinegar
Sunflower seeds as needed
1 small onion, diced

DIRECTIONS (Ready in about: 35 min)
Preheat your outdoor grill to medium-high heat. Punch the eggplant several times with a knife/fork. Cook the eggplants on the grill for about 15 minutes until they are charred. Set them aside and let them cool. Remove the skin from the eggplant and cut the pulp into cubes. Transfer the pulp to a bowl and add the parsley, onion, tomato, olive oil, parmesan cheese, and vinegar. Mix well and let cool for 1 hour. Sprinkle with sunflower seeds and enjoy!

Per serving: Kcal 99, Sodium 163 mg, Protein 3.5 g, Carbs 7 g, Fat 7 g

77. Lentil and Sausage Soup

INGREDIENTS (Servings: 15)

1 tbsp. olive oil
1 large yellow onion, chopped (2 cups)
2 medium celery ribs, chopped
2 medium carrots, chopped
4 cloves garlic, minced
1-pound lentils, sorted, rinsed, and drained
1 pound of sweet or hot turkey sausage, casings removed
1 tsp. kosher salt
¼ Homemade Chicken Broth or canned low-sodium chicken broth 1-quart water, plus more as needed
½ tsp. dried rosemary
½ tsp. crushed hot red pepper
1 can (14.5 oz.) no-salt-added diced tomatoes in juice, undrained 2 cups wholewheat rotini or other tubular pasta

DIRECTIONS (Ready in about: 2 h)
Heat the oil in a big saucepan over medium heat. Add the onion, carrots, celery, and garlic and cook, occasionally stirring, until just tender, about 5 minutes. Include the turkey sausage and cook, stirring occasionally and breaking the meat with the side of a wooden spoon, until the sausage loses its raw appearance, about 6 minutes. Combine the lentils, broth, water, rosemary, salt, and pepper and bring to a boil over high heat. Reduce heat and simmer, occasionally stirring, until lentils are tender, about 45 minutes. Include the tomatoes and their juice and simmer until the lentils are tender, adding enough hot water to just barely cover the lentils, about 45 more minutes. Add up enough hot water to cover the lentils by ½ inch and bring to a boil. Add the pasta and cook until the pasta is very tender about 15 minutes. Pour the ladle into the bowls and serve hot.

Per serving: Kcal 271, Sodium 619 mg, Protein 19 g, Carbs 34 g, Fat 7 g

78. Lentil Soup

INGREDIENTS (Servings: 4)

½ onion, diced
1 cup lentils
7 cups chicken broth
1 tsp. chili flakes
½ tsp. chili powder
1 bell pepper, chopped
1 tbsp. margarine
1 tbsp. tomato paste

DIRECTIONS (Ready in about: 30 min)
Pour the margarine into the saucepan and melt it. Then add the pepper and onion. Cook the vegetables until the onion is lightly browned. Then add the lentils and the tomato paste. Mix the ingredients. Add the chicken broth, chili powder, and chili flakes. Stir the soup well and close the lid. Cook the soup for 15 minutes over medium heat.

Per serving: Kcal 240, Sodium 167 mg, Protein 16.5 g, Carbs 35 g, Fat 3.5 g

79. Low Sodium Vegetable Soup

INGREDIENTS (Servings: 3)

3 cups low-sodium vegetable broth
½ cup spinach, chopped
⅓ cup broccoli, chopped
2 potatoes, chopped
¼ cup low-fat yogurt
2 oz. green beans, cooked
1 tsp. cayenne pepper
1 tomato, roughly chopped

DIRECTIONS (Ready in about: 25 min)
In an enormous bowl, add the chickpeas, vegetable juice, tomatoes, cucumber, onion, cilantro, chili sauce, garlic, and lime juice and mix them very well. Cover and refrigerate until chilled or for at least 1 hour. To serve, pour the chilled soup into individual chilled bowls and garnish with a lemon wedge. Serve immediately.

Per serving: Kcal 144, Sodium 102 mg, Protein 6.5 g, Carbs 28 g, Fat 0.5 g

80. Minestrone Soup

INGREDIENTS (Servings: 4)

½ cup chopped onion
1 tbsp. olive oil
⅓ cup chopped celery
1 garlic clove, minced
1 carrot, diced
4 cups fat-free, low-sodium chicken broth
½ cup chopped spinach
2 large tomatoes, seeded and chopped
1 can (16 oz.) no-salt-added kidney beans, drained
1 small zucchini, diced (about 1 cup)
2 tbsp. chopped fresh basil
½ cup uncooked whole grain small shell pasta

DIRECTIONS (Ready in about: 45 min)
In an enormous saucepan, heat olive oil over medium heat. Add the onion, celery, and carrots. Sauté until tender, about 5 minutes. Include the garlic and cook for another minute. Combine the broth, tomatoes, spinach, beans, and pasta. Bring to a boil over high heat. Reduce the heat and simmer for 10 minutes and add the zucchini. Cover and cook for another 5 minutes. Take it away from the heat and add the basil. Pour into individual bowls and serve immediately.
Per serving: Kcal 200, Sodium 99 mg, Protein 11 g, Carbs 30.5 g, Fat 4 g

81. Mixed Greens Soup

INGREDIENTS (Servings: 6)
1 medium onion, diced
2 slices bacon, diced
2 cloves garlic, minced
4 cups low-sodium chicken broth
¼ tsp. black pepper
¼ tsp. kosher salt
3 cups chopped combined greens (spinach, collards, turnip greens, Swiss chard, or others)
4 cups water

DIRECTIONS (Ready in about: 40 min)
In an enormous pot over medium-high heat, add the bacon, and stir until cooked but not crisp, 4 to 6 minutes. Add the onion and cook, stirring, until translucent, 2 to 3 minutes. Add the garlic and the greens, and cook briefly until the garlic is golden and the greens are wilted for 1 to 2 minutes. Add the chicken broth, water, salt, and pepper. Increase the pressure of the heat to high and bring the soup to a boil. Reduce the heat, and simmer until the flavors have melded about 15 to 20 minutes. Carefully transfer half of the soup to a food processor. Puree until smooth, about 1 minute. Return the pureed soup to the pot. Season to taste, and reheat the soup if necessary
Per serving: Kcal 41, Sodium 333 mg, Protein 4 g, Carbs 4 g, Fat 1 g

82. Mushroom Barley Soup

INGREDIENTS (Servings: 9)
1 tbsp. canola oil
1½ cups chopped onions
1 cup sliced mushrooms
¾ cup chopped carrots
1 tsp. dried thyme
⅛ tsp. black pepper
½ tsp. chopped garlic
8 cups vegetable stock
½ small potato, chopped
¼ cup thinly sliced onions
¾ cup pearl barley
3 oz. dry sherry

DIRECTIONS (Ready in about: 1 h 25 min)
In an enormous saucepan, heat oil over medium-high heat. Add the onion, mushrooms, carrot, thyme, bell pepper, and garlic. Sauté until onion becomes translucent, about 5 minutes. Add the vegetable broth and barley and bring to a boil. Reduce the heat and simmer for about 20 minutes or until the barley is tender. Add the sherry and the potatoes. For about 15 minutes, continue to boil until the potato is fully cooked. Garnish with chopped green onions and serve.
Per serving: Kcal 121, Sodium 112 mg, Protein 4 g, Carbs 19 g, Fat 7 g

83. Potato Leek Soup

INGREDIENTS (Servings: 8)
2 tbsp. olive oil
3 leeks, washed and sliced
¼ tsp. red pepper flakes
6 cups water (could substitute with low-sodium chicken broth)
1¼ pounds golden Yukon potatoes, peeled and cubed
2 bay leaves
⅛ tsp. of salt
Black pepper, to taste
1 tsp. thyme

DIRECTIONS (Ready in about: 60 min)
In an enormous saucepan, heat olive oil over medium heat. Add the leeks and sauté for 5 to 6 minutes, until the leeks are tender and wilted. Add thyme and red pepper, mix. Add the water, potatoes, and bay leaf. Bring to a boil. Cover, reduce heat, and simmer until potatoes are tender for about 20 minutes. Remove the bay leaves and discard them. Season with salt and black pepper. Using an immersion blender, blend the soup to desired consistency. It can also be mixed, in batches of 2 cups, in the blender.
Per serving: Kcal 150, Sodium 161 mg, Protein 9 g, Carbs 24 g, Fat 6 g

84. Potato-Fennel Soup

INGREDIENTS (Servings: 8)
1 tsp. olive oil
1 large fennel bulb, chopped
1 cup chopped red onion
2 large russet potatoes, peeled and sliced
1 cup fat-free milk
2 tsp. lemon juice
2 tsp. fennel seeds, toasted
3 cups low-sodium chicken broth

DIRECTIONS (Ready in about: 55 min)
In an enormous saucepan, heat olive oil over medium heat. Add the fennel and onion. Sauté until vegetables are tender, about 5 minutes. Add the potatoes, chicken broth, milk, and lemon juice. Cover, reduce heat and cook until potatoes are tender about 15 minutes. In a blender or food processor, beat the soup in batches until smooth. Fill the blender or food processor at most ⅓ full to avoid burns. Return the soup to the pot and heat until heated through. Pour into individual bowls and garnish with toasted fennel seeds. Serve immediately.
Per Serving: Kcal 149, Sodium 104 mg, Protein 6 g, Carbs 28 g, Fat 1.5 g

85. Pumpkin Cream Soup

INGREDIENTS (Servings: 5)

1-pound pumpkin, chopped	1 tsp. ground turmeric
1 tsp. ground cumin	½ tsp. ground nutmeg
½ cup cauliflower, chopped	1 tbsp. fresh dill, chopped
4 cups of water	1 tsp. olive oil
	½ cup skim milk

DIRECTIONS (Ready in about: 30 min)
Grill the pumpkin with olive oil in the pan for 3 minutes. Then mix well and add the cauliflower, cumin, turmeric, nutmeg, and water. Close the lid and cook the soup over medium heat for 15 minutes or until the squash is tender. Then beat the mixture until smooth and add the skimmed milk. Remove the soup from the heat and top with the dill.
Per serving: Kcal 56, Sodium 28 mg, Protein 2 g, Carbs 10 g, Fat 1.5 g

86. Pumpkin Soup

INGREDIENTS (Servings: 4)

¾ cup water, divided	½ tsp. ground cinnamon
1 small onion, chopped	½ tsp. ground nutmeg
1 can (15 oz.) pumpkin puree	1 cup fat-free milk
2 cups unsalted vegetable broth	⅛ tsp. black pepper
	1 green onion top, chopped

DIRECTIONS (Ready in about: 75 min)
In a big pot, heat ¼ cup of water over medium heat. Include the onion and cook until tender, about 3 minutes. Do not let the onion dry out. Add the remaining water, pumpkin, broth, cinnamon and nutmeg. Bring to a boil, lower the heat and simmer for 5 minutes. Add milk and cook until heated through. Do not boil. Garnish with black pepper and green onions and pour the soup into serving bowls. Serve immediately.
Per serving: Kcal 77, Sodium 58 mg, Protein 3 g, Carbs 14 g, Fat 1 g

87. Quibebe Soup

INGREDIENTS (Servings: 8)

1 tbsp. olive oil	1 butternut squash, cubed
2 cups chopped onions	¾ tsp. salt
1½ cups diced tomatoes	¾ tsp. ground black pepper
2 Fresno chili peppers, chopped	½ tsp. sugar
1½ garlic cloves, diced	2½ tbsp. chopped fresh parsley
8 cups low-sodium vegetable stock	

DIRECTIONS (Ready in about: 25 min)
In an enormous saucepan over medium heat, add the oil. Sauté onions, tomatoes, Fresno peppers, and garlic for about 15 minutes, stirring frequently. Add the vegetable broth and pumpkin. Bring the mix to a boil on low heat and simmer. Once the squash is tender (about 15 minutes), place the soup in a small blender and beat until smooth. Return the soup to the pot. Combine the salt, pepper, and sugar. Sprinkle with parsley before serving.
Per serving: Kcal 106, Sodium 280 mg, Protein 2 g, Carbs 12 g, Fat 4 g

88. Roasted Squash Soup

INGREDIENTS (Servings: 4)

1 small butternut squash, cut into half-inch pieces	2 cloves garlic, minced
2 tsp. canola oil, divided	1 cup diced carrot
1 cup diced celery	4 cups unsalted vegetable stock
1½ cups diced yellow onion	1 tsp. sage
1½ cups spinach	½ tsp. nutmeg
	1 tsp. black pepper

DIRECTIONS (Ready in about: 1 h 25 min)
Heat up the oven to 400°F. In a roasting pan, toss the pumpkin with 1 tsp. of oil. Bake for 40 minutes or until golden brown. Set aside. In a large saucepan, add the remaining oil, celery, onion, spinach, garlic, and carrot.

Sauté over medium heat until the vegetables are lightly browned. Add the broth, sage, nutmeg, pepper, and roasted pumpkin to the pot and simmer for a few minutes. Mix the soup well with an immersion blender or mix the soup in batches in a blender or food processor. Return the mashed soup to the pot and bring it to a boil. Serve immediately.
Per serving: Kcal 213, Sodium 139 mg, Protein 5 g, Carb 37 g, Fat 7 g

89. Sausage Minestrone with Kale
INGREDIENTS (Servings: 8)
1¼ pounds sweet turkey sausage, casings removed
1 large yellow onion, chopped
2 medium carrots, cut into ½-inch dice
2 medium celery ribs, cut into ½-inch dice
2 medium zucchini, trimmed and cut into ½-inch dice
2 cloves garlic, minced
1 (15 oz.) can no-salt-added cannellini beans, drained and rinsed
1-quart Homemade Chicken Broth 2 cups of water
1 (14.5 oz.) can no-salt-added diced tomatoes in juice, undrained
1 tsp. dried oregano
½ tsp. crushed hot red pepper
1 bay leaf
4 packed cups thinly sliced black kale (wash well and remove tough stems before slicing)
1 tbsp. olive oil

DIRECTIONS (Ready in about: 60 min)
Heat the oil in a big saucepan over medium heat. Include the turkey sausage and cook, stirring occasionally and breaking up the sausage with the side of a wooden spoon, until the sausage loses its raw appearance, about 6 minutes. Add onion, carrots, celery, zucchini, and garlic and cook, occasionally stirring, until onion is tender, about 5 minutes. Combine the broth, water, tomatoes with their juice, oregano, red pepper, and bay leaf and bring to a boil over high heat. Lower the warmth and simmer for 30 minutes. Add the cabbage and beans and simmer until the vegetables are very tender, about 15 minutes more. Discard the bay leaf. Pour the ladle into the bowls and serve hot.
Per serving: Kcal 205, Sodium 659 mg, Protein 16 g, Carbs 19 g, Fat 8 g

90. Steamy Salmon Chowder
INGREDIENTS (Servings: 8)
1 tsp. olive oil
½ cup chopped celery
1 clove garlic, minced
1 15 oz. can reduced-sodium chicken broth
2½ cups frozen country-style hash browns with green pepper and onion
1 cup frozen peas and carrots
½ tsp. dill
½ tsp. ground pepper
6 oz. pouched or canned pink salmon (bones removed)
1 12 oz. can evaporate skim milk
1 can (14¾ oz.) no-salt-added, cream-style corn

DIRECTIONS (Ready in about: 55 min)
In an enormous saucepan over medium heat, brown the olive oil and celery for about 10 minutes. Include the garlic and sauté for another minute. Add the chicken broth, hash browns, peas and carrots, dill, and pepper, and bring to a boil. Reduce the heat and simmer, about 10 minutes, until the vegetables are cooked but not overcooked. Add the salmon and break it into pieces with a fork. Add evaporated milk and corn and cook until heated through. Serve hot.
Per serving: Kcal 166, Sodium 207 mg, Protein 11 g, Carbs 26 g, Fat 2.5 g

91. Summer Berry Soup
INGREDIENTS (Servings: 2)
½ cup apple juice
¼ cup strawberries
¼ cup raspberries
¼ cup blackberries
¼ cup blueberries
1 tsp. potato starch
¼ tsp. ground cinnamon

DIRECTIONS (Ready in about: 20 min)
Pour the apple juice into the saucepan. Add all the berries and ground cinnamon. Close the lid and bring the ingredients to a boil. Pour 3 tbsp. of the apple juice mixture into the glass, add the potato starch, and beat until smooth. Then pour the starch mixture into the berry soup and stir until the soup thickens. Close the lid and let the soup steep for 10 minutes. Serve.
Per serving: Kcal 71, Sodium 3 mg, Protein 0.5 g, Carbs 11 g, Fat 3 g

92. Sweet Black-Eyed Pea Soup

INGREDIENTS (Servings: 8)

1 tbsp. canola oil
1 (7 oz.) ham steak, cut into bite-sized pieces
1 large yellow onion, chopped
2 cloves garlic, minced
1-quart Homemade Chicken Broth
3 cups of water
½ tsp. salt
1-pound sweet potatoes (yams), peeled and cut into ½-inch dice
½ tsp. hot red pepper
4 packed cups thinly sliced collard greens (wash well and remove thick stems before slicing)
1 cup frozen black-eyed peas

DIRECTIONS (Ready in about: 80 min)

Heat the oil in a big saucepan over medium heat. Add the ham and cook, occasionally stirring, until lightly browned, about 3 minutes. Add onion and garlic and cook, constantly stirring, until onion is tender about 5 minutes. Add the broth, water, sweet potatoes, salt, and pepper and bring to a boil over high heat. Return the heat to medium and simmer until the sweet potatoes begin to soften for about 10 minutes. Add the collards and black-eyed peas and cook until the vegetables and sweet potatoes are tender, about 10 minutes more. Ladle into the bowls and serve hot.

Per serving: Kcal 172, Sodium 548 mg, Protein 11 g, Carbs 24 g, Fat 7 g

93. Turkey Bean Soup

INGREDIENTS (Servings: 6)

1-pound turkey breast
2 onions, chopped
1 clove garlic, minced
¼ cup ketchup
1 can (14.5 oz.) unsalted diced tomatoes
3 cubes low-sodium chicken bouillon
7 cups of water
1½ tsp. dried basil
¼ tsp. black pepper
2 cups shredded cabbage
1 can (15 oz.) unsalted cannellini beans, rinsed and drained
2 stalks celery, chopped

DIRECTIONS (Ready in about: 50 min)

In a large pot, cook the ground turkey, onion, celery, and garlic until the vegetables are tender and the turkey is cooked through. Add the ketchup, tomatoes, bouillon, water, basil, pepper, cabbage, and beans. Bring to a boil and lower the heat. Cover and simmer for 30 minutes and serve hot.

Per serving: Kcal 242, Sodium 204 mg, Protein 26 g, Carbs 30 g, Fat 2 g

94. Turkey Soup

INGREDIENTS (Servings: 3)

1 potato, diced
1 cup ground turkey
1 tsp. cayenne pepper
1 onion, diced
1 tbsp. olive oil
¼ carrot, diced
2 cups of water

DIRECTIONS (Ready in about: 35 min)

Heat the olive oil in the pan and add the chopped onion and carrot. Cook the vegetables for 3 minutes. Mix well and add the ground turkey and cayenne pepper. Add the chopped potato and mix the ingredients well. Cook them for another 2 minutes. Then add the water. Check if you put all the ingredients. Cover and cook the soup for approximately 20 minutes and serve hot.

Per serving: Kcal 187, Sodium 131 mg, Protein 14 g, Carbs 17 g, Fat 8 g

95. Vegetable Garbanzo Bean Stew

INGREDIENTS (Servings: 8)

3 cups butternut squash, cut into 1-inch cubes
3 large carrots, cut into ½-inch pieces
2 large onions, chopped
3 garlic cloves, minced
4 cups vegetable stock
1 cup red lentils
1 can (16 oz.) garbanzo beans, drained and rinsed
2 tbsp. tomato paste
2 tbsp. peeled and minced fresh ginger
2 tsp. ground cumin
1 tsp. turmeric
¼ tsp. saffron
1 tsp. ground pepper
¼ cup lemon juice
½ cup chopped roasted unsalted peanuts
½ cup chopped cilantro

DIRECTIONS (Ready in about: 5 h 25 min)

In a Dutch oven, slowly melt the vegetables (squash, carrots, onions, and garlic) over medium-low heat until the onions begin to brown. Add the vegetable broth and scrape the pieces of golden vegetables from the bottom of the pan. Add the lentils, tomato paste, and seasonings. Cover and cook over medium-low heat until the lentils and squash are tender (about 1 to 1 ½ hours). Stir it from time to time. At this point, transfer the ingredients to the slow cooker and cook for 4-6 hours over low heat. Combine the lemon juice and the chickpeas. Serve hot and top with chopped peanuts and cilantro.

Per serving: Kcal 287, Sodium 258 mg, Protein 13 g, Carbs 41 g, Fat 7.5 g

96. Vegetarian Chilli

INGREDIENTS (Servings: 8)

1 cup diced celery
2 cups diced onion
1 cup diced bell pepper
2 tbsp. water
2 cloves garlic, minced
2 diced Fresno peppers
2 quarts of crushed tomatoes (no salt added)
1 tbsp. dried oregano
2 cups of cooked pinto beans (no salt added; if canned, rinse underwater)
2 tbsp. ground cumin
1 tbsp. chipotle pepper (or smoked paprika)
1 tbsp. ground black pepper
1 tbsp. balsamic vinegar

DIRECTIONS (Ready in about: 2 h)

In a saucepan over low heat, cook the onion, celery, bell pepper, and garlic in 2 tbsp. of water until the onions turn translucent, about 10 minutes. Add the other ingredients. Close the cover and cook over low heat for 1 to 2 hours, stirring occasionally. If the chilli becomes too thick, dilute with a little water.

Per serving: Kcal 161, Sodium 116 mg, Protein 7 g, Carbs 31 g, Fat 1 g

97. White Chicken Chilli

INGREDIENTS (Servings: 8)

2 cans (15 oz. each) of low-sodium white beans, drained
1 can (10 oz.) white chunk chicken
1 can (14.5 oz.) of low sodium diced tomatoes
1 medium onion, chopped
4 cups low-sodium chicken broth
1 tsp. dried oregano
1 tsp. ground cumin
½ medium green pepper, chopped
2 garlic cloves, minced
1 medium red pepper, chopped
2 tsp. chili powder
Cayenne pepper, to taste
3 tbsp. chopped fresh cilantro
8 tbsp. shredded reduced-fat Monterey Jack cheese

DIRECTIONS (Ready in about: 50 min)

In a big pot, add the chicken, beans, tomatoes, and chicken broth. Cover and cook over medium heat. Meanwhile, spray a nonstick skillet with cooking spray. Add onions, peppers, and garlic and sauté until vegetables are tender, 3 to 5 minutes. Include the onion and pepper mixture in the pot. Add the chilli powder, cumin, oregano, and cayenne pepper to taste. Cook on low heat for approximately 10 minutes or until all the vegetables are tender. Pour into hot bowls. Sprinkle each serving with a tbsp. of cheese and garnish with cilantro. Serve hot.

Per serving: Kcal 212, Sodium 241 mg, Protein 19 g, Carbs 25 g, Fat 4 g

98. Wild Rice Mushroom Soup

INGREDIENTS (Servings: 4)

Half a white onion, chopped
¼ cup chopped celery
1½ cups of sliced fresh white mushrooms
¼ cup chopped carrots
½ cup of white wine, or ½ cup low-sodium, fat-free chicken broth
1 cup fat-free half-and-half
2½ cups of low-sodium, fat-free chicken broth
2 tbsp. flour
Black pepper
¼ tsp. dried thyme
1 cup cooked wild rice
1 tbsp. olive oil

DIRECTIONS (Ready in about: 60 min)

Put olive oil in a saucepan and bring to medium heat. Add the diced onion, celery, and carrots. Cook until tender. Add the mushrooms, white wine, and chicken broth. Cover and heat. In a bowl, combine half and half, flour, thyme, and pepper. Then add the cooked wild rice. Pour the rice mixture into a saucepan with the vegetables. Cook over medium heat. Stir continuously until thick and bubbly and serve hot.

Per serving: Kcal 170, Sodium 120 mg, Protein 8 g, Carbs 23 g, Fat 5 g

99. Zesty Tomato Soup

INGREDIENTS (Servings: 2)

1 can (10.5 oz.) of fat-free milk
1 can (10.5 oz.) of condensed low-sodium, low-fat tomato soup
2 tbsp. croutons
1½ tbsp. freshly grated Parmesan cheese
1 tbsp. chopped fresh basil or cilantro
1 medium tomato, chopped

DIRECTIONS (Ready in about: 25 min)

In a portable saucepan, add the soup and milk. Beat until smooth. Heat over medium heat for 7 to 10 minutes, stirring frequently. Add the chopped tomato and the herbs. Cook for another 5 minutes, stirring occasionally. Pour equal amounts into individual bowls and top each serving with 1 tbsp. croutons and 1½ tsp. Parmesan cheese. Serve immediately.

Per serving: Kcal 178, Sodium 221 mg, Protein 9 g, Carbs 31 g, Fat 2 g

100. Zucchini Noodles Soup

INGREDIENTS (Servings: 4)

4 cups low-sodium chicken stock
2 oz. fresh parsley, chopped
½ tsp. chilli flakes
1 oz. carrot, shredded
1 tsp. canola oil
2 zucchinis, trimmed

DIRECTIONS (Ready in about: 35 min)

Grill the carrot with the canola oil in the pan for 5 minutes over medium-low heat. Mix well and add the chicken broth. Bring the mixture to a boil. Meanwhile, prepare the zucchini noodles using the spiralizer. Add them to the hot soup liquid. Add the parsley and chilli flakes. Bring the soup to a boil and take it away from the heat. Let it stand for 10 minutes. Serve.

Per serving: Kcal 39, Sodium 158 mg, Protein 2 g, Carbs 5 g, Fat 1.5 g

SALADS

101. Ambrosia Toasted Almonds

INGREDIENTS (Servings: 8)

½ cup slivered almonds
½ cup unsweetened shredded coconut
1 small pineapple, cubed (about 3 cups)
5 oranges, segmented
2 tbsp. cream sherry
2 red apples, cored and diced
1 banana, halved lengthwise, peeled, and sliced crosswise
Fresh mint leaves for garnish

DIRECTIONS (Ready in about: 35 min)

Heat oven to 325°F. Spread almonds out on a baking sheet and bake, occasionally stirring, until golden and fragrant, about 10 minutes. Immediately transfer to a plate to cool. Add the coconut to the batter and bake, frequently stirring, until lightly browned, about 10 minutes. Immediately transfer to a plate to cool. In an enormous bowl, combine the pineapple, oranges, apples, banana, and sherry. Stir gently to mix well. Divide the fruit mixture evenly among the individual bowls. Sprinkle evenly with toasted almonds and coconut and garnish with mint. Serve immediately.

Per serving: Kcal 177, Sodium 2 mg, Protein 3 g, Carbs 30 g, Fat 5 g

102. Apple Blue Cheese Salad

INGREDIENTS (Servings: 4)

3 apples, peeled, cored, and cubed
1 tbsp. lemon juice
1 cup plain low-fat or nonfat yogurt, preferable Greek-style
¼ tsp. cayenne pepper
½ tsp. black pepper
⅓ cup blue cheese crumbled
⅓ cup pistachios

DIRECTIONS (Ready in about: 40 min)

Spot the apples in a bowl and sprinkle with lemon juice. Add yogurt and pepper to apples and toss to combine. Put in the refrigerator and let cool for at least 30 minutes. When ready to serve, add the blue cheese and pistachios and mix well.

Per serving: Kcal 200, Sodium 240 mg, Protein 8.5 g, Carbs 25 g, Fat 8 g

103. Apple Lettuce Salad

INGREDIENTS (Servings: 4)

¼ cup unsweetened apple juice
2 tbsp. lemon juice
1 tbsp. canola oil
2¼ tsp. brown sugar
½ tsp. Dijon mustard
¼ tsp. apple pie spice
1 medium red apple, chopped
8 cups mixed salad greens

DIRECTIONS (Ready in about: 20 min)

Combine apple juice, lemon juice, oil, brown sugar, mustard, and apple pie spice in a large bowl. Add the apple and toss to coat. Add the green salad and toss just before serving.

Per serving: Kcal 124, Sodium 45 mg, Protein 2 g, Carbs 20 g, Fat 4 g

104. Apple Salad with Figs

INGREDIENTS (Servings: 6)

6 dried figs, chopped
2 large red apples, cored and diced
2 carrots, peeled and grated
½ cup fat-free lemon yogurt
2 ribs of celery, diced
2 tbsp. slivered almonds

DIRECTIONS (Ready in about: 15 min)

In a portable bowl, combine the apples, figs, carrots, and celery. Add the yogurt and mix well. Top it with the slivered almonds and serve.

Per serving: Kcal 93, Sodium 33 mg, Protein 2 g, Carbs 19 g, Fat 1 g

105. Apple-Fennel Slaw

INGREDIENTS (Servings: 4)

1 medium-sized fennel bulb, thinly sliced
1 large Granny Smith apple, cored and thinly sliced
2 carrots, grated
2 tbsp. raisins
1 tsp. sugar
½ cup apple juice
2 tbsp. apple cider vinegar
4 lettuce leaves
1 tbsp. olive oil

39

DIRECTIONS (Ready in about: 25 min)
In an enormous bowl, combine the fennel, apple, carrots, and raisins to make the slaw. Drizzle with olive oil, cover, and refrigerate while you prepare the rest of the ingredients. In a saucepan, combine the sugar and apple juice. Put on medium heat and cook until reduced to about ¼ cup, about 10 minutes. Remove from heat and let cool. Include the apple cider vinegar. Pour the apple juice mixture over the slaw and mix well. Let cool completely. Serve on lettuce leaves.
Per serving: Kcal 124, Sodium 61 mg, Protein 2 g, Carbs 22 g, Fat 1 g

106. Arugula Peach Almond Salad

INGREDIENTS (Servings: 4)

1 tbsp. balsamic vinegar	3 ripe peaches, pitted and sliced
1 tbsp. olive oil, preferably extra-virgin	½ cup sliced natural almonds, toasted
1 tbsp. water	Freshly ground black pepper
⅛ tsp. of kosher salt	
6 cups baby arugula, well washed and dried	

DIRECTIONS (Ready in about: 5 min)
In an enormous bowl, combine the vinegar, oil, water, and salt. Add the arugula, peaches, and almonds and mix. Season with pepper and serve immediately.
Per serving: Kcal 152, Sodium 73 mg, Protein 4 g, Carbs 15 g, Fat 10 g

107. Asian Vegetable Salad

INGREDIENTS (Servings: 4)

½ cup julienned red bell pepper	1 tbsp. thinly sliced cilantro
1½ cup julienned bok choy	1 tbsp. minced garlic
½ cup julienned yellow onion	1½ tbsp. chopped cashews
1 cup thinly sliced red cabbage	1½ cups snow peas
1½ cup thinly sliced spinach	2 tsp. toasted sesame oil
	2 tsp. low-sodium soy sauce
	1½ cup julienned carrot

DIRECTIONS (Ready in about: 25 min)
Rinse all the vegetables under cold running water. Leave to drain. Julienne (cut into very thin strips like matches) carrot, pepper, bok choy, and onion. Chiffonade (cut along the grain into very thin strips) the cabbage, spinach, and cilantro. In a large bowl, combine the chopped vegetables, garlic, cashews, and peas. Dress the salad with sesame oil and soy sauce. Toss again to combine and serve.
Per serving: Kcal 113, Sodium 168 mg, Protein 3 g, Carbs 14 g, Fat 4 g

108. Baby Beet and Orange Salad

INGREDIENTS (Servings: 4)

2 ribs celery, chopped (½ cup)	1 orange, peeled, and cut into segments
¼ head Napa cabbage, chopped	Juice and zest of 1 orange
1 chopped small yellow onion, chopped (½ cup)	black pepper to taste
½ tbsp. olive oil	2 bunches baby beets with greens

DIRECTIONS (Ready in about: 1 h 25 min)
Warm the oven to 400°F. Cut the greens from the beets. Rinse the greens under cold water, drain well, and set aside. Wash the beets. Pour a drizzle of olive oil on your hands and rub the beets to coat them lightly. Wrap beets in foil and cook for about 45 minutes or until tender. Allow it to cool until you can be able to handle it, then peel off the outer skin. Cut and reserve. Cut the beets into strips and put them in the bowl. Chop the celery, cabbage, and onion and add them to the bowl. Zest and juice one orange in the bowl. Cut the already peeled orange into quarters. Add to bowl. Pour half tbsp. of olive oil over the salad. Top with black pepper and toss to combine. Place the salad on cold plates and garnish with sliced beets. Serve immediately.
Per serving: Kcal 118, Sodium 135 mg, Protein 3 g, Carbs 22 g, Fat 2 g

109. Bean Salad with Vinaigrette

INGREDIENTS (Servings: 6)

For the vinaigrette:	4 garlic cloves, finely chopped
⅓ cup of fresh parsley, chopped	**For the Salad:**
Ground black pepper, to taste	1 can (15 oz.) of low-sodium garbanzo beans, rinsed and drained
¼ cup of extra-virgin olive oil	1 medium red onion, diced
2 tbsp. balsamic vinegar	

1 can (15 oz.) of black beans (low sodium), rinsed and drained
6 lettuce leaves
½ cup celery, finely chopped

DIRECTIONS (Ready in about: 25 min)
To make the dressing, in a portable bowl, combine the parsley, garlic, balsamic vinegar, and pepper. While whisking, add the olive oil slowly. Set aside. Combine the beans and onion in an enormous bowl. Pour the dressing over the mixture and toss gently to combine well and evenly coat. Cover and refrigerate until serving. To serve, place 1 lettuce leaf on each plate. Divide the salad between individual plates and garnish with chopped celery. Serve immediately.
Per serving: Kcal 206, Sodium 174 mg, Protein 7 g, Carbs 22 g, Fat 10 g

110. Beet Walnut Salad

INGREDIENTS (Servings: 8)
1 small bunch of beets, or enough canned beets (no salt added) to make 3 cups, drained
¼ cup red wine vinegar
3 tbsp. balsamic vinegar
1 tbsp. olive oil
1 tbsp. water
8 cups fresh salad greens
¼ cup chopped apple
¼ cup chopped celery
Freshly ground pepper
3 tbsp. chopped walnuts
¼ cup gorgonzola cheese, crumbled

DIRECTIONS (Ready in about: 1 h 20 min)
Steam the raw beets in water in a saucepan until tender. Remove the skins. Rinse to cool. Cut into ½-inch slices. In a medium bowl, season with red wine vinegar. In an enormous bowl, combine the balsamic vinegar, olive oil, and water. Add the salad greens and mix. Arrange the salad greens on individual salad plates. Garnish with sliced beets and chopped apples and celery. Sprinkle with pepper, nuts, and cheese. Serve immediately.
Per serving: Kcal 105, Sodium 131 mg, Protein 3 g, Carbs 12 g, Fat 5 g

111. Blue Cheese Spinach Salad

INGREDIENTS (Servings: 12)
Dressing:
4 tsp. olive oil
2 tbsp. balsamic vinegar
1 tbsp. maple syrup
¼ tsp. nutmeg
1 tbsp. plain low-fat yogurt

Salad:
2 pounds spinach, roughly chopped (or 3 10 oz. packages)
1½ cups sliced cucumbers
1½ cups grape tomatoes
¼ cup chopped walnuts
¼ cup blue cheese crumbles
½ cup sliced red onion

DIRECTIONS (Ready in about: 20 min)
Combine all the ingredients for the seasoning in a blender or food processor. Toss spinach with seasoning and whisk 2 generous cups on cold plates. Place the grated vegetables, nuts, and blue cheese on the spinach and serve.
Per serving: Kcal 70, Sodium 95 mg, Protein 4 g, Carbs 7.5 g, Fat 4 g

112. Braised Celery Root

INGREDIENTS (Servings: 6)
1 cup vegetable stock or broth
1 celery root (celeriac), peeled and diced (about 3 cups)
¼ cup sour cream
1 tsp. Dijon mustard
¼ tsp. salt
¼ tsp. freshly ground black pepper
2 tsp. fresh thyme leaves

DIRECTIONS (Ready in about: 1 h 25 min)
In an enormous saucepan, bring the stock to a boil over high heat. Add the celeriac. When the stock comes back to a boil, reduce the heat to low. Cover and cook over low heat, occasionally stirring, until the celery root is tender, 10 to 12 minutes. With a slotted spoon, transfer the celeriac to a bowl, cover, and keep warm. Increase the heat to high heat and bring the cooking liquid to a boil. Cook, uncovered until reduced to 1 tbsp., about 5 minutes. Remove from heat and add sour cream, mustard, salt, and pepper. Add the celeriac and thyme to the sauce and stir over medium heat until heated through. Move to a warm plate and serve right away.
Per serving: Kcal 54, Sodium 206 mg, Protein 2 g, Carbs 7 g, Fat 2 g

113. Butternut Squash Apple Salad

INGREDIENTS (Servings: 6)
Dressing:
½ cup low-fat plain yogurt
2 tsp. balsamic vinegar
1½ tsp. honey

Salad:
A butternut squash, seeded and peeled, cut into ½ inch pieces
2 big apples, cored and cut ½-inch pieces
2 cups chopped carrots
1½ cups chopped celery
6 cups spinach, chopped
6 cups arugula, chopped
2 tsp. of olive oil

DIRECTIONS (Ready in about: 25 min)
Heat oven to 400°F. Stirs squash in olive oil, roast in the oven for 20-30 minutes until golden and tender. Let it cool completely. Mix all the vegetables in a large bowl. Prepare the vinaigrette by mixing yogurt, vinegar, and honey. Beat until smooth. Pour the vinaigrette over the salad. Toss and serve immediately.
Per serving: Kcal: 215, Sodium 97 mg, Protein 5 g, Carbs 42 g, Fat 3 g

114. Chicken Salad with Pineapple

INGREDIENTS (Servings: 8)
4 boneless, skinless chicken breasts, each about 5 oz.
1 tbsp. olive oil
1 can (8 oz.) unsweetened pineapple chunks, drained except for 2 tbsp. juice
2 cups broccoli florets
4 cups fresh baby spinach leaves
½ cup thinly sliced red onions
For the Vinaigrette:
¼ cup olive oil
2 tbsp. balsamic vinegar
2 tsp. sugar
¼ tsp. ground cinnamon

DIRECTIONS (Ready in about: 30 min)
Cut each chicken breast into cubes. In an enormous nonstick skillet, heat olive oil over medium heat. Add the chicken and cook until golden brown, about 10 minutes. In a large bowl, combine the cooked chicken, pineapple chunks, broccoli, spinach, and onion. To prepare the vinaigrette, combine the olive oil, vinegar, reserved pineapple juice, sugar, and cinnamon in a small bowl. Pour over the salad. Stir gently to coat evenly. Serve immediately.
Per serving: Kcal 186, Sodium 50 mg, Protein 17 g, Carbs 7 g, Fat 10 g

115. Chopped Greek Salad

INGREDIENTS (Servings: 4)
1 small red onion, cut into very thin half-moons
1 tbsp. red wine vinegar
1 tsp. dried oregano
1 tbsp. extra-virgin olive oil
1-pint grape tomatoes, cut in halves
1 tbsp. water
1 clove garlic, minced
⅛ tsp. freshly ground black pepper
2 oz. (½ cup) crumbled regular rindless goat cheese
1 medium cucumber, peeled, halved lengthwise, seeded, and cut into thin half-moons
½ cup diced (½-inch) green bell pepper

DIRECTIONS (Ready in about: 35 min)
Soak the red onion in a portable bowl of cold water for 30 minutes; drain and dry. (This step is optional, but it helps soften the strong onion flavor.) In a large bowl, combine the vinegar, water, oregano, garlic, and pepper. Gradually add the oil. Add the drained onion, tomatoes, cucumber, and bell pepper and mix well. Sprinkle with goat cheese and serve immediately.
Per serving: Kcal 95, Sodium 81 mg, Protein 5 g, Carbs 10 g, Fat 5 g

116. Classic Chicken Salad

INGREDIENTS (Servings: 2)
2 tbsp. light mayonnaise
2 tbsp. plain low-fat yogurt
⅛ tsp. freshly ground black pepper
8 oz. Basic Roast Chicken Breast
2 small celery ribs, finely diced
1 finely chopped scallion, white and green parts
4 romaine lettuce leaves, for serving
¼ tsp. kosher salt

DIRECTIONS (Ready in about: 30 min)
In a medium-sized bowl, combine mayonnaise, yogurt, and pepper. Add the chicken, celery, and scallion and mix well. Divide equal portions of the chicken salad between two plates, add the lettuce, and serve.
Per serving: Kcal 197, Sodium 276 mg, Protein 25 g, Carbs 4 g, Fat 8 g

117. Corn Salad

INGREDIENTS (Servings: 4)
¼ cup coarsely chopped cilantro
6 ears corn, shucked
¼ cup nicely chopped red onion
2 roasted red bell peppers, diced (about 1 cup)
1-pint grape tomatoes, cut in half
¼ tsp. kosher salt
Juice of 1 lime
¼ tsp. freshly ground black pepper
1-½ tbsp. extra-virgin olive oil

DIRECTIONS (Ready in about: 30 min)
In an enormous pot of boiling water, cook the ears of corn until the kernels have turned bright yellow, 3 to 4 minutes. Drain and let cool. When cool enough to handle, remove the corn kernels from the cob using a knife. Put the corn in a large bowl, and add the cilantro, red onion, tomatoes, bell peppers, salt, black pepper, lime juice, and olive oil. Mix the salad, taste, and adjust the seasonings as needed. Serve.
Per serving: Kcal 243, Sodium 153 mg, Protein 6 g, Carbs 43 g, Fat 7 g

118. Couscous Salad

INGREDIENTS (Servings: 8)
1 cup whole-wheat couscous
1 cup zucchini, cut into ¼-inch pieces
1 normal red bell pepper, cut into ¼-inch pieces
½ cup finely chopped red onion
¾ tsp. ground cumin
½ tsp. ground black pepper
2 tbsp. extra virgin olive oil
1 tbsp. lemon juice
Chopped fresh parsley, basil, or oregano for garnish (optional)

DIRECTIONS (Ready in about: 25 min)
Cook couscous according to package directions. When the couscous is cooked, peel it with a fork. Stir in the zucchini, peppers, onion, cumin, and black pepper and set aside. In a portable bowl, combine the olive oil and lemon juice. Pour over couscous mixture and toss to combine. Cover and refrigerate. Serve cold. Garnish with fresh herbs.
Per serving: Kcal 136, Sodium 3 mg, Protein 4 g, Carbs 21 g, Fat 4 g

119. Cucumber Pineapple Salad

INGREDIENTS (Servings: 4)
¼ cup sugar
⅔ cup rice wine vinegar
2 tbsp. water
1 cup canned no-sugar-added pineapple chunks
1 carrot, peeled and cut into thin strips
1 cucumber, peeled and thinly sliced
4 cups torn salad greens
⅓ cup thinly sliced red onion
1 tbsp. sesame seeds, toasted

DIRECTIONS (Ready in about: 25 min)
In a heavy-bottomed saucepan, bring the vinegar, sugar, and water to a boil. Stir evenly until reduced to about ½ cup, about 5 minutes. Move to a large bowl and refrigerate until chilled. Add the cucumber, pineapple, carrot, and red onion to the mixture. Mix it out very well. To serve, divide the greens among individual plates. Top with pineapple mixture and sprinkle with toasted sesame seeds. Serve immediately.
Per serving: Kcal 129, Sodium 102 mg, Protein 2 g, Carbs 28 g, Fat 1 g

120. Dilled Pasta Salad

INGREDIENTS (Servings: 8)
For the Dressing:
¼ cup olive oil
2 tbsp. lemon juice
2 tbsp. rice or white wine vinegar
2 tsp. of dill weed
Black pepper, to taste
For the Salad:
8 asparagus spears, cut into a ½-inch piece
3 cups uncooked whole-grain shell pasta, medium-sized
1 cup halved cherry tomatoes
½ cup chopped green (spring) onions
1 cup sliced green peppers

DIRECTIONS (Ready in about: 25 min)
To prepare the dressing, add olive oil, lemon juice, vinegar, dill, and black pepper to a small bowl. Beat to mix evenly and set aside. To prepare the salad, fill a large saucepan ¾ full with water and bring to a boil. Add pasta and cook until tender (al dente), 10 to 12 minutes, or according to package directions. Drain the pasta very well and rinse with cold water. In a saucepan, cover the asparagus with water. Bring to a boil and cook until crispy and tender, about 3 to 5 minutes. Drain and rinse with cold water. In a big bowl, add the pasta, asparagus, tomatoes, green peppers, onion, and seasoning. Stir to mix evenly. Cover and refrigerate. Serve cold.
Per serving: Kcal 160, Sodium 11 mg, Protein 4 g, Carbs 23 g, Fat 8 g

121. Dilled Shrimp Salad

INGREDIENTS (Servings: 2)

- 2 cups uncooked farfalle (bow-tie) pasta
- 4 fresh asparagus stalks, cut into ½-inch pieces
- ¼ cup reduced-sodium or light vinaigrette salad dressing
- ½ pound cooked shrimp
- 8 cherry tomatoes, halved
- 4 scallions or green onions, diced
- 4 cups watercress
- 1½ tsp. fresh dill

DIRECTIONS (Ready in about: 1 h 25 min)

Fill a large saucepan ¾ full with water and bring to a boil. Add pasta and cook until tender, 10 to 12 minutes, or according to package directions. Drain the pasta very well and rinse with cold water. In a saucepan, cover the asparagus with water. Bring to a boil and cook until crispy and tender, about 3 to 5 minutes. Drain and rinse with cold water. In a small bowl, add the vinaigrette and dill. Beat to mix evenly. In a large bowl, add the pasta, asparagus, shrimp, tomatoes, and scallions. Add the dressing mixture and toss to coat evenly. Cover and refrigerate until completely cold, about 1 hour. To serve, divide the watercress between the plates. Garnish with dill salad and serve.

Per serving: Kcal 329, Sodium 215 mg, Protein 35 g, Carbs 45 g, Fat 4 g

122. English Cucumber Salad

INGREDIENTS (Servings: 4)

- 1 English cucumber with peel (8 to 9 inches in length), washed and thinly sliced
- 1 tbsp. finely chopped fresh rosemary
- Black pepper, to taste
- **For the Dressing:**
- 2 tbsp. balsamic vinegar
- 1½ tbsp. olive oil
- 1 tbsp. low-salt Dijon mustard

DIRECTIONS (Ready in about: 25 min)

In a portable saucepan, add the vinegar, rosemary, and olive oil. Heat to mix and enhance the flavors over very low heat, approximately 5 minutes. Take it out from the heat and add the mustard until well combined. In a serving bowl, add the cucumber slices. Pour the dressing over the cucumbers and toss to coat evenly. Add black pepper to taste. Refrigerate until ready to serve.

Per serving: Kcal 67, Sodium 90 mg, Protein 0.5 g, Carbs 5 g, Fat 5 g

123. Fattoush

INGREDIENTS (Servings: 8)

For the Dressing:
- ¼ cup fresh lemon juice
- 3 garlic cloves, minced
- 1 tsp. ground cumin
- 1 tsp. ground sumac (or lemon zest to taste)
- ½ tsp. salt
- ½ tsp. red pepper flakes
- ¼ tsp. freshly ground black pepper
- 2 tbsp. extra-virgin olive oil

For the Salad:
- 1 head romaine lettuce, chopped
- 2 whole-wheat pitas, 6 inches in diameter
- 2 small cucumbers, peeled, seeded, and diced
- 2 tomatoes, seeded and diced
- 3 green onions including tender green tops, minced
- 1 red bell pepper, diced and seeded
- 1 tbsp. of chopped fresh mint
- ¼ cup of chopped fresh parsley

DIRECTIONS (Ready in about: 25 min)

Start by preparing the dressing. In a blender or food processor, combine the lemon juice, garlic, cumin, sumac (or lemon zest), salt, red pepper flakes, and black pepper. Blend until smooth. With the engine running, slowly add olive oil until it is emulsified. Set aside. Then prepare the pita croutons. Heat oven to 400°F. Cut each pita into ½-inch pieces (or cut into 8 triangles). Spread the pieces in a single layer on a baking sheet and bake until crisp and lightly browned, about 8 minutes. Let it cool. You are now ready to prepare the salad. In a big bowl, combine the lettuce, tomatoes, cucumbers, peppers, chives, mint, and parsley and toss. Add dressing and toss lightly to evenly coat. Divide the salad among individual plates. Complete with the croutons.

Per serving: Kcal 108, Sodium 230 mg, Protein 3 g, Carbs 15 g, Fat 4 g

124. French Green Lentil Salad

INGREDIENTS (Servings: 6)

- ½ yellow onion, finely chopped
- 4 tbsp. olive oil, divided
- 4-inch-piece celery stalk, finely chopped
- 3 cloves garlic, minced
- 1 tsp. mustard seed
- ¼ tsp. freshly ground black pepper
- 1 tsp. fennel seed
- ½ cup water
- 1 tbsp. of freshly chopped thyme or 1 tsp. dried thyme
- 1 cup of French green lentils, picked over, rinsed, then drained
- 1 bay leaf

4-inch-piece carrot, peeled and finely chopped
2 cups of vegetable stock or chicken stock
1 tbsp. Dijon mustard
1 tbsp. sherry vinegar or red wine vinegar
2 tbsp. fresh flat-leaf (Italian) parsley, cut into

DIRECTIONS (Ready in about: 60 min)
In a large saucepan, heat 2 tsp. of olive oil over medium heat. Add onion, celery, and carrot, and sauté until vegetables are tender for about 5 minutes. Add the garlic, mustard seeds, and fennel seeds, and sauté until the spices are fragrant about 1 minute. Add the broth, water, lentils, thyme, and bay leaf. Increase the heat to medium-high and bring it to a boil. Reduce heat to low, partially cover, and simmer until lentils are tender but still firm, 25 to 30 minutes. Drain the lentils, to conserve the liquid for cooking. Move the lentils to a large bowl and discard the bay leaf. In a portable bowl, combine the vinegar, mustard, and ¼ cup of the reserved cooking liquid. (Discard remaining liquid or set aside for another use.) Add remaining olive oil. Add the dressing, parsley, and pepper to the lentils and toss gently to combine and evenly coat. Serve hot.
Per serving: Kcal 189, Sodium 185 mg, Protein 11 g, Carbs 25 g, Fat 5 g

125. Grilled Chicken Salad

INGREDIENTS (Servings: 4)
For the Salad:
4 boneless, skinless chicken breasts, each 4 oz.
2 garlic cloves
8 cups leaf lettuce, washed and dried
16 large ripe (black) olives
2 navel oranges, peeled and sliced

For the Dressing:
½ cup red wine vinegar
4 garlic cloves, minced
1 tbsp. extra-virgin olive oil
1 tbsp. finely chopped red onion
1 tbsp. finely chopped celery
Cracked black pepper, to taste

DIRECTIONS (Ready in about: 35 min)
To make the dressing, mix the vinegar, garlic, olive oil, onion, celery, and pepper in a small bowl. Stir to mix evenly. Cover and refrigerate until needed. Build a hot fire in a charcoal grill or heat up a grill or gas grill. Away from sources of heat, coat the grill or pan lightly with cooking spray. Place the cooking grid 4 to 6 inches from the heat source. Rub the chicken breasts with the garlic, then remove the cloves. Grill or broil the chicken until golden brown and cooked through, about 5 minutes per side. Transfer the chicken to a cutting board and let it rest for 5 minutes before cutting into strips. Place 2 cups of lettuce, 4 olives, and ¼ of the sliced oranges on 4 plates. Garnish each plate with a chicken breast cut into strips and season with dressing. Serve immediately.
Per serving: Kcal 237, Sodium 199 mg, Protein 27 g, Carbs 12 g, Fat 9 g

126. Lentil and Goat Cheese Salad

INGREDIENTS (Servings: 6)
1 cup of brown lentils
2 tbsp. sherry or cider vinegar
2 tbsp. water
Freshly grated zest of 1 lemon
½ tsp. kosher salt
¼ tsp. freshly ground black pepper
2 tbsp. olive oil, preferably extra-virgin

1 medium red bell pepper, cored and cut into ¼-inch dice
2 celery ribs, cut into ¼-inch dice
1 medium carrot, peeled and cut into ¼-inch dice
2 tbsp. finely chopped fresh basil or oregano
4 oz. (1 cup) crumbled goat cheese

DIRECTIONS (Ready in about: 55 min)
Bring a portable pot of water to a boil over high heat. Add the lentils and cook (like pasta) until tender, about 30 minutes. Drain in a metal colander, rinse under cold running water and drain well. In a large bowl, combine the vinegar, water, lemon zest, salt, and pepper. Gradually add the oil. Add the lentils, bell pepper, celery, carrot, and basil and mix well. Sprinkle with goat cheese and serve cold or at room temperature.
Per serving: Kcal 170, Sodium 21 mg, Protein 9 g, Carbs 22 g, Fat 5 g

127. Lentil Salad with Mango

INGREDIENTS (Servings: 4)
1 cup diced mango
1 cup dried green lentils
1½ tbsp. chopped red onion

½ tbsp. freshly squeezed lemon juice
¼ cup chopped cilantro
1 tbsp. olive oil

DIRECTIONS (Ready in about: 40 min)
In a portable saucepan, add the lentils and enough water to cover them by an inch or two. Bring to a boil, reduce the heat to low, and simmer, covered, until tender, about 20 minutes. Drain and let cool to room temperature. In a medium bowl, add the lentils, mango, onion, and cilantro. Toss to combine. Drizzle with the lemon juice and the olive oil and toss again.
Per serving: Kcal 235, Sodium 14 mg, Protein 13 g, Carbs 15 g, Fat 4 g

128. Mango Tango Salad

INGREDIENTS (Servings: 6)

3 ripe mangoes, pitted and cubed	2 tbsp. chopped of fresh cilantro leaves
Juice of 1 lime	½ jalapeno pepper, seeded and minced
1 tsp. minced red onion	

DIRECTIONS (Ready in about: 20 min)
Combine all ingredients in a mixing bowl. Let stand 10 minutes. Toss just before serving.
Per serving: Kcal 68, Sodium 10 mg, Protein 1 g, Carbs 16 g, Fat 0.5 g

129. Mixed Bean Salad

INGREDIENTS (Servings: 8)

1 can (15 oz.) of unsalted wax beans, drained	1 can (15 oz.) of unsalted kidney beans, drained
½ cup cider vinegar	1 can (15 oz.) of unsalted garbanzo beans, drained
1 can (15 oz.) of unsalted green beans, drained	¼ cup orange juice
¼ cup chopped white onion	

DIRECTIONS (Ready in about: 40 min)
In a big bowl, mix the beans and onion. Stir gently to mix evenly. In another bowl, combine the orange juice and vinegar. Add a sugar substitute for the desired sweetness. Spurt the orange juice mixture over the bean mixture. Stir to evenly coat. Let it stand 30 minutes before serving.
Per serving: Kcal 113, Sodium 139 mg, Protein 6 g, Carbs 19 g, Fat 1.5 g

130. Pasta Salad with Vegetables

INGREDIENTS (Servings: 8)

12 oz. whole-wheat rotini (spiral-shaped) pasta	1-pound mushrooms, sliced
1 tbsp. olive oil	1 red bell pepper, sliced
¼ cup low-sodium chicken broth	1 green bell pepper, sliced
1 garlic clove, chopped	2 medium zucchini, shredded
2 medium onions, chopped	½ tsp. basil
1 can (28 oz.) unsalted diced tomatoes in juice	½ tsp. oregano
	8 romaine lettuce leaves

DIRECTIONS (Ready in about: 1 h 25 min)
Cook pasta according to package directions. Drain the pasta well. Put the pasta in an enormous serving bowl. Add olive oil and mix and set aside. In a bid skillet, heat the chicken broth over medium heat. Add the garlic, onion, and tomatoes. Sauté until onions are translucent, about 5 minutes. Add remaining vegetables and sauté until tender, about 5 minutes. Add the basil and oregano. Add the vegetable mixture to the pasta. Stir to mix evenly. Cover and chill in a refrigerator for approximately an hour. Arrange the lettuce leaves on individual plates. Top with the pasta salad and serve immediately.
Per serving: Kcal 251, Sodium 60 mg, Protein 10 g, Carbs 46 g, Fat 3 g

131. Pickled Onion Salad

INGREDIENTS (Servings: 4)

2 large red onions, thinly sliced (about 2 cups)	2 tbsp. sugar
4 spring (green) onions with tops, chopped	½ cup fresh cilantro, chopped
½ cup cider vinegar	1 tbsp. lime juice
2 tsp. olive oil	4 lettuce leaves

DIRECTIONS (Ready in about: 75 min)
In a portable bowl, mix the onion, vinegar, oil, and sugar. Stir to mix evenly. Cover and refrigerate until chilled, about 60 minutes. Just before serving, add the cilantro and sprinkle with lime. Serve the mounded on a lettuce leaf.
Per serving: Kcal 86, Sodium 21 mg, Protein 1 g, Carbs 16 g, Fat 2 g

132. Potato Salad

INGREDIENTS (Servings: 4)
1-pound potatoes, diced and boiled or steamed
1 large yellow onion, chopped (1 cup)
1 large carrot, diced (½ cup)
2 ribs celery, diced (½ cup)
2 tbsp. minced fresh dill (or ½ tbsp. dried)
1 tsp. ground black pepper
¼ cup low-calorie mayonnaise
1 tbsp. Dijon mustard
2 tbsp. red wine vinegar

DIRECTIONS (Ready in about: 40 min)
Combine all the ingredients in a normal size bowl and mix them very well. Refrigerate before serving.
Per serving: Kcal 77, Sodium 128 mg, Protein 1 g, Carbs 14 g, Fat 1 g

133. Quick Bean and Tuna Salad

INGREDIENTS (Servings: 4)
2 tbsp. olive oil
½ whole-grain baguette, torn into 2-inch pieces (about 1 cup)
1 can (16 oz.) cannellini beans, no salt added, drained and rinsed
1 small red onion, thinly sliced (about ½ cup)
¼ tsp. pepper
2 small dill pickles, cut into bite-size pieces (about 2 tbsp.)
2 tbsp. red wine vinegar
1 can (7 oz.) water-packed tuna, no salt added, drained, and rinsed
2 tbsp. finely chopped fresh parsley

DIRECTIONS (Ready in about: 20 min)
Heat the grill. Place the baguette pieces on a heavy baking sheet and brush with 1 tbsp. of oil. Place under the broiler for about 1 to 2 minutes, until golden brown. Turn the bread pieces over and toast for another 1 to 2 minutes. In a large bowl, combine the remaining oil, beans, pickles, onion, vinegar, and pepper. Stir in the toasted baguette pieces. Split the mixture among four bowls and garnish with the tuna and parsley.
Per serving: Kcal 316, Sodium 171 mg, Protein 23 g, Carbs 21 g, Fat 10 g

134. Rice and Beans Salad

INGREDIENTS (Servings: 10)
1½ cups uncooked brown rice
3 cups of water
½ cup of chopped shallots or spring onions
½ cup chopped fresh parsley
15 oz. can unsalted garbanzo beans
¼ cup olive oil
15 oz. can unsalted dark kidney beans
⅓-½ cup rice vinegar, according to your taste

DIRECTIONS (Ready in about: 3 h)
Put the rice and water in the pot. Cover and cook over medium heat until the rice is tender, about 45 to 50 minutes. Let cool to room temperature. Add the other ingredients. Let cool for 2 hours or more.
Per serving: Kcal 227, Sodium 110 mg, Protein 7 g, Carbs 34 g, Fat 7 g

135. Roasted Beet Salad

INGREDIENTS (Servings: 4)
1½ pounds beets (6 medium) without leaves or stems, scrubbed but unpeeled
½ cup plain nonfat yogurt
1 tbsp. cider vinegar
1 tbsp. finely chopped fresh dill, tarragon, or parsley
½ tsp. kosher salt
¼ tsp. freshly ground black pepper
1 clove garlic, crushed through a press
1 cup halved grape tomatoes
2 scallions, white and green parts, trimmed and thinly sliced

DIRECTIONS (Ready in about: 1 h 55 min)
Preheat the oven to 400°F. Wrap each beet in foil. Place and roast on a rimmed baking sheet until tender, about 1¼ hour, depending on the size and age of the beets. Discard and let cool until easy to handle. Peel the beets and cut them into ½ inch-thick wedges. In a medium bowl, combine yogurt, vinegar, dill, salt, pepper, and garlic. Add the tomatoes, beets, and chives and toss to coat. Cover the lid and refrigerate until chilled for at least one hour and up to 12 hours. Serve cold.
Per serving: Kcal 83, Sodium 325 mg, Protein 4 g, Carbs 17 g, Fat 1 g

136. Salad Greens with Pears

INGREDIENTS (Servings: 6)

6 cups mixed salad greens
1 medium fennel bulb, trimmed and thinly sliced
2 medium pears, cored, quartered, and thinly sliced
2 tbsp. grated Parmesan cheese
¼ cup toasted walnuts, coarsely chopped
2 tbsp. olive oil
3 tbsp. balsamic vinegar
Freshly ground black pepper, to taste

DIRECTIONS (Ready in about: 25 min)

Divide the salad greens among 6 plates. Divide the fennel and pear slices over the greens. Sprinkle with Parmesan and walnuts. Drizzle with olive oil and vinegar. Add black pepper to taste. Serve immediately.

Per serving: Kcal 144, Sodium 51 mg, Protein 3 g, Carbs 15 g Fat 8 g

137. Salad Greens with Squash

INGREDIENTS (Servings: 4)

2 tbsp. brown sugar
1 tbsp. olive oil
2 small acorn squash (approx. 2 pounds total)
4 cups of leaf lettuce, such as spring mix
2 tbsp. sunflower seeds
4 tsp. of honey

DIRECTIONS (Ready in about: 1 h 25 min)

Punch the squash several times with a sharp knife to allow the steam to escape during cooking. Microwave each squash until tender, approximately five minutes. Turn the squash after three minutes to ensure proper cooking. Place the squash on a cutting board and cut it in half. Scrape the seeds from the center of each half and discard them. Remove the pulp and put it in a bowl. Repeat the same process with the other squash. There should be about two cups of pulp. Sprinkle the squash with brown sugar and add olive oil. Blend until smooth. Cool slightly. Split the lettuce among four salad plates. Top each with ½ cup of the squash mixture, ½ tbsp. of sunflower seeds and 1 tsp. of honey. Serve immediately.

Per serving: Kcal 210, Sodium 18 mg, Protein 3 g, Carbs 36 g, Fat 6 g

138. Salmon and Peaches Salad

INGREDIENTS (Servings: 4)

2 smoked salmon fillets, boneless, skinless, and cubed
2 peaches, stones removed and cubed
1 tsp. olive oil
A pinch of black pepper
2 cups baby spinach
½ tbsp. balsamic vinegar
1 tbsp. lemon juice
1 tbsp. cilantro, chopped

DIRECTIONS (Ready in about: 10 min)

In a salad bowl, combine the salmon with the peaches and the other ingredients, toss, and serve cold.

Per serving: Kcal 133, Sodium 263 mg, Protein 1.5 g, Carbs 8 g, Fat 7 g

139. Shrimp and Black Bean Salad

INGREDIENTS (Servings: 4)

2 tbsp. olive oil, plus more in a pump sprayer
¾ pound large shrimp (16 to 20), peeled and deveined
2 tbsp. fresh lime juice
2 ripe mangoes, pitted, peeled, and cut into ½-inch dice
1 can (15 oz.) reduced-sodium black beans, drained and rinsed
½ jalapeño, seeded and minced
2 tbsp. chopped fresh cilantro or mint
2 tbsp. minced red onion

DIRECTIONS (Ready in about: 1 h 15 min)

Drizzle an enormous roasting pan with oil and heat over medium heat. Add the shrimp to the pan. (Or place a rack about 4 inches from the heat source and preheat the grill. Spray the grill with oil and spread the shrimp on the rack.) 3 to 5 minutes. Refrigerate to cool completely, about 20 minutes. In an enormous serving bowl, combine the lemon juice and 2 tbsp. of oil. Add the shrimp, mango, beans, jalapeño, cilantro, and onion and mix gently. Serve immediately.

Per serving: Kcal 213, Sodium 679 mg, Protein 18 g, Carbs 36 g, Fat 2 g

140. Spiced Melon Salad

INGREDIENTS (Servings: 4)

½ cup of plain or vanilla low-fat or nonfat yogurt
2 cups of diced assorted melon, such as cantaloupe, honeydew, or watermelon (or any fruit you like)
¼ tsp. nutmeg
⅛ tsp. clove
¼ tsp. mace
Orange zest (about 1 tbsp.) and juice (about 3 tbsp.)
⅛ tsp. cinnamon

DIRECTIONS (Ready in about: 15 min)

In an enormous bowl, combine all the ingredients to mix. Serve.

Per serving: Kcal 52, Sodium 31 mg, Protein 2.5 g, Carbs 11 g, Fat 0.5 g

141. Spinach Berry Salad

INGREDIENTS (Servings: 4)

4 packed cups torn fresh spinach
1 cup sliced fresh strawberries
1 cup fresh or frozen blueberries
1 small, sweet onion, sliced
¼ cup chopped pecans, toasted

For the Dressing:
2 tbsp. white wine vinegar or cider vinegar
2 tbsp. balsamic vinegar
2 tbsp. honey
2 tsp. Dijon mustard
1 tsp. curry powder (can be omitted)
⅛ tsp. pepper

DIRECTIONS (Ready in about: 15 min)

In a large bowl, combine the spinach, strawberries, blueberries, onion, and pecans. In a jar with a tight-fitting lid, combine the ingredients for the seasoning. Shake well. Pour over salad and toss to coat. Serve immediately.

Per serving: Kcal 158, Sodium 198 mg, Protein 4 g, Carbs 25 g, Fat 5 g

142. Steak and Berry Salad

INGREDIENTS (Servings: 4)

2 tsp. olive oil
2 tbsp. lime juice
¼ tsp. pepper
1 beef top sirloin steak
½ tsp. salt

For the Salad:
¼ cup crumbled blue cheese
¼ cup chopped walnuts
1 bunch romaine, torn
¼ cup red onion (thinly sliced)
2 cups fresh strawberries (halved)
Reduced-fat balsamic vinaigrette

DIRECTIONS (Ready in about: 25 min)

Rub meat with pepper and salt. Heat up the oil in a pan over medium flame. Cook each side of meat for up to 7 minutes. Transfer to a plate and leave for 5 minutes. Cut into small strips and add lime juice. Place onion, strawberries, and romaine on a platter. Add steak, walnuts, and cheese. Drizzle with vinaigrette before serving.

Per serving: Kcal 289, Sodium 452 mg, Protein 29 g, Carbs 11 g, Fat 26.5 g

143. Sweet Persimmon Salad

INGREDIENTS (Servings: 4)

⅓ cup pomegranate seeds
5 cups baby arugula
4 navel oranges, peeled and cut into segments
3 tbsp. pine nuts
2 tbsp. orange juice
¼ tsp. ground cinnamon
1 tbsp. honey
2 persimmons, chopped

DIRECTIONS (Ready in about: 10 min)

Put all ingredients in a big salad bowl and mix it up.

Per serving: Kcal: 182, Sodium 6 mg, Protein 4 g, Carbs 33 g, Fat 5 g

144. Tabbouleh Salad

INGREDIENTS (Servings: 8)

¾ cup of bulgur (cracked wheat), rinsed and drained
1½ cups water
1 cup diced, seeded tomatoes
½ cup of chopped scallions or green onions
1 tsp. dill weed
1 cup chopped parsley
¼ cup raisins
4 black olives, sliced
¼ cup lemon juice
Freshly ground black pepper, to taste
2 tbsp. extra-virgin olive oil

DIRECTIONS (Ready in about: 2 h 30 min)

In a portable saucepan, bring the water to a boil. Take it away from the heat and add the bulgur. Cover and let stand until bulgur is tender and liquid is completely absorbed approximately 15 to 20 minutes. In a big bowl, add the bulgur and the other ingredients. Stir gently until the ingredients are properly distributed. Cover and refrigerate for 2 hours to allow flavors to blend. Serve cold.

Per serving: Kcal: 108, Sodium 28 mg, Protein 2 g, Carbs 16 g, Fat 4 g

145. Tarragon Chicken Salad

INGREDIENTS (Servings: 2)

3 tbsp. plain low-fat yogurt
2 tsp. finely chopped fresh tarragon
⅛ tsp. of kosher salt
¼ tsp. freshly ground black pepper
8 oz. Basic Roast Chicken Breast, cut into ½-inch dice (1 ½ cups)
2 tbsp. light mayonnaise
1 cup halved red or green seedless grapes
2 medium celery ribs, thinly sliced
¼ cup sliced almonds, toasted
2 cups (2 oz.) mixed salad greens
Lemon wedges, for serving

DIRECTIONS (Ready in about: 25 min)

In a portable bowl, whisk together yogurt, mayonnaise, tarragon, salt, and pepper. Add the chicken, grapes, celery, and almonds and mix well. Divide the salad greens between 2 salad bowls. Top each with half the chicken mixture. Serve immediately with the lemon wedges to squeeze the juice over the salad.

Per serving: Kcal 352, Sodium 658 mg, Protein 20 g, Carbs 22 g, Fat 17 g

146. Thai Cobb Salad

INGREDIENTS (Servings: 6)

¾ cup Asian toasted sesame salad dressing
2 tbsp. creamy peanut butter
¼ cup fresh cilantro leaves
1 cup fresh snow peas (halved)
½ cup unsalted peanuts
1 medium sweet red pepper
1 medium ripe avocado (peeled and thinly sliced)
1 medium carrot (shredded)
3 hard-boiled large eggs (coarsely chopped)
1 bunch romaine (torn)
2 cups rotisserie chicken (shredded)

DIRECTIONS (Ready in about: 15 min)

Arrange romaine in a platter. Add cilantro, peanuts, veggies, avocado, eggs, and chicken. Put peanut butter and salad dressing in a bowl. Whisk until combined. Serve salad along with the sauce.

Per serving: Kcal 382, Sodium 472 mg, Protein 5 g, Carbs 12 g, Fat 12.5 g

147. Tossed Greens with Pasta

INGREDIENTS (Servings: 6)

For the Dressing:
1 tsp. dried rosemary or 1 tbsp. fresh rosemary
¼ tsp. ground cinnamon
¼ tsp. salt
3 tbsp. balsamic vinegar
¼ cup olive oil
For the Salad:
½ cup golden raisins
4 oz. uncooked whole-wheat spiral pasta
6 cups mixed greens
2 large fresh pears, cored and sliced
½ cup sliced water chestnuts
3 tbsp. roasted unsalted soy nuts

DIRECTIONS (Ready in about: 25 min)

Use a portable bowl to prepare the dressing. Add the rosemary, cinnamon, salt, balsamic vinegar, and olive oil; beat well to combine. Fill a large saucepan ¾ full with water and bring to a boil. Add pasta and cook until tender (al dente), 10 to 12 minutes, or according to package directions. Drain the pasta very well and rinse with cold water. In a large bowl, combine the cooked pasta, mixed green, pears, water chestnuts, and raisins. Whisk the dressing again briefly and add it to the salad. Toss to coat evenly. Split the salad among individual plates and garnish it with soy nuts. Serve immediately.

Per serving: Kcal 274, Sodium 137 mg, Protein 6 g, Carbs 40 g, Fat 10 g

148. Watermelon Shrimp Salad

INGREDIENTS (Servings: 4)

½ medium red onion, cut into thin half-moons
24 large basil leaves, cut into thin shreds (¼ cup packed)
Olive oil in a pump sprayer
1-pound large shrimp (peeled and deveined
6 cups seedless watermelon cubes, cut into 1-inch squares, chilled
Lime Vinaigrette to taste

DIRECTIONS (Ready in about: 1 h 15 min)

Spray a large nonstick skillet with oil and heat over medium-high heat. Add the shrimp and cook, occasionally stirring, until completely opaque, about 3 minutes. Move it to a plate and leave it to cool. Cover and refrigerate until chilled, at least 1 hour. In a large serving bowl, combine the watermelon, onion, and basil. Add the shrimp and the vinaigrette and mix gently. Serve cold.

Per serving: Kcal 234, Sodium 696 mg, Protein 17 g, Carbs 23 g, Fat 9 g

149. Yellow Pear Salad

INGREDIENTS (Servings: 6)

2 tbsp. sherry vinegar or red wine vinegar
1 tbsp. minced shallot
1 tbsp. extra-virgin olive oil
4 big fresh basil leaves, cut into slender ribbons
¼ tsp. salt
⅛ tsp. freshly ground black pepper
1½ cups of orange cherry tomatoes, halved
1½ cups yellow pear tomatoes, halved
1½ cups of red cherry tomatoes, halved

DIRECTIONS (Ready in about: 25 min)

To prepare the vinaigrette, in a portable bowl, combine the vinegar and shallot and let steep for 15 minutes. Add olive oil, salt, and pepper and mix until smooth. In a large bowl or salad bowl, combine all the tomatoes. Spill the vinaigrette over the tomatoes, add the basil pieces and toss gently to combine well and evenly coat. Serve immediately.

Per serving: Kcal 47, Sodium 125 mg, Protein 1 g, Carbs 4 g, Fat 3 g

PLANT-BASED MAINS

150. Aromatic Spaghetti

INGREDIENTS (Servings: 2)

¼ cup of soy milk
6 oz. whole-grain spaghetti
2 cups of water
1 tsp. ground nutmeg
1 tsp. dried basil

DIRECTIONS (Ready in about: 15 min)

You first boil the water, then add the spaghetti and cook for 8 to 10 minutes. Meanwhile, boil the soy milk. Drain the cooked spaghetti and mix it with soy milk, ground nutmeg, and dried basil. Mix well and serve immediately.

Per serving: Kcal 128, Sodium 25 mg, Protein 5.5 g, Carbs 25 g, Fat 1.5 g

151. Baked Falafel

INGREDIENTS (Servings: 6)

2 cups chickpeas, cooked
3 tbsp. olive oil
1 cup fresh parsley, chopped
1 tsp. ground cumin
½ tsp. coriander
2 garlic cloves, diced
1 yellow onion, diced

DIRECTIONS (Ready in about: 35 min)

All the ingredients should be put together in the food processor and mix until smooth. Preheat the oven to 375°F. Then cover the pan with parchment paper. With the chickpea mixture, make the balls and gently press them into a falafel. Put the falafels in the pan and bake for 25 minutes. Serve immediately.

Per serving: Kcal 200, Sodium 240 mg, Protein 8.5 g, Carbs 25 g, Fat 8 g

152. Baked Tempeh

INGREDIENTS (Servings: 6)

¼ cup low-sodium tamari
1 tsp. nutritional yeast
1-pound tempeh, cubed

DIRECTIONS (Ready in about: 24 min)

Combine tamari and nutritional yeast. Then dip the tempeh cubes in the liquid and transfer them to the lined parchment paper. Bake the tempeh for 14 minutes at 385°F. Turn the tempeh cubes over to the other side after 7 minutes of cooking. Serve hot.

Per serving: Kcal 154, Sodium 361 mg, Protein 15 g, Carbs 8.5 g, Fat 8 g

153. Bean Hummus

INGREDIENTS (Servings: 6)

1 cup chickpeas, soaked
6 cups of water
1 tbsp. tahini paste
2 garlic cloves
¼ cup olive oil
¼ cup lemon juice
1 tsp. harissa

DIRECTIONS (Ready in about: 50 min)

Pour the water into the pot. Add the chickpeas and close the lid. Cook the chickpeas for 40 minutes over low heat or until tender. Then transfer the cooked chickpeas to the food processor. Add olive oil, lemon juice, harissa, garlic cloves, and tahini paste. Mix the hummus until you get a smooth mixture.

Per serving: Kcal 215, Sodium 30 mg, Protein 7 g, Carbs 21 g, Fat 12 g

154. Bow Ties and Beans

INGREDIENTS (Servings: 4)

¾ tsp. freshly ground pepper
½ cup crumbled feta cheese
1 2 oz. can sliced ripe olives (drained)
1 15 oz. can cannellini beans (rinsed and drained)
2 large tomatoes (chopped)
1 medium zucchini (sliced)
2½ cups uncooked whole wheat bow tie pasta
1 tbsp. olive oil
2 garlic cloves (minced)

DIRECTIONS (Ready in about: 30 min)

Check package about how to cook your pasta. Reserve half a cup of cooking water and drain the rest. Put oil in a pan over medium-high flame. Once heated, add zucchini to the pan and cook for 4 minutes or until crisp. Include the garlic and cook for 30 seconds. Add pepper, olives, beans, and tomatoes. Turn the heat to low and simmer for 5 minutes while occasionally stirring. Add pasta and enough of the reserved water to get it moist. Add cheese and gently mix until combined. Serve.

Per serving: Kcal 348, Sodium 394 mg, Protein 6 g, Carbs 23 g, Fat 4 g

155. Briam

INGREDIENTS (Servings: 4)
2 zucchinis, sliced
2 potatoes, sliced
1 red onion, sliced
1 tsp. dried oregano
½ tsp. dried rosemary
½ cup fresh cilantro, chopped
1 cup marinara sauce
1 tbsp. olive oil

DIRECTIONS (Ready in about: 75 min)
Combine zucchini, potatoes, and onion in the bowl. Sprinkle the vegetables with dried oregano, rosemary, and cilantro. Add the olive oil and mix the vegetables well. Then place them one by one in the pan and top with the marinara sauce. Cover the vegetables with foil and bake in a preheated 385°F oven for 55 minutes. Serve hot.
Per serving: Kcal 187, Sodium 276 mg, Protein 4.5 g, Carbs 31 g, Fat 5.5 g

156. Broccoli Balls

INGREDIENTS (Servings: 4)
1 cup broccoli, shredded
¼ cup quinoa, cooked
1 tsp. nutritional yeast
½ tsp. ground coriander
1 tbsp. flax meal
1 egg, beaten
2 tbsp. avocado oil

DIRECTIONS (Ready in about: 25 min)
Combine broccoli, quinoa, nutritional yeast, ground coriander, flax meal, and eggs. Stir the mixture until it is smooth. Then make medium-sized balls. Heat the avocado oil for 1 minute. Place the broccoli balls in the hot avocado oil and cook for 2 minutes per side or until golden brown. Serve immediately.
Per serving: Kcal 82, Sodium 24 mg, Protein 4 g, Carbs 9 g, Fat 3.5 g

157. Carrot Cakes

INGREDIENTS (Servings: 4)
1 cup carrot, grated
1 tbsp. semolina
1 egg, beaten
1 tsp. Italian seasonings
1 tbsp. sesame oil

DIRECTIONS (Ready in about: 20 min)
In the bowl, combine the grated carrot, semolina, egg, and Italian seasonings. Heat the sesame oil in the pan. Prepare the carrot cakes with the help of 2 tbsp. and put them in the pan. Bake the cakes for 4 minutes per side. Serve.
Per serving: Kcal 70, Sodium 35 mg, Protein 2 g, Carbs 4.5 g, Fat 5 g

158. Cauliflower Steaks

INGREDIENTS (Servings: 4)
1-pound cauliflower head
1 tsp. ground turmeric
½ tsp. cayenne pepper
2 tbsp. olive oil
½ tsp. garlic powder

DIRECTIONS (Ready in about: 40 min)
Cut the cauliflower head into the fillets and rub with the ground turmeric, cayenne pepper, and garlic powder. Then line the baking sheet with baking paper and place the cauliflower fillets inside. Sprinkle with olive oil and bake at 375°F for 25 minutes or until the vegetable fillets are tender. Serve immediately.
Per serving: Kcal 92, Sodium 34 mg, Protein 2.5 g, Carbs 7 g, Fat 7 g

159. Cauliflower Tots

INGREDIENTS (Servings: 4)
1 cup cauliflower, shredded
3 oz. vegan Parmesan, grated
⅓ cup flax seeds meal
1 egg, beaten
1 tsp. Italian seasonings
1 tsp. olive oil

DIRECTIONS (Ready in about: 35 min)
In the bowl, combine the grated cauliflower, vegan parmesan, flaxseed meal, egg, and Italian seasonings. Knead the cauliflower mixture. Add water if necessary. Next, prepare the cauliflowers tots from the mixture. Line the mold with parchment paper and put the cauliflower tots in it. Sprinkle with olive oil and transfer to preheated 375°F oven. Cook the meal for 15-20 minutes or until golden brown. Serve.
Per serving: Kcal 109, Sodium 72 mg, Protein 6 g, Carbs 6.5 g, Fat 6.5 g

160. Chana Masala

INGREDIENTS (Servings: 4)
1 jalapeno pepper, chopped
1 tsp. minced garlic
1 tsp. minced ginger
3 tbsp. fresh cilantro, chopped
1 tbsp. garam masala
1 cup tomatoes, chopped
1 onion, diced
1 tbsp. olive oil
2 cups of water
1 cup chickpeas, cooked

DIRECTIONS (Ready in about: 20 min)
Combine the jalapeño pepper, minced garlic, ginger, and fresh cilantro. Then heat the olive oil in the pan. Add the onion and grill until it turns golden brown.

Add the jalapeño mixture, garam masala, and chopped tomatoes. Bring the mixture to a boil. Add the chickpeas and water. Simmer the food for 10 minutes. Serve immediately.
Per serving: Kcal 235, Sodium 24 mg, Protein 10.5 g, Carbs 35 g Fat 6 g

161. Chickpea Curry

INGREDIENTS (Servings: 4)

1½ cup chickpeas, boiled	1 tsp. coconut oil
1 tsp. curry powder	¼ cup of soy milk
½ tsp. garam masala	1 tbsp. tomato paste
1 cup spinach, chopped	½ cup of water

DIRECTIONS (Ready in about: 20 min)
Heat the coconut oil in the pan. Add the curry powder, garam masala, tomato paste, and soy milk. Beat the mixture until smooth and bring to a boil. Add the water, spinach, and chickpeas. Add the meal and close the lid. Cook for 5 minutes over medium heat. Serve.
Per serving: Kcal 298, Sodium 37 mg, Protein 15.5 g, Carbs 47 g, Fat 6 g

162. Chile Rellenos

INGREDIENTS (Servings: 2)

2 chili peppers	2 tbsp. whole-grain wheat flour
2 oz. vegan mozzarella cheese, shredded	1 tbsp. potato starch
2 oz. tomato puree	¼ cup of water
1 tbsp. coconut oil	½ tsp. chili flakes

DIRECTIONS (Ready in about: 40 min)
Bake the peppers for 15 minutes in the oven preheated to 375°F. Meanwhile, pour the tomato puree into the pan. Add the chili flakes and bring the mixture to a boil. Remove from the heat. After that, mix the potato starch, flour, and water. When the peppers are cooked, cut them and remove the seeds. Then fill the peppers with grated cheese and secure the cuts with toothpicks. Heat the coconut oil in the pan. Dip the peppers in the flour mixture and toast in coconut oil until golden brown. Sprinkle the cooked chili peppers with the tomato puree mixture.
Per serving: Kcal 187, Sodium 123 mg, Protein 4 g, Carbs 16 g, Fat 12 g

163. Chunky Tomatoes

INGREDIENTS (Servings: 3)

2 cups plum tomatoes, roughly chopped	1 tsp. Italian seasonings
½ cup onion, diced	1 tsp. canola oil
½ tsp. garlic, diced	1 chili pepper, chopped

DIRECTIONS (Ready in about: 20 min)
Heat the canola oil in the pan. Add the chili and onion. Cook the vegetables for 5 minutes. Mix them from time to time. Then add the tomatoes, garlic, and Italian seasonings. Close the lid and sauté the food for 10 minutes.
Per serving: Kcal 550, Sodium 17 mg, Protein 1.5 g, Carbs 2 g, Fat 1.5 g

164. Corn Patties

INGREDIENTS (Servings: 4)

½ cup chickpeas, cooked	1 tsp. chili powder
1 cup corn kernels, cooked	½ tsp. ground coriander
	1 tbsp. tomato paste
1 tbsp. fresh parsley, chopped	1 tbsp. almond meal
	1 tbsp. olive oil

DIRECTIONS (Ready in about: 25 min)
Crush the cooked chickpeas and combine them with the corn kernels, parsley, chili powder, ground cilantro, tomato paste, and almond meal. Stir the mixture until it is smooth. Prepare the patties. Then heat the olive oil in the pan. Place prepared patties in boiling oil and cook for 3 minutes per side or until golden brown. Pat the cooked patties dry with a paper towel if necessary. Serve.
Per serving: Kcal 168, Sodium 23 mg, Protein 6.5 g, Carbs 25 g, Fat 6 g

165. Dill Zucchini Patties

INGREDIENTS (Servings: 6)

3 cups zucchinis, grated	1 tsp. black pepper
½ cup fresh dill, chopped	1 tbsp. canola oil
½ cup oatmeal, grinded	1 tbsp. dairy-free yogurt

DIRECTIONS (Ready in about: 20 min)
Combine the grated zucchini, dill, yogurt, and ground black pepper. Then add the oatmeal and mix the mixture until smooth. Heat the canola oil in the pan for 2 minutes. Prepare the patties with the spoon and put them in the hot oil. Cook the patties for 4 minutes per side or until golden brown.

166. Eggplant Croquettes

INGREDIENTS (Servings: 4)

1 eggplant, peeled, boiled
2 potatoes, mashed
2 tbsp. almond meal
1 tsp. chili pepper
1 tbsp. coconut oil
1 tbsp. olive oil
¼ tsp. ground nutmeg

DIRECTIONS (Ready in about: 20 min)

Blend the eggplants until smooth. Then mix it with mashed potatoes, chili pepper, coconut oil, and nutmeg. Prepare the croquettes with the eggplant mixture. Heat the olive oil in the pan. Place the croquettes in the boiling oil and cook for 2 minutes per side or until golden brown. Serve immediately.

Per serving: Kcal 180, Sodium 9 mg, Protein 3.5 g, Carbs 24 g, Fat 8.5 g

167. Garbanzo Stir Fry

INGREDIENTS (Servings: 4)

1 cup garbanzo beans, cooked
1 zucchini, diced
5 oz. cremini mushrooms, chopped
1 tbsp. coconut oil
1 tsp. ground black pepper
1 tbsp. fresh parsley, chopped
1 tbsp. lemon juice

DIRECTIONS (Ready in about: 40 min)

Heat the coconut oil in the pan. Add the mushrooms and grill for 10 minutes. Then add the cooked zucchini and garbanzo beans. Mix the ingredients well and cook for another 10 minutes. After that, sprinkle the vegetables with ground black pepper and lemon juice. Cook the food for 5 minutes. Add the parsley and mix. Cook for another 5 minutes. Serve hot.

Per serving: Kcal 231, Sodium 21 mg, Protein 11 g, Carbs 34 g, Fat 6.5 g

168. Garden Stuffed Squash

INGREDIENTS (Servings: 4)

12 oz. butternut squash halved
1 bell pepper, chopped
5 oz. leek, chopped
1 tsp. dried sage
1 tbsp. coconut oil
2 oz. vegan mozzarella, shredded

DIRECTIONS (Ready in about: 60 min)

Melt the coconut oil in the pan. Add the pepper and leek. Roast the vegetables for 3 minutes. After that, add the dried sage and mix well. Fill the butternut with the vegetable mixture and top with the vegan mozzarella. Bake the squash halves at 360°F for 40 minutes. Serve immediately.

Per serving: Kcal 289, Sodium 233 mg, Protein 4.5 g, Carbs 41 g, Fat 13 g

169. Garlic Shells

INGREDIENTS (Servings: 5)

10 oz. jumbo shells pasta, cooked
5 oz. firm tofu, crumbled
1 tsp. garlic powder
½ cup spinach, grinded
1 tbsp. olive oil
1 cup marinara sauce

DIRECTIONS (Ready in about: 25 min)

In the bowl, combine the olive oil, crumbled tofu, garlic powder, and spinach. Then fill the giant shell pasta with the garlic mixture. Place the pasta with the stuffed shells in the casserole dish and top with the marinara sauce. Use foil to cover the pan and bake in a preheated oven at 365°F for 15 minutes. Serve.

Per serving: Kcal 303, Sodium 211 mg, Protein 10.5 g, Carbs 49.5 g, Fat 6.5 g

170. Glazed Eggplant Rings

INGREDIENTS (Servings: 4)

3 eggplants, sliced
1 tbsp. liquid honey
1 tsp. minced ginger
2 tbsp. lemon juice
3 tbsp. avocado oil
½ tsp. ground coriander
3 tbsp. water

DIRECTIONS (Ready in about: 20 min)

Rub the eggplant with the ground coriander. Then heat the avocado oil in the pan for 1 minute. When the oil is hot, add the sliced eggplants and lay them out in a layer. Cook the vegetables for 1 minute on each side. Transfer the eggplants to the bowl. Then add the minced ginger, liquid honey, lemon juice, and water to the pan. Bring to a boil and add the cooked eggplants. Grease the vegetables well with the sweet liquid and cook for another 2 minutes.

Per serving: Kcal 136, Sodium 12 mg, Protein 4 g, Carbs 30 g, Fat 2 g

171. Hasselback Eggplant

INGREDIENTS (Servings: 2)
2 eggplants, trimmed
2 tomatoes, sliced
1 tbsp. low-fat yogurt
1 tsp. curry powder
1 tsp. olive oil

DIRECTIONS (Ready in about: 40 min)
Make the cuts in the eggplant in the shape of Hasselback. Then rub the vegetables with the curry powder and fill with the tomato slices. Sprinkle the eggplant with olive oil and yogurt and wrap in plastic wrap. Cook the vegetables at 375°F for 25 minutes. Serve.
Per serving: Kcal 188, Sodium 13 mg, Protein 7 g, Carbs 38 g, Fat 3 g

172. Honey Sweet Potato Bake

INGREDIENTS (Servings: 4)
4 sweet potatoes, baked
1 tbsp. honey
1 tsp. ground cinnamon
¼ tsp. ground cardamom
⅓ cup soy milk

DIRECTIONS (Ready in about: 40 min)
Peel the sweet potatoes and mash them. Then mix the mashed potatoes with ground cinnamon, cardamom, and soy milk. Mix it very well. Transfer the mixture to the pan and mash well. Sprinkle the honey mixture and cover with foil. Cook the meal at 375°F for 20 minutes. Serve hot.
Per serving: Kcal 30, Sodium 11 mg, Protein 0.5 g, Carbs 6.5 g, Fat 0.5 g

173. Korma

INGREDIENTS (Servings: 3)
¼ cup cashews, chopped
1 cup of coconut milk
1 cup of frozen vegetables
1 onion, diced
1 tbsp. olive oil
1 tsp. garam masala
½ tsp. curry powder

DIRECTIONS (Ready in about: 30 min)
Mix the cashews and coconut milk. Heat the olive oil in the pan and add the onion. Cook for a few minutes. Stir it well. Then pour the mixture into a saucepan and bring it to a boil. Add the frozen vegetables, garam masala, and curry powder. Close the lid and cook the korma for 10 minutes over medium heat. Serve.
Per serving: Kcal 345, Sodium 38 mg, Protein 6 g, Carbs 19.5 g, Fat 29 g

174. Lentil Curry

INGREDIENTS (Servings: 3)
½ tsp. cumin seeds
¼ tsp. coriander seeds
1 tbsp. coconut oil
1 tsp. minced ginger
½ cup of coconut milk
1 tsp. curry powder
1 cup lentils
½ cup tomato puree
3 cups of water

DIRECTIONS (Ready in about: 25 min)
Put the coconut oil in the pan and let it melt. Add the cumin seeds and coriander seeds. Bring the condiments to a boil. Then add the minced ginger, curry powder, lentils, tomato puree, and water. Boil the lentils and simmer for 10 minutes. Then add the coconut milk and let the lentil curry simmer for another 10 minutes.
Per serving: Kcal 378, Sodium 30 mg, Protein 18 g, Carbs 45.5 g, Fat 15 g

175. Lentil Quiche

INGREDIENTS (Servings: 4)
1 cup green lentils, boiled
½ cup carrot, grated
1 onion, diced
1 tbsp. olive oil
¼ cup flax seeds meal
1 tsp. ground black pepper
¼ cup of soy milk

DIRECTIONS (Ready in about: 50 min)
Use olive oil to cook the onion in the pan until it turns golden brown. Then add the cooked onion, lentils, and carrots. Add the flaxseed, ground black pepper, and soy milk. Stir the mixture until it is smooth. Then transfer it to the pan and flatten it. Bake the quiche for 35 minutes at 375°F.
Per serving: Kcal 351, Sodium 29 mg, Protein 17 g, Carbs 41.5 g, Fat 13 g

176. Loaded Potato Skins

INGREDIENTS (Servings: 6)
6 potatoes
1 tsp. ground black pepper
2 tbsp. olive oil
½ tsp. minced garlic
¼ cup of soy milk

DIRECTIONS (Ready in about: 60 min)
Preheat the oven to 400°F. Prick the potatoes with the knife 2-3 times and bake for 30 minutes or until the vegetables are tender. Then cut the baked potatoes in half and scoop the potato into the bowl.

Sprinkle the scooped potato halves with olive oil and ground black pepper and return to the oven. Bake the potatoes for 15 minutes or until lightly browned. Meanwhile, crush the scooped potato meat and mix it with soy milk and minced garlic. Fill the cooked potato halves with the mashed potatoes. Serve hot.
Per serving: Kcal 196, Sodium 18 mg, Protein 4 g, Carbs 34.5 g, Fat 5 g

177. Mac Stuffed Sweet Potatoes

INGREDIENTS (Servings: 2)
1 sweet potato
¼ cup whole-grain penne pasta
1 tsp. tomato paste
1 tsp. olive oil
¼ tsp. minced garlic
1 tbsp. soy milk

DIRECTIONS (Ready in about: 45 min)
Divide the sweet potato in half and pierce it 3 to 4 times with a fork. Sprinkle the sweet potato halves with olive oil and bake in a preheated 375°F oven until the vegetables are tender. Meanwhile, combine the penne, tomato paste, minced garlic, and soy milk. When the sweet potatoes are cooked, scoop up the vegetarian meat and mix it with the penne mixture. Fill the sweet potatoes with the pasta mixture. Serve.
Per serving: Kcal: 105, Sodium 28 mg, Protein 2.5 g, Carbs 18 g, Fat 3 g

178. Marinated Tofu

INGREDIENTS (Servings: 3)
10 oz. firm tofu, cubed
1 tbsp. olive oil
1 tbsp. rice vinegar
1 tsp. Italian seasonings
1 tbsp. marinara sauce
1 tsp. coconut oil
½ tsp. chili flakes

DIRECTIONS (Ready in about: 28 min)
Prepare the marinade and mix together olive oil, rice vinegar, Italian seasonings, and marinara sauce. Add the chilli flakes and mix the mixture gently. Then sprinkle the tofu cubes with the marinade and let stand for 10 to 15 minutes in the refrigerator. Meanwhile, heat the coconut oil in the pan. Place the marinated tofu in the pan in a layer and broil for 2 minutes per side or until the tofu cubes are light brown. Serve.
Per serving: Kcal 132, Sodium 33 mg, Protein 8 g, Carbs 2.5 g, Fat 11 g

179. Marinated Tofu Skewers

INGREDIENTS (Servings: 4)
¼ cup low-fat yogurt
1 tsp. curry powder
1 onion, diced
1-pound firm tofu, cubed
½ tsp. chili flakes
1 tsp. ground paprika

DIRECTIONS (Ready in about: 45 min)
In the bowl, combine the yogurt, curry, onion, chili flakes, and ground paprika. Then mix the yogurt mixture and the diced tofu. Let the tofu marinate for 20 minutes. Then slide the tofu cubes onto the skewers and place them in the pan. Bake the tofu for 12 minutes at 375°F or until it's light brown.
Per serving: Kcal 105, Sodium 26 mg, Protein 10.5 g, Carbs 6 g, Fat 5 g

180. Minty Chickpea Tabbouleh

INGREDIENTS (Servings: 4)
2 tbsp. lemon juice
¼ cup olive oil
2 tbsp. julienned soft sun-dried tomatoes
¼ cup minced fresh mint
1 can (15 oz.) of garbanzo beans or chickpeas (rinsed and drained)
½ cup minced fresh parsley
1 cup fresh or frozen peas (thawed)
1 cup bulgur
2 cups water
½ tsp. salt
¼ tsp. pepper

DIRECTIONS (Ready in about: 30 min)
Put water and bulgur in a pan over a medium-high flame and bring to a boil. Turn heat to low, cover the pan and simmer for 10 minutes. Add peas, stir and cover the pan. Lower the pressure of the heat and simmer for 5 minutes or until the peas and bulgur are cooked. Put the cooked dish in a bowl and add the rest of the ingredients. Serve warm.
Per serving: Kcal 380, Sodium 450 mg, Protein 4 g, Carbs 21 g, Fat 3 g

181. Mushroom Cakes

INGREDIENTS (Servings: 4)
2 cups mushrooms, chopped
3 garlic cloves, chopped
1 tbsp. dried dill
1 egg, beaten
¼ cup of rice, cooked
1 tbsp. sesame oil
1 tsp. chili powder

DIRECTIONS (Ready in about: 25 min)
Grind the mushrooms in a food processor. Add the garlic, dill, egg, rice, and chili powder. Stir the mixture for 10 seconds. After that, heat the sesame oil for 1 minute. Bake medium-sized mushroom cakes and add hot sesame oil. Cook the mushroom cakes for 5 minutes per side over medium heat. Serve.
Per serving: Kcal 103, Sodium 27 mg, Protein 3.5 g, Carbs 12 g, Fat 4.5 g

182. Mushroom Florentine

INGREDIENTS (Servings: 4)

5 oz. whole-grain pasta	¼ cup of soy milk
¼ cup low-sodium chicken broth	1 tsp. olive oil
1 cup mushrooms, sliced	½ tsp. Italian seasonings

DIRECTIONS (Ready in about: 30 min)
Cook the pasta according to directions from the manufacturer. Then pour the olive oil into the pan and heat it. Add the mushrooms and Italian seasonings. Mix the mushrooms well and cook for 10 minutes. Then add the soy milk and the chicken broth. Add the cooked pasta and mix the mixture well. Cook for 5 minutes over low heat. Serve immediately.
Per serving: Kcal 287, Sodium 26 mg, Protein 12.5 g, Carbs 50.5 g, Fat 4 g

183. Mushroom Stroganoff

INGREDIENTS (Servings: 4)

2 cups mushrooms, sliced	1 tsp. dried thyme
1 tsp. whole-grain wheat flour	1 garlic clove, diced
1 tbsp. coconut oil	1 tsp. ground black pepper
1 onion, chopped	½ cup of soy milk

DIRECTIONS (Ready in about: 30 min)
Heat the coconut oil in the pan. Add the mushrooms and onion and cook for 10 minutes. Stir the vegetables from time to time. Then sprinkle them with ground black pepper, thyme, and garlic. Add the soy milk and bring the mixture to a boil. Then add the whole-grain wheat flour and mix well until smooth. Cook the stroganoff mushrooms until thickened. Serve.
Per serving: Kcal 70, Sodium 19 mg, Protein 2.5 g, Carbs 7 g, Fat 4 g

184. Paella

INGREDIENTS (Servings: 6)

1 tsp. dried saffron	6 oz. artichoke hearts, chopped
1 cup short-grain rice	½ cup green peas
1 tbsp. olive oil	1 onion, sliced
2 cups of water	1 cup bell pepper, sliced
1 tsp. chili flakes	

DIRECTIONS (Ready in about: 35 min)
Pour the water into the pot. Add the rice and cook for 15 minutes. Meanwhile, heat the olive oil in the pan. Add the dried saffron, chili flakes, onion, and bell pepper. Roast the vegetables for 5 minutes. Add them to the cooked rice. Then add the artichoke hearts and the peas. Stir the paella well and cook for 10 minutes over low heat. Serve warm.
Per serving: Kcal 170, Sodium 33 mg, Protein 4 g, Carbs 32.5 g, Fat 2.5 g

185. Pakoras

INGREDIENTS (Servings: 3)

1 potato, diced	¼ cup whole-grain wheat flour
1 onion, diced	4 tbsp. water
1 tbsp. cilantro, chopped	1 tbsp. olive oil
½ cup chickpea flour	
1 tsp. chili flakes	

DIRECTIONS (Ready in about: 30 min)
Combine the potato, onion, cilantro, chickpea flour, chili flakes, wheat flour, and water. Make the mixture homogeneous. Then heat the olive oil in the pan. Using the spoon, make small pakora-balls, and put them in the hot oil. Grill the pakora for 3.5 minutes per side over medium heat or until golden brown. Dry the meal flour with absorbent paper.
Per serving: Kcal 256, Sodium 14 mg, Protein 9.5 g, Carbs 41 g, Fat 7 g

186. Portobello Florentine

INGREDIENTS (Servings: 2)

⅛ tsp. salt	½ tsp. olive oil
¼ cup goat or feta cheese (crumbled)	Minced fresh basil
2 large eggs	⅛ tsp. pepper
1 small onion (chopped)	⅛ tsp. garlic salt
1 cup fresh baby spinach	2 large Portobello mushrooms

DIRECTIONS (Ready in about: 25 min)
Arrange mushrooms in a lightly greased baking pan with the stem side facing up. Spritz with a bit of cooking spray and sprinkle with pepper and garlic salt. Bake in a preheated oven at 425°F for 10 minutes or until tender. Heat oil in a skillet over medium-high flame. Put onion and cook for 3 minutes. Add spinach and stir until wilted. Put the eggs and salt in a bowl and whisk until combined. Add to the skillet and cook until eggs are done. Turn off the heat. Scoop the cooked egg mixture to the mushrooms. Add cheese and basil on top and serve.
Per serving: Kcal 126, Sodium 472 mg, Protein 8 g, Carbs 12 g, Fat 8 g

187. Quinoa Bowl

INGREDIENTS (Servings: 4)
1 cup quinoa
2 cups of water
1 cup tomatoes, diced
1 cup sweet pepper, diced
½ cup of rice, cooked
1 tbsp. lemon juice
½ tsp. lemon zest, grated
1 tbsp. olive oil

DIRECTIONS (Ready in about: 30 min)
Mix the water and the quinoa and cook for 15 minutes. Then remove it from the heat and let stand for 10 minutes. Transfer the cooked quinoa to the large bowl. Add the tomatoes, sweet peppers, rice, lemon juice, lemon zest, and olive oil. Mix well and transfer to serving bowls.
Per serving: Kcal 290, Sodium 11 mg, Protein 8.5 g, Carbs 50 g, Fat 6.5 g

188. Quinoa Burger

INGREDIENTS (Servings: 4)
⅓ cup chickpeas, cooked
½ cup quinoa, cooked
1 tsp. Italian seasonings
1 tsp. olive oil
½ onion, minced

DIRECTIONS (Ready in about: 35 min)
Mix the chickpeas until smooth. Then mix them with the quinoa, Italian seasonings, and chopped onion. Mix the ingredients until they are smooth. After that, make the burgers from the mixture and put them in the lined pan. Sprinkle the quinoa burger with olive oil and bake at 275°F for 20 minutes.
Per serving: Kcal 158, Sodium 6 mg, Protein 6.5 g, Carbs 25 g, Fat 4 g

189. Seitan Patties

INGREDIENTS (Servings: 3)
¼ onion, diced
1 bell pepper, chopped
8 oz. seitan chunks
1 tsp. coconut oil
1 tsp. ground cumin
¼ cup oatmeal
1 oz. walnuts, chopped
¼ tsp. cayenne pepper

DIRECTIONS (Ready in about: 35 min)
Mix onion, pepper, seitan pieces, coconut oil, ground cumin, oatmeal, walnuts, and cayenne pepper. Transfer the mixture to the bowl when it's smooth. Preheat the oven to 365F. Prepare 3 meatballs and transfer them to a lined skillet. Cook the meatballs for 25 minutes at 360°F until they are lightly browned and slightly crispy.
Per serving: Kcal 133, Sodium 44 mg, Protein 3 g, Carbs 13 g, Fat 8 g

190. Spinach Casserole

INGREDIENTS (Servings: 3)
2 cups spinach, chopped
4 oz. artichoke hearts, chopped
¼ cup low-fat yogurt
1 tsp. Italian seasonings
2 oz. vegan mozzarella, shredded

DIRECTIONS (Ready in about: 35 min)
Put the ingredients together in the pot and cover with aluminum foil. Then transfer to a preheated 365°F oven and bake for 30 minutes. Serve hot.
Per serving: Kcal 102, Sodium 206 mg, Protein 3.5 g, Carbs 11 g, Fat 5 g

191. Stuffed Portobello

INGREDIENTS (Servings: 4)
4 Portobello mushroom caps
½ zucchini, grated
1 tomato, diced
1 tsp. olive oil
½ tsp. dried parsley
¼ tsp. minced garlic

DIRECTIONS (Ready in about: 30 min)
In the bowl, combine the chopped tomato, grated zucchini, dried parsley, and minced garlic. Next, fill the mushroom caps with the zucchini mixture and transfer them to the parchment-lined baking sheet. Cook the vegetables until soft or for 20 minutes.
Per serving: Kcal 24, Sodium 5 mg, Protein 1 g, Carbs 3 g, Fat 1 g

192. Sweet Brussel Sprouts

INGREDIENTS (Servings: 2)

1 cup Brussel sprouts, sliced
1 tsp. white pepper
3 tbsp. soy sauce
1 tbsp. olive oil
1 tbsp. pumpkin seeds, chopped
1 tsp. liquid honey

DIRECTIONS (Ready in about: 28 min)

Heat the olive oil in the pan. Add the sliced Brussels sprouts and sauté for 10 minutes. From time to time, stir the vegetables. After that, sprinkle them with white pepper, soy sauce, and liquid honey. Mix the vegetables well and cook for 3 minutes. Add the pumpkin seeds and mix well. Cook the food for another 2 minutes.

Per serving: Kcal 109, Sodium 134 mg, Protein 5 g, Carbs 7.5 g, Fat 7 g

193. Sweet Potato Balls

INGREDIENTS (Servings: 2)

1 cup sweet potato, mashed, cooked
1 tbsp. cilantro, chopped
1 egg, beaten
3 tbsp. ground oatmeal
1 tsp. ground paprika
½ tsp. ground turmeric
2 tbsp. coconut oil

DIRECTIONS (Ready in about: 25 min)

In the bowl, combine the mashed sweet potatoes, fresh cilantro, eggs, ground oatmeal, paprika, and turmeric. Blend the mixture until smooth and make the small balls. Heat the coconut oil in the pan. Add the sweet potato balls to the hot coconut oil. Cook them until golden brown.

Per serving: Kcal 122, Sodium 4 mg, Protein 8 g, Carbs 21 g, Fat 10.5 g

194. Taco Casserole

INGREDIENTS (Servings: 2)

1 tsp. taco seasonings
1 cup black beans, cooked
¼ cup long-grain rice, cooked
1 zucchini, grated
1 cup salsa verde
½ cup vegan mozzarella, shredded
1 tsp. olive oil

DIRECTIONS (Ready in about: 35 min)

Brush the casserole dish with olive oil. After that, add the black beans, rice, and taco seasoning. Put the mixture in the casserole dishes, flatten it well, and decorate with salsa verde and vegan mozzarella. Cook the meal at 375°F for 25 minutes. Serve immediately.
Then add the water, the rest of the soy sauce mixture, and the chopped spinach. Close the lid and cook the flour for another 5 minutes. Serve.

Per serving: Kcal 113, Sodium 242 mg, Protein 9 g, Carbs 19.5 g, Fat 2.5 g

195. Tempeh Reuben

INGREDIENTS (Servings: 4)

10 oz. tempeh
½ cup low-sodium vegetable broth
1 tsp. apple cider vinegar
1 tsp. garlic powder
1 tbsp. olive oil

DIRECTIONS (Ready in about: 35 min)

In the bowl, combine the vegetable broth, apple cider vinegar, and garlic powder. Then put the tempeh in the liquid and marinate for 15-20 minutes. Next, cut the tempeh into portions and place it in the well-preheated pan. Add olive oil and cook for 4 minutes per side or until golden brown.

Per serving: Kcal 171, Sodium 47 mg, Protein 13.5 g, Carbs 7.5 g, Fat 11 g

196. Tofu Parmigiana

INGREDIENTS (Servings: 2)

6 oz. firm tofu, roughly sliced
1 tsp. coconut oil
1 tsp. tomato sauce
½ tsp. Italian seasonings

DIRECTIONS (Ready in about: 25 min)

In the mixing bowl, mix tomato sauce and Italian seasonings. Then, spread the tofu slices well with the tomato mixture and let it marinate for 10 minutes. Heat the coconut oil. Then put the tofu slices in the hot oil and grill for 3 minutes on both sides or until it turns golden brown.

Per serving: Kcal 83, Sodium 24 mg, Protein 7 g, Carbs 1.5 g, Fat 6 g

197. Tofu Stir Fry

INGREDIENTS (Servings: 2)

9 oz. firm tofu, cubed
3 tbsp. low-sodium soy sauce
1 tsp. sesame seeds
1 tbsp. sesame oil
1 cup spinach, chopped
¼ cup of water

DIRECTIONS (Ready in about: 35 min)

In the bowl, combine the soy sauce and sesame oil. Dip the tofu cubes in the soy sauce mixture and marinate for 10 minutes. Heat a skillet and put the tofu cubes in it. Cook them for 1.5 minutes on each side.

Per serving: Kcal 118, Sodium 406 mg, Protein 8.5 g, Carbs 3 g, Fat 8.5 g

198. Tofu Stroganoff

INGREDIENTS (Servings: 2)

4 oz. egg noodles	1 tbsp. coconut oil
6 oz. firm tofu, chopped	1 tsp. ground black pepper
1 tbsp. whole-wheat flour	½ tsp. smoked paprika
1 onion, sliced	½ cup of soy milk
½ cup of water	

DIRECTIONS (Ready in about: 40 min)

Grill the chopped onion with the coconut oil in the pan until golden brown. Then add the ground black pepper, smoked paprika, water, and egg paste. Boil the mixture for 8 minutes. Then mix the flour and soy milk and pour the liquid into the stroganoff mixture. Add the tofu and mix the mixture well. Close the lid and cook the tofu stroganoff for 5 minutes. Let the cooked food rest for 10 minutes and serve.

Per serving: Kcal 270, Sodium 49 mg, Protein 13 g, Carbs 28.5 g, Fat 12 g

199. Tofu Tikka Masala

INGREDIENTS (Servings: 2)

8 oz. tofu, chopped	1 tsp. ground paprika
½ cup of soy milk	½ cup tomatoes, chopped
1 tsp. garam masala	
1 tsp. olive oil	½ onion, diced

DIRECTIONS (Ready in about: 35 min)

Heat the olive oil in the pan. Add the chopped onion to the already heated oil and cook until golden brown. Then add the tomatoes, ground paprika, and garam masala. Bring the mixture to a boil. Add soy milk and mix well. Simmer for 5 minutes. Then add the chopped tofu and cook the food for 3 minutes. Let the cooked food rest for 10 minutes and serve.

Per serving: Kcal 155, Sodium 51 mg, Protein 12 g, Carbs 20.5 g, Fat 8.5 g

200. Tofu Turkey

INGREDIENTS (Servings: 6)

1 cup mushrooms, chopped	1 tsp. dried rosemary
1 bell pepper, chopped	1 tbsp. avocado oil
12 oz. firm tofu, crumbled	½ cup marinara sauce
	1 tsp. miso paste
	1 onion, diced

DIRECTIONS (Ready in about: 90 min)

Sauté onion, mushrooms, bell pepper, rosemary, miso paste, and avocado oil in a saucepan until all ingredients are cooked through (about 10 to 15 minutes). Then put half of the tofu in the round pan. Press down well and make the whole half in the center. Spread the mushroom mixture over the tofu and toss with the marinara sauce. Add the remaining tofu and mash it well. Cover the food with foil. Cook the turkey tofu for 60 minutes at 395°F. Let the turkey rest for 5 minutes and serve.

Per serving: Kcal 80, Sodium 130 mg, Protein 6 g, Carbs 8 g, Fat 3.5 g

201. Turmeric Cauliflower Florets

INGREDIENTS (Servings: 4)

2 cups cauliflower florets	1 tsp. smoked paprika
1 tbsp. ground turmeric	1 tbsp. olive oil

DIRECTIONS (Ready in about: 35 min)

Sprinkle the cauliflower florets with ground turmeric, smoked paprika, and olive oil. Then line the pot with baking paper and place the cauliflower florets in the pan in a single layer. Cook the food for 25 minutes at 375°F or until the cauliflower florets are tender. Serve immediately.

Per serving: Kcal 50, Sodium 16 mg, Protein 1 g, Carbs 4.5 g, Fat 4 g

202. Vegan Chili

INGREDIENTS (Servings: 4)

½ cup bulgur	2 cups low-sodium chicken broth
1 cup tomatoes, chopped	
1 chili pepper, chopped	1 tsp. tomato paste
1 cup red kidney beans, cooked	½ cup celery stalk, chopped

DIRECTIONS (Ready in about: 35 min)
Put all the ingredients in the large saucepan and mix well. Close the lid and simmer the pepper for 25 minutes over medium-low heat. Serve.
Per serving: Kcal 234, Sodium 57 mg, Protein 14 g, Carbs 44.5 g, Fat 0.9 g

203. Vegan Meatballs

INGREDIENTS (Servings: 8)
½ cup white beans, cooked
½ cup quinoa, cooked
2 oz. vegan Parmesan, grated
1 oz. fresh cilantro, chopped
1 tbsp. coconut oil
½ tsp. chili flakes
1 tbsp. tomato paste
½ cup tomato puree
1 tsp. ground black pepper

DIRECTIONS (Ready in about: 35 min)
Put the white beans, quinoa, and vegan Parmesan cheese in the blender. Add the cilantro, chili flakes, and tomato paste and mix until smooth. Prepare the meatballs with the mixture and grill them in preheated coconut oil for 3 minutes per side or until golden brown. Then add the tomato puree and ground black pepper. Close the lid and cook the meatballs for 5 minutes over medium heat. Serve.
Per serving: Kcal 109, Sodium 27 mg, Protein 5.5 g, Carbs 17 g, Fat 2.5 g

204. Vegan Meatloaf

INGREDIENTS (Servings: 6)
1 cup chickpeas, cooked
1 onion, diced
1 tbsp. ground flax seeds
½ tsp. chili flakes
1 tbsp. coconut oil
½ cup carrot, diced
½ cup celery stalk, chopped
1 tbsp. tomato paste

DIRECTIONS (Ready in about: 40 min)
Heat the coconut oil in the pan. Add the carrot, onion, and celery stalk. Cook vegetables for 8 minutes or until tender. Then add the chickpeas, pepper flakes, and ground flax seeds. Stir the mixture until a homogeneous mixture is obtained using the immersion blender. Then cover the loaf pan with parchment paper and transfer the mixed mixture inside. Flatten it well and spread it with the tomato paste. Bake the meatloaf in the preheated 365°F oven for 20 minutes. Serve.
Per serving: Kcal 162, Sodium 25 mg, Protein 7 g, Carbs 24 g, Fat 4.5 g

205. Vegan Shepherd Pie

INGREDIENTS (Servings: 4)
½ cup quinoa, cooked
½ cup tomato puree
½ cup carrot, diced
1 shallot, chopped
1 tbsp. coconut oil
½ cup potato, cooked, mashed
1 tsp. chili powder
½ cup mushrooms, sliced

DIRECTIONS (Ready in about: 50 min)
Place the carrot, shallot, and mushrooms in the pot. Add the coconut oil and cook the vegetables for 10 minutes or until tender but not mushy. Then mix the cooked vegetables with the chili powder and the tomato puree. Transfer the mixture to the saucepan and mash well. Then top the vegetables with mashed potatoes. Cover the shepherd's pie with foil and bake in a preheated 375°F oven for 25 minutes. Serve.
Per serving: Kcal 136, Sodium 27 mg, Protein 4 g, Carbs 20 g, Fat 4.5 g

206. Vegetarian Kebabs

INGREDIENTS (Servings: 4)
2 tbsp. balsamic vinegar
1 tbsp. olive oil
1 tsp. dried parsley
2 tbsp. water
2 sweet peppers
2 red onions, peeled
2 zucchinis, trimmed

DIRECTIONS (Ready in about: 16 min)
Cut the sweet peppers and onions into medium squares. Then cut the zucchini. Put all the vegetables on the skewers. Then, in a shallow bowl, combine the olive oil, dried parsley, water, and balsamic vinegar. Sprinkle the vegetable skewers with the olive oil mixture and transfer them to a preheated 390°F grill. Cook the skewers on both sides for 3 minutes, or until the vegetables are golden brown. Serve immediately.
Per serving: Kcal 88, Sodium 14 mg, Protein 2.5 g, Carbs 4 g, Fat 4 g

207. Vegetarian Lasagna

INGREDIENTS (Servings: 6)
1 cup carrot, diced
½ cup bell pepper, diced
1 cup spinach, chopped
1 tbsp. olive oil
1 tsp. chili powder
1 eggplant, sliced
1 cup tomatoes, chopped
4 oz. low-fat cottage cheese
1 cup low-sodium chicken broth

DIRECTIONS (Ready in about: 40 min)
Place the carrot, pepper, and spinach in the pot. Add olive oil and chili powder and mix the vegetables well. Cook them for 5 minutes. Then place the sliced eggplant layer in the casserole dish and garnish with the vegetable mixture. Add the tomatoes and cottage cheese. Bake the lasagna for 30 minutes at 375°F. Serve hot.
Per serving: Kcal 77, Sodium 113 mg, Protein 4.5 g, Carbs 9.5 g, Fat 3 g

208. Vegetarian Sloppy Joes

INGREDIENTS (Servings: 2)
½ cup green lentils
1 white onion, diced
1 tsp. chili pepper
½ tsp. smoked paprika
2 tbsp. tomato paste
1 tbsp. sesame oil
1 tsp. liquid honey
2 cups of water
½ cup of coconut milk

DIRECTIONS (Ready in about: 60 min)
Pour the sesame oil into the pan. Add the white onion, chili, and smoked paprika and cook the ingredients for 4 minutes. Then add the green lentils, tomato paste, liquid honey, and water. Add the coconut milk and mix the mixture well. Close the lid and cook over medium heat for 40 minutes. Then remove the flour from the heat and leave it to stand for 10 minutes before serving.
Per serving: Kcal 416, Sodium 38 mg, Protein 15 g, Carbs 44 g, Fat 22 g

209. White Beans Stew

INGREDIENTS (Servings: 4)
1 cup white beans, soaked
1 cup low-sodium chicken broth
1 cup zucchini, chopped
1 tsp. tomato paste
4 cups of water
½ tsp. peppercorns
½ tsp. ground black pepper
¼ tsp. ground nutmeg
1 tbsp. avocado oil

DIRECTIONS (Ready in about: 65 min)
In the pan, heat the avocado oil, add the zucchini, and cook for 5 minutes. Then add the white beans, chicken broth, tomato paste, water, peppercorns, ground black pepper, and nutmeg. Cover the lid and cook the stew on low heat for 50 minutes.
Per serving: Kcal 184, Sodium 37 mg, Protein 13 g, Carbs 32 g, Fat 8,5 g

210. Zucchanoush

INGREDIENTS (Servings: 6)
4 zucchinis, chopped
2 tbsp. olive oil
1 tsp. harissa
1 tbsp. tahini paste
1 tsp. pine nuts, roasted
¼ tsp. garlic powder
½ tsp. dried mint

DIRECTIONS (Ready in about: 45 min)
Preheat the oven to 365°F. Place the zucchini in the pan, sprinkle with olive oil and bake for 35 minutes or until the vegetables are tender. Then transfer the zucchini to the food processor. Add the harissa, tahini paste, pine nuts, garlic powder, and dried mint. Mix the food until smooth. Serve.
Per serving: Kcal 123, Sodium 39 mg, Protein 3 g, Carbs 8.5 g, Fat 10 g

211. Zucchini Grinders

INGREDIENTS (Servings: 2)
¼ cup marinara sauce
2 oz. vegan mozzarella, grated
1 tsp. olive oil
1 tsp. chili powder
1 zucchini, diced

DIRECTIONS (Ready in about: 30 min)
Roast the zucchini in olive oil for 4 minutes. From time to time, stir the vegetables. Then transfer the vegetables to the baking pan flatten well. Add the marinara sauce and the mozzarella. Use the foil to cover the baking pan and bake for 15 minutes at 365°F. Serve.
Per serving: Kcal 157, Sodium 261 mg, Protein 3 g, Carbs 15 g, Fat 9.5 g

212. Zucchini Soufflé

INGREDIENTS (Servings: 4)
2 cups zucchini, grated
½ tsp. baking powder
½ cup oatmeal, grinded
1 onion, diced
3 tbsp. water
1 tsp. cayenne pepper
1 tsp. dried thyme

DIRECTIONS (Ready in about: 65 min)
Combine all the ingredients in the casserole mold. Flatten the zucchini mixture well and cover it with plastic wrap. Bake the soufflé at 365°F for 60 minutes. Serve.

POULTRY

213. Artichoke Spinach Chicken

INGREDIENTS (Servings: 4)

2 tbsp. olive oil
14 oz. artichoke hearts, chopped
4 chicken breasts, boneless and skinless
28 oz. tomato sauce, no-salt-added
½ tsp. red pepper flakes, crushed
10 oz. baby spinach

DIRECTIONS (Ready in about: 30 min)

Bring the pan to medium heat -high heat, add chicken and red pepper flakes and cook for 5 minutes on each side. Add spinach, artichokes, and tomato sauce, toss, cook for 10 minutes more, divide between plates and serve.

Per serving: Kcal 212, Sodium 346 mg, Protein 20 g, Carbs 16 g, Fat 3 g

214. Avocado and Chicken Mix

INGREDIENTS (Servings: 4)

2 chicken breasts, skinless, boneless, and halved
2 tbsp. olive oil
½ cup low-sodium veggie stock
A pinch of black pepper
2 garlic cloves, minced
1 avocado, peeled, pitted, and cut into wedges
Juice of ½ lemon

DIRECTIONS (Ready in about: 30 min)

Warm a pan with the oil over medium heat, add the garlic and the meat, and brown for 2 minutes on each side. Add the lemon juice and the other ingredients, bring to a simmer, and cook over medium heat for 15 minutes. Divide the whole mix between plates and serve.

Per serving: Kcal 436, Sodium 230 mg, Protein 42 g, Carbs 5.5 g, Fat 27 g

215. Baked Chicken and Apples

INGREDIENTS (Servings: 4)

2 pounds chicken thighs, boneless and skinless
1 tsp. thyme, dried
A pinch of black pepper
1 tsp. basil, dried
2 garlic cloves, minced
2 tbsp. olive oil
1 cup green apples, cored and roughly cubed
1 tbsp. cilantro, chopped
2 cups low-sodium chicken stock
1 cup tomatoes, cubed
2 red onions, sliced
1 tbsp. lemon juice

DIRECTIONS (Ready in about: 60 min)

Warm a pan with the oil over medium-high heat, add the onions and garlic and sauté for 5 minutes. Add the chicken and brown for another 5 minutes. Add the thyme, basil, and the other ingredients, toss gently, introduce in the oven and bake at 390°F for 40 minutes. Divide the chicken and apple mix between plates and serve.

Per serving: Kcal 290, Sodium 280 mg, Protein 10 g, Carbs 15.5 g, Fat 12 g

216. Baked Chicken and Wild Rice

INGREDIENTS (Servings: 6)

1-pound boneless, skinless chicken breast halves
1½ cups chopped celery
1½ cups whole pearl onions
2 cups chicken broth
¾ cup uncooked long-grain white rice
¾ cup uncooked wild rice
1½ cups dry white wine
1 tsp. fresh tarragon

DIRECTIONS (Ready in about: 2 h)

Heat up the oven to 300°F. Cut the chicken breasts into 1-inch pieces. In a nonstick skillet, combine the chicken, celery, onion, and tarragon with 1 cup of unsalted chicken broth. Cook over medium heat until chicken and vegetables are tender, about 10 minutes. Set aside to cool. In a baking dish, combine the rice, wine, and the remaining cup of chicken broth. Let it soak for 30 minutes. Add the chicken and vegetables to the pan. For 60 minutes, cover and bake. Check regularly and if the rice is too dry, add more broth. Serve immediately.

Per serving: Kcal 313, Sodium 104 mg, Protein 2.5 g, Carbs 38 g, Fat 8 g

217. Balsamic Roast Chicken

INGREDIENTS (Servings: 8)

1 tbsp. fresh of rosemary or 1 tsp. dried rosemary
1 whole chicken, about 4 pounds
1 garlic clove
⅛ tsp. black pepper
1 tbsp. olive oil
8 sprigs of fresh rosemary
1 tsp. brown sugar
½ cup balsamic vinegar

DIRECTIONS (Ready in about: 2 h 20 min)
Heat up the oven to 350°F. Chop the rosemary and garlic together. Peel the chicken skin off the meat and rub the meat with olive oil and then the herb mixture. Sprinkle with black pepper. Place 2 sprigs of rosemary in the chicken cavity. Truss the chicken. Place the chicken on a baking sheet and roast for 20-25 minutes per pound, about 1 hour and 20 minutes. Whole chicken should be cooked to a minimum core temperature of 165°F. Baste frequently with the juice from the pan. When the chicken is browned, and the sauce is clear, transfer the chicken to a serving plate. In a saucepan, combine the balsamic vinegar and the brown sugar. Warm until the mixture is warmed and brown sugar dissolves, but do not boil. Cut the chicken into slices and remove the skin. Cover the pieces with the vinegar mixture. Garnish with the remaining rosemary and serve immediately.
Per serving: Kcal 301, Sodium 131 mg, Protein 43 g, Carbs 3.5 g, Fat 4 g

218. Balsamic Turkey Peach Mix

INGREDIENTS (Servings: 4)
1 turkey breast, skinless, boneless, and sliced
1 tbsp. avocado oil
A pinch of black pepper
2 tbsp. chives, chopped
¼ cup balsamic
4 peaches, stones removed and cut into wedges
1 yellow onion, chopped

DIRECTIONS (Ready in about: 35 min)
Warmth up a pan with the oil over medium-high heat, add the meat and the onion, toss, and brown for approximately five minutes. Include the rest of the ingredients except the chives, toss gently, and bake at 390°F for 20 minutes. Divide everything between plates and serve with the chives sprinkled on top.
Per serving: Kcal 123, Sodium 230 mg, Protein 9 g, Carbs 19 g, Fat 1.5 g

219. Barbecue Chicken Pizza

INGREDIENTS (Servings: 4)
1 12-inch thin, whole-grain pizza crust
1 cup tomato sauce, no salt added
4 oz. of cooked chicken breast, sliced about 1-inch thick, with all visible fat, removed
1 green pepper, cut into rings
1 cup mushrooms, sliced
1 tomato, sliced
1 cup shredded, reduced-fat mozzarella cheese
4 tbsp. barbecue sauce

DIRECTIONS (Ready in about: 1 h 25 min)
Heat up the oven to 400°F. Spread the sauce uniformly over the crust of the pizza. Add pepper, tomato, chicken, and mushrooms. Drizzle over the pizza with barbecue sauce and cover with cheese. Cook for 12 to 14 minutes, roughly. Break into 8 slices of pizza and serve.
Per serving: Kcal 261, Sodium 475 mg, Protein 21.5 g, Carbs 28 g, Fat 7 g

220. Buffalo Chicken Salad Wrap

INGREDIENTS (Servings: 4)
2 whole chipotle peppers
3 4-oz. chicken breasts (12 oz. total)
¼ cup white wine vinegar
¼ cup low-calorie mayonnaise
2 whole-grain tortillas (12-inch diameter)
2 stalks celery, diced
4 oz. raw spinach
3 4-oz. chicken breasts (12 oz. total)
2 carrots, cut into matchsticks
½ cup of raw rutabaga or jicama, cut into matchsticks
1 small diced yellow onion (about ½ cup)

DIRECTIONS (Ready in about: 40 min)
Heat the oven to 375°F or turn on the grill. Broil or grill the chicken breasts for about 10 minutes per side until the core temperature is 165°F. Remove, cool, and cube the chicken. In a blender, combine the chipotle peppers with the white wine vinegar and mayonnaise. Put all ingredients together except spinach and tortillas in a bowl and mix well. Place 2 oz. of spinach and half the chicken mixture on each tortilla and wrap. Cut each wrap in half to serve.
Per serving: Kcal 247, Sodium 374 mg, Protein 25 g, Carbs 21 g, Fat 7 g

221. Chicken and Asparagus Mix

INGREDIENTS (Servings: 4)
2 tbsp. avocado oil
2 chicken breasts, skinless, boneless, and cubed
2 spring onions, chopped
½ tsp. sweet paprika
14 oz. canned tomatoes, no-salt-added, drained and chopped
1 bunch asparagus, trimmed and halved
A pinch of black pepper

DIRECTIONS (Ready in about: 35 min)
Warmth up a pan with the oil over medium-high heat, add the meat and the spring onions, stir and cook for 5 minutes. Add the asparagus and the other ingredients, toss, cover the pan and cook over medium heat for 20 minutes. Divide everything between plates and serve.
Per serving: Kcal 171, Sodium 396 mg, Protein 22 g, Carbs 6.5 g, Fat 6.5 g

222. Chicken and Asparagus Penne

INGREDIENTS (Servings: 2)
1 cup asparagus, cut into 1-inch pieces
1 can (14.5 oz.) diced tomatoes, without salt, including juice
2 cloves garlic, minced
2 tsp. dried basil or oregano
1 tbsp. Parmesan cheese
6 oz. of boneless, skinless chicken breasts, cut into 1-inch cubes
1 oz. soft goat cheese, crumbled
1½ cups of uncooked whole-grain penne pasta

DIRECTIONS (Ready in about: 35 min)
Fill a large saucepan ¾ full with water and bring to a boil. Add pasta and cook until tender, 10 to 12 minutes, or according to package directions. Drain the pasta well and set it aside. In a saucepan fitted with a steamer basket, bring 1 inch of water to a boil. Add the asparagus. Cover and steam until tender and crisp, about 2-3 minutes. Spray an enormous nonstick skillet with cooking spray. Add chicken and garlic and sauté over medium-high heat. Cook for about 5 to 7 minutes, until the chicken is golden brown. Add the tomatoes and their juice, basil or oregano, and cook for another 1 minute. Put the cooked pasta, steamed asparagus, chicken mixture, and goat cheese in a large dish. Stir gently to blend uniformly. Divide the pasta mixture into 2 plates in order to serve. Sprinkle ½ tbsp. of Parmesan cheese on each serving. Serve immediately.
Per serving: Kcal 433, Sodium 240 mg, Protein 34 g, Carbs 54 g, Fat 9.5 g

223. Chicken and Celery Mix

INGREDIENTS (Servings: 4)
2 pounds chicken breast, skinless, boneless, and cubed
1 poblano pepper, chopped
2 tbsp. chives, chopped
A pinch of black pepper
2 tbsp. olive oil
3 garlic cloves, minced
1 cup celery, chopped
1 tsp. chili powder
1 cup low-sodium veggie stock

DIRECTIONS (Ready in about: 45 min)
Warm a pan with the oil over medium heat, add the garlic, celery, and poblano pepper, toss and cook for 5 minutes. Add the meat, toss and cook for another 5 minutes. Include the rest of the ingredients except the chives, bring to a simmer and cook over medium heat for 25 minutes more. Divide the whole mix between plates and serve with the chives sprinkled on top.
Per serving: Kcal 305, Sodium 332 mg, Protein 6 g, Carbs 22.5, Fat 18 g

224. Chicken and Chili Zucchini

INGREDIENTS (Servings: 4)
1 cup low-sodium chicken stock
1-pound chicken breasts, skinless, boneless and cubed
2 zucchinis, roughly cubed
1 cup canned tomatoes, no-salt-added, chopped
1 tbsp. olive oil
1 yellow onion, chopped
1 tbsp. cilantro, chopped
1 tsp. chili powder

DIRECTIONS (Ready in about: 30 min)
Warm a pan with the oil over medium-high heat, add the meat and the onion, toss, and brown for 5 minutes. Add the zucchinis and the rest of the ingredients, toss gently, reduce the heat to medium and cook for 20 minutes. Divide everything between plates and serve.
Per serving: Kcal 284, Sodium 310 mg, Protein 35 g, Carbs 8 g, Fat 12.5 g

225. Chicken and Dill Green Beans

INGREDIENTS (Servings: 4)
10 oz. green beans, trimmed and halved
1 yellow onion, chopped
2 chicken breasts, skinless, boneless, and halved
½ tsp. red pepper flakes, crushed
1 tbsp. dill, chopped
2 cups tomato sauce, no-salt-added
2 tbsp. olive oil

DIRECTIONS (Ready in about: 35 min)
Warm a pan with the oil over medium-high heat, add the onion and the meat and brown it for 2 minutes on each side.

Add the green beans and the other ingredients, toss, introduce in the oven and bake at 380°F for 20 minutes. Divide between plates and serve right away.
Per serving: Kcal 391, Sodium 280 mg, Protein 44 g, Carbs 15.5 g, Fat 18 g

226. Chicken and Mustard Sauce

INGREDIENTS (Servings: 4)
1 cup asparagus, cut into 1-inch pieces
1 can (14.5 oz.) diced tomatoes, without salt, including juice
2 cloves garlic, minced
2 tsp. dried basil or oregano
1 tbsp. Parmesan cheese
6 oz. of boneless, skinless chicken breasts, cut into 1-inch cubes
1 oz. soft goat cheese, crumbled
1½ cups of uncooked whole-grain penne pasta

DIRECTIONS (Ready in about: 45 min)
Warm a pan with the oil over medium heat, add the shallot, garlic, and the chicken, and brown everything for 5 minutes. Add the mustard and the rest of the ingredients, toss gently, bring to a simmer and cook over medium heat for 30 minutes. Divide everything between plates and serve hot.
Per serving: Kcal 299, Sodium 150 mg, Protein 12.5 g, Carbs 30 g, Fat 15.5 g

227. Chicken and Olives Pan

INGREDIENTS (Servings: 4)
A pinch of black pepper
1-pound chicken breasts, skinless, boneless, and roughly cubed
1 tbsp. avocado oil
1 cup of coconut milk
1 red onion, chopped
1 tbsp. lemon juice
¼ cup cilantro, chopped
1 cup kalamata olives, pitted and sliced

DIRECTIONS (Ready in about: 35 min)
Warmth up a pan with the oil over medium-high heat, add the onion and the meat, and brown for 5 minutes. Add the rest of the ingredients, toss, bring to a simmer and cook over medium heat for 20 minutes more. Divide between plates and serve.
Per serving: Kcal 409, Sodium 280 mg, Protein 35 g, Carbs 8 g, Fat 26.5 g

228. Chicken and Veggies

INGREDIENTS (Servings: 4)
1 cup low-sodium chicken stock
1-pound chicken breasts, skinless, boneless, and cubed
2 zucchinis, roughly cubed
1 cup canned tomatoes, no-salt-added, chopped
1 tbsp. olive oil
1 yellow onion, chopped
1 tbsp. cilantro, chopped
1 tsp. chili powder

DIRECTIONS (Ready in about: 35 min)
Bring the pan to medium heat -high heat, add chicken, black pepper, onion, and Italian seasoning, toss, and cook for 5 minutes. Add tomatoes and cauliflower, toss, cover the pan and cook over medium heat for 20 minutes. Toss again, divide everything between plates and serve.
Per serving: Kcal 310, Sodium 314 mg, Protein 20 g, Carbs 16.5 g, Fat 6 g

229. Chicken Brats

INGREDIENTS (Servings: 6)
4 cloves garlic, minced
1 cup minced yellow onion
1-pound ground chicken breast
1 cup cooked brown rice
2 tsp. fennel seed
1 tsp. ground paprika
1 tsp. cumin seed (or caraway, which has a milder flavor)
1 tsp. black pepper
½ tsp. ground cayenne pepper
1 tsp. of minced fresh rosemary (or ¼ tsp. dried)
½ tsp. ground white pepper
¼ tsp. nutmeg
1 tsp. ground mustard seed
1 tsp. celery seed
½ tsp. canola oil

DIRECTIONS (Ready in about: 25 min)
In a skillet, brown the onion and garlic in canola oil until golden brown. Transfer to a large bowl and toss with the cooked rice, minced chicken breast, and other ingredients. Refrigerator for 1 hour. Divide the mixture into 6 equal parts. Roll into a sausage shape. Or, if you like, you can pipe the mixture into 6 sausage shapes. Put on the baking sheet. Bake at 350°F for 5 to 10 minutes, until internal temperature is 125°F. Then transfer to the grill to finish cooking. The brats are not fully cooked until they reach a core temperature of 165°F.

Per serving: Kcal 147, Sodium 37 mg, Protein 18 g, Carbs 12 g, Fat 3 g

230. Chicken Burritos

INGREDIENTS (Servings: 4)

1 red bell pepper, chopped
1 tsp. oil
1 jalapeno pepper, seeded and chopped
1 yellow onion, chopped
2 ribs celery, chopped
2 tbsp. cumin seed
2 tbsp. fresh oregano
2 cups grape tomatoes
2 cloves garlic, chopped
2 cups shredded green cabbage
4 whole-wheat tortillas
8 oz. cooked chicken breast meat
½ cup canned black beans, drained and rinsed

DIRECTIONS (Ready in about: 55 min)

In an enormous skillet over medium-high heat, add the oil and peppers, celery, onion, and cumin until lightly browned, about 10 to 15 minutes. Add the tomatoes, oregano, and garlic. Continue to sauté until the tomatoes are bubbling and popping, about 5 to 10 minutes. Move the contents to a blender and mix to the desired consistency. Separate the chicken breast and divide it between the tortillas. Garnish with beans, cabbage, and sauce. Roll up and serve.

Per serving: Kcal 286, Sodium 382 mg, Protein 20.5 g, Carbs 38 g, Fat 6 g

231. Chicken Cutlets with Fruit

INGREDIENTS (Servings: 6)

1 cup chopped pineapple
2 Ruby Red grapefruits
1 mango, chopped
1 to 3 jalapeño chiles, seeded and chopped
¼ cup sliced red onion
¼ cup chopped cilantro
2 tsp. canola oil
¼ tsp. freshly ground black pepper
½ tsp. kosher salt, divided
1-½ pounds chicken breast tenders

DIRECTIONS (Ready in about: 35 min)

Make the salsa: Supreme the grapefruits into a large bowl and cut into bite-size pieces. Add the pineapple, mango, onion, jalapeño, cilantro, and ¼ tsp. of the salt, and stir to combine. Set aside. Season the chicken tenders with the remaining ¼ tsp. salt and pepper. Heat the canola oil in a medium sauté pan or skillet over medium-high heat. Working in batches if necessary, add chicken and sauté until browned on one side, 2 to 3 minutes. Flip the chicken and cook the other side until golden, 2-3 minutes more. Cut off the thicker piece to determine that it is no longer pink. Serve the chicken fillets with a dollop of fruit sauce.

Per serving: Kcal 389, Sodium 502 mg, Protein 37 g, Carbs 37.5 g, Fat 19 g

232. Chicken Quesadillas

INGREDIENTS (Servings: 6)

1 cup chopped onions
4 boneless and skinless chicken breasts, each 4 oz.
½ cup smoky or hot salsa
1 cup shredded reduced-fat cheddar cheese
1 cup chopped fresh cilantro
1 cup chopped fresh tomatoes
6 whole-wheat tortillas, every 8 inches in diameter

DIRECTIONS (Ready in about: 55 min)

Heat oven to 425°F. Lightly coats a baking sheet with cooking spray. Cut each chicken breast into cubes. In a large nonstick skillet, add the chicken and onions and sauté until the onions are tender and the chicken is cooked for about 5-7 minutes. Keep away from heat. Add the sauce, tomatoes, and cilantro. To assemble, lay out a flat tortilla and rub the outer edge with water. Spread about a half cup of the chicken mixture over the tortilla, leaving about ½ inch free around the outer edge. Sprinkle with a tbsp. of shredded cheese. Fold the tortilla in half and close it. Put it on a baking sheet. Repeat with the remaining tortillas. Cover the tops of tortillas lightly with cooking spray. Cook until quesadillas are lightly browned and crispy, about 5 to 7 minutes. Cut in half and serve immediately.

Per serving: Kcal 298, Sodium 524 mg, Protein 27 g, Carbs 25.3 g, Fat 5 g

233. Chicken Salad with Pineapple

INGREDIENTS (Servings: 8)

1 tbsp. olive oil
4 boneless and skinless chicken breasts, each about 5 oz.
1 can (8 oz.) of unsweetened pineapple chunks, drained except for 2 tbsp. juice
2 cups broccoli florets
4 cups fresh baby spinach leaves
½ cup thinly sliced red onions

For the Vinaigrette:
¼ cup olive oil
2 tbsp. balsamic vinegar
2 tsp. sugar
¼ tsp. ground cinnamon

DIRECTIONS (Ready in about: 35 min)
Cut each chicken breast into cubes. Heat the olive oil in an enormous nonstick skillet over medium heat. Add the chicken and cook until golden brown, about 10 minutes. In a large bowl, combine the cooked chicken, pineapple chunks, broccoli, spinach, and onion. To prepare the dressing, combine the olive oil, vinegar, reserved pineapple juice, sugar, and cinnamon in a small bowl. Pour over the salad. Stir gently to coat evenly. Serve immediately.
Per serving: Kcal 186, Sodium 50 mg, Protein 17 g, Carbs 7 g, Fat 3 g

234. Chicken Sliders

INGREDIENTS (Servings: 4)

10 oz. ground chicken breast	1 fresh chili pepper, minced
1 tbsp. black pepper	1 tbsp. fennel seed, crushed
1 tbsp. minced garlic	
1 tbsp. balsamic vinegar	4 whole-wheat mini buns
½ cup minced onion	
4 tomato slices	4 lettuce leaves

DIRECTIONS (Ready in about: 30 min)
Mix the first 7 items and refrigerate for 1 hour. Form into 4 patties. Roast or broil in the oven until it reaches a minimum internal temperature of 165°F. Serve on small whole-wheat buns with lettuce and tomatoes.
Per serving: Kcal 224, Sodium 173 mg, Protein 22 g, Carbs 25 g, Fat 4 g

235. Chicken with Mustard Greens

INGREDIENTS (Servings: 4)

3 cups mustard greens	1 red onion, chopped
2 chicken breasts, skinless, boneless, and cubed	1 tsp. oregano, dried
	A pinch of black pepper
	1 tbsp. chives, chopped
1 cup canned tomatoes, no-salt-added, chopped	2 garlic cloves, minced
	1 tbsp. balsamic vinegar
2 tbsp. avocado oil	

DIRECTIONS (Ready in about: 35 min)
Warm a pan with the oil over medium-high heat, add the onion and the garlic and sauté for 5 minutes. Add the meat and brown it for 5 minutes more. Add the greens, tomatoes, and the other ingredients, toss, cook for 20 minutes over medium heat, divide between plates and serve.
Per serving: Kcal 290, Sodium 156 mg, Protein 14 g, Carbs 22.5 g, Fat 12.5 g

236. Chicken with Paprika Scallions

INGREDIENTS (Servings: 4)

4 scallions, chopped	1 tbsp. ginger, grated
1-pound chicken breast, skinless, boneless, and sliced	1 tsp. cumin, ground
	1 tsp. oregano, dried
	1 tsp. allspice, ground
1 tbsp. olive oil	A pinch of black pepper
1 cup low-sodium chicken stock	½ cup cilantro, chopped
	1 tbsp. sweet paprika

DIRECTIONS (Ready in about: 40 min)
Warm a pan with the oil over medium heat, add the scallions and the meat, and brown for 5 minutes. Add the rest of the ingredients, toss, introduce in the oven and bake at 390°F for 25 minutes. Divide the chicken and scallions, mix between plates and serve.
Per serving: Kcal 295, Sodium 200 mg, Protein 15.5 g, Carbs 22 g, Fat 12.5 g

237. Chicken with Red Onion Mix

INGREDIENTS (Servings: 4)

3 red onions, sliced	1 tbsp. chives, chopped
2 chicken breasts, skinless, boneless, and roughly cubed	A pinch of black pepper
	1 cup low-sodium veggie stock
2 tbsp. olive oil	1 tbsp. cilantro, chopped

DIRECTIONS (Ready in about: 35 min)
Warm a pan with the oil over medium heat, add the onions and a pinch of black pepper and sauté for 10 min, stirring often. Include the chicken and cook for 3 min more. Add the rest of the ingredients, bring to a simmer and cook over medium heat for 12 min more. Divide the chicken and onions between plates. Serve.
Per serving: Kcal 364, Sodium 160 mg, Protein 41.5 g, Carbs 9 g, Fat 17.5 g

238. Chipotle Chicken

INGREDIENTS (Servings: 6)

1 yellow onion, chopped	1 tsp. cumin, ground
	1 tbsp. coriander, chopped
2 pounds chicken thighs, boneless and skinless	4 tbsp. chipotle chili paste
	1 cup low-sodium chicken stock
2 tbsp. olive oil	3 garlic cloves, minced
1 tbsp. coriander seeds	A pinch of black pepper

DIRECTIONS (Ready in about: 1 h 10 min)
Warm a pan with the oil over medium heat, add the onion and the garlic and sauté for 5 minutes. Add the meat and brown for 5 minutes more. Add the rest of the ingredients, toss, introduce everything in the oven, and bake at 390°F for 50 minutes. Divide the whole mix between plates and serve.
Per serving: Kcal 280, Sodium 369.5 mg, Protein 12 g, Carbs 15.5 g, Fat 12 g

239. Cinnamon Roasted Chicken

INGREDIENTS (Servings: 4)

2 tbsp. unsalted butter, at room temperature	1 (3-¼ to 3-½-pound) whole chicken
3 Red Delicious apples, sliced	½ tsp. kosher salt
2 tsp. of grated orange zest (about 1 orange)	1 tsp. ground cinnamon
	¼ tsp. freshly ground black pepper

DIRECTIONS (Ready in about: 2 h)
Preheat the oven to 425°F. Spread the apples in the baking dish. Combine the butter, orange zest, cinnamon, salt, and pepper in a small bowl. Rinse the chicken and blot dry. Using a knife, cut the backbone out. Place the chicken split-side down on top of the apples. Divide the butter mixture into two and rub half underneath the skin. Rub the remaining half on the skin. Cook the chicken until the temperature reaches 180°F, or the juices run clear when pricked, about 40 minutes. Tent the chicken with aluminum foil to keep warm and let rest for about 5 minutes. Cut the chicken into pieces and serve with the roasted apples and juices.
Per serving: Kcal 329, Sodium 387 mg, Protein 19 g, Carbs 19 g, Fat 14 g

240. Coconut Chicken and Spinach

INGREDIENTS (Servings: 4)

1-pound chicken breast, skinless, boneless, and cubed	2 cups baby spinach
	2 garlic cloves, minced
	2 shallots, chopped
1 tbsp. avocado oil	½ tsp. sweet paprika
½ tsp. basil, dried	2 tbsp. cilantro, chopped
¼ cup low-sodium veggie stock	⅔ cup coconut cream
A pinch of black pepper	

DIRECTIONS (Ready in about: 35 min)
Warm a pan with the oil over medium-high heat, add the meat, basil, black pepper, and brown for 5 minutes. Add the shallots and the garlic and cook for another 5 minutes. Add the rest of the ingredients, toss, bring to a simmer and cook over medium heat for 15 minutes more. Divide between plates and serve hot.
Per serving: Kcal 237, Sodium 327 mg, Protein 26 g, Carbs 4.5 g, Fat 13 g

241. Garlic Turkey and Mushrooms

INGREDIENTS (Servings: 4)

½ pound white mushrooms halved	1 tbsp. rosemary, chopped
	2 garlic cloves, minced
1 turkey breast, boneless, skinless, and cubed	A pinch of black pepper
	3 tbsp. garlic sauce
	2 green onion, chopped
⅓ cup coconut aminos	2 tbsp. olive oil

DIRECTIONS (Ready in about: 50 min)
Warmth up a pan with the oil over medium heat, add the green onions, garlic sauce, and the garlic, and sauté for 5 minutes. Add the meat and brown it for 5 minutes more. Add the rest of the ingredients, introduce them into the oven, and bake at 390°F for 30 minutes. Divide the mix between plates and serve.
Per serving: Kcal 154, Sodium 22 mg, Protein 10 g, Carbs 11.5 g, Fat 8 g

242. Honey Crusted Chicken

INGREDIENTS (Servings: 2)

8 saltine crackers, each about 2 inches square	2 boneless, skinless chicken breasts, each 4 oz.
1 tsp. paprika	4 tsp. honey

DIRECTIONS (Ready in about: 50 min)
Heat oven to 375°F. Lightly coats a baking sheet with cooking spray. Crush the crackers. Put the crackers in a small bowl and add the paprika. Stir to mix well. In another bowl, add the chicken and honey. Launch evenly. Add the cookie mixture. Stir and press chicken into the crackers mixture until evenly coated on both sides. Place the chicken in the prepared pan. Cook until it turns lightly browned and cooked through, about 20-25 minutes. Serve immediately.
Per serving: Kcal 224, Sodium 204 mg, Protein 27.5 g, Carbs 20 g, Fat 4 g

243. Hot Turkey and Rice

INGREDIENTS (Servings: 4)
1 cup white rice
1 turkey breast, skinless, boneless, and cubed
2 cups low-sodium veggie stock
2 small Serrano peppers, chopped
A pinch of black pepper
1 tsp. hot paprika
2 garlic cloves, minced
½ red bell pepper chopped
2 tbsp. olive oil

DIRECTIONS (Ready in about: 52 min)
Warm a pan with the oil over medium heat, add the Serrano peppers and garlic and sauté for 2 minutes. Add the meat and brown it for 5 minutes. Add the rice and the other ingredients, bring to a simmer, and cook over medium heat for 35 minutes. Stir, divide between plates, and serve.

Per serving: Kcal 271, Sodium 230 mg, Protein 8 g, Carbs 42 g, Fat 7.5 g

244. Italian Chicken and Vegetable

INGREDIENTS (Servings: 1)
1 skinless, boneless chicken breast (3 oz.)
½ cup diced zucchini
½ cup scrubbed and diced potato
¼ cup diced onion
¼ cup sliced baby carrots
¼ cup sliced mushrooms
⅛ tsp. garlic powder
¼ tsp. Italian seasoning or oregano

DIRECTIONS (Ready in about: 50 min)
Heat oven to 350°F. Cut a 12-inch sheet of aluminum foil or parchment paper. Fold the foil or parchment paper in half, unfold and spray with cooking spray. Center the chicken breast on the foil. Complete with zucchini, potatoes, onions, carrots, and mushrooms. Sprinkle garlic powder and Italian seasoning over the chicken and vegetables. Gather the foil and make small, overlapping folds on the wrapper to seal. Twist the two ends several times to make a tight seal so that the liquid does not leak out during cooking. Arrange the packet on a baking sheet and bake for 45 minutes, until the chicken and vegetables are tender.

Per serving: Kcal 207, Sodium 72 mg, Protein 23 g, Carbs 23 g, Fat 2.5 g

245. Lemon or Lime Glaze

INGREDIENTS (Servings: 4)
1 tsp. lemon or lime juice
1 tbsp. chopped parsley
2 tsp. cornstarch
1 tsp. grated lemon or lime zest
½ cup unsalted chicken broth
1 tbsp. sugar

DIRECTIONS (Ready in about: 5 min)
In a microwave-safe bowl, combine all the ingredients. Beat to mix evenly. Microwave over high heat until clear and thickened, about 1 to 2 minutes. Serve immediately.

Per serving: Kcal 24, Sodium 10.5 mg, Protein 1 g, Carbs 5 g, Fat 4 g

246. Lemony Leek and Chicken

INGREDIENTS (Servings: 4)
A pinch of black pepper
1-pound chicken breast, skinless, boneless, and cubed
2 tbsp. avocado oil
½ cup lemon juice
1 cup low-sodium veggie stock
1 tbsp. tomato sauce, no-salt-added
4 leek, roughly chopped

DIRECTIONS (Ready in about: 50 min)
Warm a pan with the oil over medium heat, add the leeks, toss and sauté for 10 minutes. Add the chicken and the other ingredients, toss, cook over medium heat for 20 minutes more, divide between plates and serve.

Per serving: Kcal 199, Sodium 310 mg, Protein 17.5 g, Carbs 7.5 g, Fat 13 g

247. Lime Turkey with Potatoes

INGREDIENTS (Servings: 4)
2 tbsp. olive oil
1 turkey breast, skinless, boneless, and sliced
1-pound baby potatoes, peeled and halved
1 yellow onion, chopped
1 tbsp. sweet paprika
1 tsp. chili powder
2 cups low-sodium chicken stock
1 tbsp. cilantro, chopped
1 tsp. Rosemary, dried
A pinch of black pepper
1 tbsp. lime juice
Zest of 1 lime, grated

DIRECTIONS (Ready in about: 50 min)
Warm a pan with the oil over medium heat, add the onion, chili powder, and rosemary, toss and sauté for 5 minutes. Add the meat and brown for 5 minutes more. Add the potatoes and the rest of the ingredients except the cilantro, toss gently, bring to a simmer and cook over medium heat for 30 minutes. Split the mix between plates and serve with the cilantro sprinkled on top.
Per serving: Kcal 345, Sodium 322 mg, Protein 16.5 g, Carbs 34.5 g, Fat 22 g

248. Orange Chicken

INGREDIENTS (Servings: 4)
1-pound chicken breast, skinless, boneless, and halved
1 tbsp. avocado oil
2 garlic cloves, minced
½ cup of orange juice
2 shallots, chopped
1 tbsp. orange zest, grated
1 tsp. rosemary, chopped
3 tbsp. balsamic vinegar

DIRECTIONS (Ready in about: 45 min)
Warm a pan with the oil over medium-high heat, add the shallots and the garlic, toss and sauté for 2 minutes. Add the meat, toss gently, and cook for 3 minutes more. Add the rest of the ingredients, toss, introduce the pan to the oven and bake at 340°F for 30 minutes. Divide between plates and serve.
Per serving: Kcal 159, Sodium 198 mg, Protein 24.5 g, Carbs 5.5 g, Fat 3.5 g

249. Orange-Rosemary Chicken

INGREDIENTS (Servings: 6)
2 garlic cloves, minced
3 skinless and bone-in chicken breast halves, 8 oz. each
3 tsp. fresh rosemary or 1 tsp. dried rosemary, minced
1½ tsp. olive oil
3 skinless, bone-in chicken legs with thigh pieces, 8 oz. each
⅛ tsp. of fresh ground black pepper
⅓ cup orange juice

DIRECTIONS (Ready in about: 45 min)
Heat oven to 450°F. Lightly coats a baking sheet with cooking spray. Rub each piece of chicken with garlic. Dab your fingers in oil and rub them with oil and sprinkle with rosemary and pepper. Place the chicken pieces in the pan. Pour the orange juice over the chicken. Cover and cook for 30 minutes. Using tongs, flip chicken and return to oven until golden brown, about 10 to 15 minutes more. Soak the chicken in the orange juice from the pan enough to keep it from drying out. Transfer the chicken to individual plates. Pour the orange juice from the pan over the chicken and serve immediately.
Per serving: Kcal 204, Sodium 95 mg, Protein 31 g, Carbs 2.5 g, Fat 8 g

250. Oregano Turkey Mix

INGREDIENTS (Servings: 4)
1 red onion, chopped
2 tbsp. avocado oil
2 garlic cloves, minced
1 tbsp. oregano, chopped
A pinch of black pepper
1 big turkey breast, skinless, boneless, and cubed
1 tbsp. chives, chopped
1½ cups low-sodium beef stock

DIRECTIONS (Ready in about: 40 min)
Warm a pan with the oil over medium heat, add the onion, stir and sauté for 3 minutes. Add the garlic and the meat, toss and cook for 3 minutes more. Add the rest of the ingredients, toss, simmer everything over medium heat for 25 minutes, divide between plates and serve.
Per serving: Kcal 76, Sodium 450 mg, Protein 8 g, Carbs 6.5 g, Fat 2 g

251. Paella with Chicken

INGREDIENTS (Servings: 4)
1 tsp. olive oil
1 small onion, sliced
2 leeks (whites only), thinly sliced
3 garlic cloves, minced
1 pound of boneless and skinless chicken breast, cut into strips ½ inch wide and 2 inches long
2 large tomatoes, chopped
1 red pepper, sliced
⅔ cup long-grain brown rice
1 tsp. tarragon, or to taste
2 cups fat-free, unsalted chicken broth
1 cup frozen peas
¼ cup chopped parsley
1 lemon, cut into 4 wedges

DIRECTIONS (Ready in about: 45 min)
Warm olive oil over medium heat in a large nonstick skillet. Add the onions, leeks, garlic, and chicken strips. Sauté until vegetables are translucent and chicken is lightly browned for about 5 minutes. Add the tomatoes and red pepper slices and continue to brown for another 5 minutes.

Add the rice, tarragon, and broth and mix well. Just bring it to a boil. Reduce the heat for about 10 minutes, cover, and simmer. Add the peas and simmer until the broth is absorbed and the rice is tender for 45 to 60 minutes. To serve, divide into individual plates. Garnish each with 1 tbsp. of parsley and 1 lemon wedge.

Per serving: Kcal 378, Sodium 182 mg, Protein 35.5 g, Carbs 46 g, Fat 6 g

252. Pasta with Grilled Chicken

INGREDIENTS (Servings: 6)

2 boneless, skinless chicken breasts, each 4 oz.
1 tbsp. olive oil
½ cup chopped white onion
1 cup sliced mushrooms
1 cup white beans, canned or cooked (no salt added)
2 tbsp. chopped garlic
¼ cup chopped fresh basil
12 oz. uncooked rotelle pasta
¼ cup grated Parmesan cheese
Ground black pepper, to taste

DIRECTIONS (Ready in about: 45 min)

In a coal grill, prepare a hot fire or heat up a broiler or gas grill. Away from sources of heat, coat grill or pan lightly with cooking spray. Place the cooking rack 4 to 6 inches from the heat source. Broil or grill the chicken until golden brown and just cooked through, about 5 minutes per side. Shift the chicken to a cutting board before cutting it into strips and let it rest for 5 minutes. In an enormous nonstick skillet, heat olive oil over medium heat. Add onions and mushrooms and sauté until tender, about 5 minutes. Add the white beans, garlic, basil, and grilled chicken strips. Keep warm. Fill ¾ of a large saucepan with water and bring it to a boil. Add the pasta and cook until tender, for 10 to 12 minutes or as directed by the packet. Drain the pasta well. Return the pasta to the pot and add the chicken mixture. Stir to mix evenly. Divide the pasta between the plates. Garnish each with 1 tbsp. of Parmesan and black pepper. Serve immediately.

Per serving: Kcal 341, Sodium 74 mg, Protein 21 g, Carbs 53.5 g, Fat 5 g

253. Turkey and Artichokes Mix

INGREDIENTS (Servings: 4)

1 turkey breast, skinless, boneless, and sliced
2 tbsp. olive oil
A pinch of black pepper
3 garlic cloves, minced
14 oz. canned artichokes, no-salt-added, chopped
¾ cup low-fat mozzarella, shredded
1 cup of coconut cream
1 tbsp. basil, chopped

DIRECTIONS (Ready in about: 30 min)

Warm a pan with the oil over medium-high heat, add the meat, garlic, and black pepper, toss and cook for 5 minutes. Include the rest of the ingredients except the cheese, toss and cook over medium heat for 15 minutes. Sprinkle the cheese, cook everything for 5 minutes more, divide between plates and serve.

Per serving: Kcal 300, Sodium 320 mg, Protein 13.5 g, Carbs 16.5 g, Fat 22 g

254. Turkey and Bok Choy

INGREDIENTS (Servings: 4)

2 scallions, chopped
1 turkey breast, boneless, skinless, and roughly cubed
1-pound bok choy, torn
½ tsp. ginger, grated
½ cup low-sodium veggie stock
2 tbsp. olive oil
A pinch of black pepper

DIRECTIONS (Ready in about: 30 min)

Warm a pot with the oil over medium-high heat, add the scallions and the ginger and sauté for 2 minutes. Include the meat and brown for 5 minutes more. Add the rest of the ingredients, toss, simmer for 13 minutes more, divide between plates and serve.

Per serving: Kcal 125, Sodium 250 mg, Protein 9.3 g, Carbs 5.5 g, Fat 8 g

255. Turkey and Broccoli Crepe

INGREDIENTS (Servings: 4)

4 prepackaged crepes, 8 inches each
4 oz. reduced-sodium turkey breast, sliced
½ cup finely shredded reduced-fat Colby jack cheese
2 cups chopped broccoli

DIRECTIONS (Ready in about: 60 min)
Heat the oven to 350°F. Lightly coat a baking sheet with cooking spray. In a saucepan equipped with a steamer basket, bring 1 inch of water to a boil. Add the broccoli. Cover and steam until crisp, about 5-7 minutes. Microwave crepes for 30 seconds to 1 minute or as per package directions. Place ¼ of turkey, ¼ cup of steamed broccoli, and 2 tbsp. of cheese on each crepe. Roll up and place the seam face down on the prepared baking sheet. Cook until the cheese has melted, about 5 minutes. Serve immediately.
Per serving: Kcal 223, Sodium 200 mg, Protein 17 g, Carbs 23 g, Fat 7 g

256. Turkey and Creamy Broccoli

INGREDIENTS (Servings: 4)

1 big turkey breast, skinless, boneless and cubed	2 shallots, chopped
	1 tbsp. basil, chopped
	½ cup coconut cream
1 tbsp. olive oil	1 tbsp. cilantro, chopped
2 cups broccoli florets	
2 garlic cloves, minced	

DIRECTIONS (Ready in about: 35 min)
Warmth up a pan with the oil over medium-high heat, add the meat, shallots, and the garlic, toss and brown for 5 minutes. Add the broccoli and the other ingredients, toss everything, cook for 20 minutes over medium heat, divide between plates and serve.
Per serving: Kcal 165, Sodium 210 mg, Protein 9.5 g, Carbs 8 g, Fat 11.5 g

257. Turkey Stove Casserole

INGREDIENTS (Servings: 4)

½ cup diced celery	½ green bell pepper, chopped and seeded
1½ cups low-sodium chicken broth	
	3 tbsp. all-purpose (plain) flour
4 slices whole-wheat toast	
	½ cup chopped fresh parsley
⅓ cup diced onions	
2 cups cooked turkey or chicken, cubed	3 tbsp. white wine
	2 tbsp. fresh rosemary
Black pepper to taste	

DIRECTIONS (Ready in about: 60 min)
In an enormous nonstick saucepan, heat ¼ cup of the chicken broth over medium-high heat until boiling. Include celery, onion, and bell pepper, and cook until vegetables are tender and crisp about 4 to 5 minutes. Reduce the heat to low and let the mixture cool slightly. In a medium bowl, add the diced turkey or chicken and flour. Stir gently until the flour coats the meat. Add to vegetables and broth, simmering for about 5 minutes. Increase the pressure of the heat to medium-high and slowly add the remaining broth, wine, parsley, rosemary, and black pepper. Cook and stir until the sauce thickens a bit. To serve, pour ¼ of the saucepan over each toast.
Per serving: Kcal: 236, Sodium 236 mg, Protein 27 g, Carbs 23 g, Fat 4 g

258. Turkey Wrap

INGREDIENTS (Servings: 4)

12 oz. sliced deli turkey (low sodium)	1 cup shredded green cabbage
¼ cup low-sodium sauce (choose your favorite)	½ cup thinly sliced carrots
2 whole-wheat tortillas (12-inch diameter)	½ cup sliced tomatoes
	¼ cup avocado

DIRECTIONS (Ready in about: 20 min)
Mash the avocado with the sauce, mix well, and set aside. Divide the avocado salsa evenly over two tortillas. Distribute the cabbage, carrots, tomato slices, and turkey evenly between the two tortillas. Place the ingredients in the center, sliding the tortilla along the entire length. Fold the side closest to the tortilla towards you. Then fold the sides and roll them, leaving the seam at the bottom. Cut each tortilla in half and serve.
Per serving: Kcal 226, Sodium 253 mg, Protein 28.5 g, Carbs 15 g, Fat 6 g

BEEF, PORK, AND LAMB

259. Asian Pork Tenderloin

INGREDIENTS (Servings: 4)

1 tsp. ground coriander
2 tbsp. sesame seeds
⅛ tsp. cayenne pepper
1 pound of pork tenderloin, sliced into 4 portions
¼ tsp. ground cumin
1 tbsp. sesame oil
⅛ tsp. ground cinnamon
½ tsp. minced onion
⅛ tsp. celery seed

DIRECTIONS (Ready in about: 45 min)

Heat up the oven to 400°F. Coat the baking sheet lightly with cooking spray. In a heavy-bottomed pan, include the sesame seeds in a single layer. Cook the seeds over low heat, stirring constantly, until golden brown and a noticeably roasted aroma, approximately 1 to 2 minutes. Take out the seeds from the pan to cool them. In a bowl, add the cilantro, cayenne pepper, celery seeds, diced onion, cumin, cinnamon, sesame oil, and toasted sesame seeds. Stir to mix evenly. Place the pork tenderloin in the prepared pan. On both sides of the pork bits, rub the spices. Cook until no longer pink, approximately 15 minutes. Or cook until a meat thermometer reaches 165°F (medium) or 170°F (well done).

Per serving: Kcal 176, Sodium 161 mg, Protein 25 g, Carbs 1 g, Fat 8 g

260. Beef and Vegetable Stew

INGREDIENTS (Servings: 6)

1-pound beef round steak
2 tsp. canola oil
2 cups diced yellow onions
1 cup diced celery
1 cup diced Roma tomatoes
½ cup diced sweet potato
½ cup diced white potato with skin
¼ cup uncooked barley
¼ cup red wine vinegar
1 tsp. balsamic vinegar
3 cups low-sodium vegetable or beef stock
1 tsp. dried sage, crushed
1 tsp. minced fresh thyme
1 tbsp. minced fresh parsley
1 tbsp. dried oregano
½ cup diced mushrooms
1 cup diced carrot
4 cloves of garlic, chopped
1 tsp. dried rosemary, minced
Black pepper, to taste
1 cup chopped kale

DIRECTIONS (Ready in about: 1 h 40 min)

Heat grill or broiler (medium heat). Trim fat and gristle from steak. Grill or broil steak for 12 to 14 minutes, turning once. Don't overcook it. Remove from heat and let rest while preparing vegetables. In a large stockpot, sauté vegetables in oil over medium-high heat until lightly brown, about 10 minutes. Add barley and cook for an additional 5 minutes. Pat steak dry with paper towels. Cut into half-inch pieces and add to the pot. Then add vinegar, stock, herbs, and spices. Bring to a boil and simmer for 1 hour, until barley is cooked and the stew has thickened considerably. Serve.

Per serving: Kcal 216, Sodium 138 mg, Protein 21 g, Carbs 24 g, Fat 4 g

261. Beef Brisket

INGREDIENTS (Servings: 8)

2½ pounds beef brisket, trimmed of fat and cut into 8 pieces of roughly equal size
1 tbsp. olive oil
Course ground pepper
4 garlic cloves, smashed and peeled
1 cup of low-sodium beef stock or red wine
1½ cups chopped onions
1 tsp. dried thyme
¼ cup red wine vinegar
1 can (14.5 oz.) no-salt-added tomatoes and

DIRECTIONS (Ready in about: 4 h 20 min)

Heat up the oven to 350°F. In a large Dutch oven or heavy pot, heat 1 tbsp. oil over medium-high heat. Season brisket with pepper. In batches, cook meat, occasionally turning, until dark brown on all sides. Transfer brisket to a plate. Add onions to the pot. Cook and stir until golden brown. Include the thyme and garlic and cook for about 1 minute and stir until fragrant. Add the (undrained) tomatoes, vinegar, and stock or wine. Bring to a boil. Return beef to the pot, cover, then place the pot in the oven. Cook until beef is tender, approximately 3 to 3½ hours.

Per serving: Kcal 229, Sodium 284 mg, Protein 31 g, Carbs 6 g, Fat 9 g

262. Beef Fajitas with Peppers

INGREDIENTS (Servings: 6)

2 tsp. olive oil, plus more in a pump sprayer
1-pound sirloin steak, excess fat trimmed, cut across the grain into ½-inch-thick slices and then into 2-inch-wide pieces 1 large red bell pepper, cored and cut into ¼-inchwide strips
Lime wedges, for serving
1 medium red onion, cut into thin half-moons
2 cloves garlic, minced
1 tbsp. Mexican Seasoning (here) 12 (8-inch) flour tortillas or Boston lettuce leaves, for serving
1 big green bell pepper, cored and cut into ¼-inch-wide strips

DIRECTIONS (Ready in about: 35 min)

Spray a large nonstick skillet with oil and heat over medium-high heat. Add half of the sirloin and cook, flipping the sirloin pieces halfway through cooking, until browned on both sides, about 2 minutes. Transfer to a plate. Repeat with the remaining sirloin. Heat the 2 tsp. oil in the skillet over medium-high heat. Add the bell peppers, onion, and garlic. Cook, occasionally stirring, until tender, about 7 minutes. Stir in the beef with any juices and the Mexican Seasoning. Transfer to a platter. To serve, fill a flour tortilla or lettuce leaf with the beef mixture and squeeze lime juice on top. Roll up and serve.

Per serving: Kcal 231, Sodium 559 mg, Protein 24 g, Carbs 6 g, Fat 12 g

263. Beef Ragù with Broccoli Ziti

INGREDIENTS (Servings: 8)

1 tbsp. olive oil
8 oz. ground sirloin
1 medium yellow onion, chopped
1 medium carrot, cut into ¼-inch dice
1 medium celery rib, cut into ¼-inch dice
2 cloves garlic, minced
1 (28 oz.) can no-salt-added crushed tomatoes
2 tsp. Italian Seasoning
¼ tsp. crushed hot red pepper
Broccoli Ziti
6 tbsp. freshly grated Parmesan cheese

DIRECTIONS (Ready in about: 60 min)

Heat up oil over medium-high heat in a medium saucepan. Add the beef and cook until the meat loses its raw appearance, stirring regularly and breaking the ground sirloin with the side of the spoon, for around 7 minutes. Add the onion, carrot, celery, and garlic and stir. Reduce the and cover it. Cook, stirring periodically, for about five minutes, until the vegetables soften. Bring to a boil, stir in the tomatoes, the Italian seasoning, and the hot pepper. Reduce the heat and simmer, often stirring, until the sauce has reduced slightly approximately 45 minutes. Divide the hot Broccoli Ziti among 6 deep bowls. Cover each with an equal amount of sauce and sprinkle with 1 tbsp. Parmesan cheese, if using. Serve amount of sauce and sprinkle with 1 tbsp. Parmesan cheese, if using. Serve hot.

Per serving: Kcal 325, Sodium 124 mg, Protein 23 g, Carbs 38 g, Fat 10 g

264. Beef Stroganoff

INGREDIENTS (Servings: 4)

½ pound of boneless beef round steak, cut ¾-inch thick, all fat removed
½ cup chopped onion
4 cups uncooked yolkless egg noodles
½ tsp. paprika
½ cup of water
½ can fat-free cream of mushroom soup (undiluted)
1 tbsp. all-purpose (plain) flour
½ cup fat-free sour cream

DIRECTIONS (Ready in about: 35 min)

In a nonstick skillet, sauté onions over medium heat until translucent, about 5 minutes. Add the meat and continue cooking for another 5 minutes or until the meat is tender and golden brown. Drain well and let stand. Fill ¾ of a large saucepan with water and bring it to a boil. Add the noodles and cook for 10 to 12 minutes, or according to package instructions, until al dente (tender). Drain well with the pasta. Whisk the broth, water, and flour over medium heat in a saucepan. Stir for about 5 minutes before the sauce thickens. Add the soup and paprika to the meat in the pan. Over medium heat, stir the mixture until heated through. Remove from heat and add sour cream. Mix until just combined. Divide the pasta between the plates to serve. Top with the meat mixture and serve immediately.

Per serving: Kcal 273, Sodium 193 mg, Protein 20 g, Carbs 37 g, Fat 5 g

265. Beef Tacos

INGREDIENTS (Servings: 4)

- 1 tbsp. chili powder
- 1 tbsp. flour
- 1 tsp. ground turmeric
- 2 tsp. canola oil
- ½ tsp. ground cumin
- 1-pound extra-lean ground beef
- ¼ cup water
- 8 taco shells

Condiments:
- 2 tomatoes, chopped
- Salsa, as needed
- 6 to 8 radishes, chopped
- 1 cup shredded lettuce

DIRECTIONS (Ready in about: 45 min)

Combine the flour, chili powder, turmeric, and cumin in a small bowl. Heat the canola oil in a medium sauté pan or skillet over medium-high heat. Add the ground beef and sauté, stirring every couple of minutes to break up the meat, until the meat is browned and cooked, 6 to 7 minutes. Add the spice mixture and the water, and cook, stirring to coat the meat with the spices, until browned, 2 to 3 minutes. To serve, pile the meat into taco shells and let each guest add their own condiments.

Per serving: Kcal 329, Sodium 567 mg, Protein 28 g, Carbs 24 g, Fat 13 g

266. Chili Lamb

INGREDIENTS (Servings: 4)

- 1 tbsp. avocado oil
- 2 pounds lamb stew meat, cubed
- 1 tsp. chili powder
- 2 red onions, roughly chopped
- 1 tsp. hot paprika
- 1 cup low-sodium veggie stock
- 1 tbsp. cilantro, chopped
- ½ cup low-sodium tomato sauce

DIRECTIONS (Ready in about: 55 min)

Heat up a pot with the oil over medium heat, add the onion and the meat, and brown for 10 minutes. Add the chili powder and the other ingredients except for the cilantro, toss, bring to a simmer and cook over medium heat for 35 minutes more. Divide the mix into bowls and serve with the cilantro sprinkled on top.

Per serving: Kcal 463, Sodium 350 mg, Protein 65 g, Carbs 8 g, Fat 17 g

267. Cumin Lamb Mix

INGREDIENTS (Servings: 4)

- 1 red onion, chopped
- 1 tbsp. olive oil
- 1 cup cherry tomatoes, halved
- 1 tbsp. chili powder
- 2 tbsp. cilantro, chopped
- 1-pound lamb stew meat, ground
- Black pepper to the taste
- 1 cup low-sodium veggie stock
- 2 tsp. cumin, ground

DIRECTIONS (Ready in about: 35 min)

Heat up a pan with the oil over medium-high heat, add the onion, lamb, and chili powder, toss and cook for 10 minutes. Add the rest of the ingredients, toss, cook over medium heat for 15 minutes more. Divide into bowls and serve.

Per serving: Kcal 320, Sodium 320 mg, Protein 22 g, Carbs 14 g, Fat 12.5 g

268. Curried Pork Tenderloin

INGREDIENTS (Servings: 4)

- 1½ tbsp. curry powder
- 1 tart apple, peeled, seeded, and cut into chunks
- 1 tbsp. extra-virgin olive oil
- 1 tbsp. cornstarch
- 2 cups apple cider, divided
- 2 medium chopped yellow onions
- 16 oz. of pork tenderloin, cut into 4 pieces

DIRECTIONS (Ready in about: 55 min)

Season the pork tenderloin with the curry powder and allow it to stand for 15 minutes. In a large, heavy-bottomed pan, heat olive oil over medium-high heat. Add the steak and cook, turning once, until browned on both sides, about 5 to 10 minutes. Remove the meat from the pan and set it aside. Include the onions to the pan and sauté until tender and golden. Add 1½ cups of cider, lower the heat and cook until the liquid is half the volume. Add the cornstarch, chopped apple, and the remaining ½ cup of cider. Stir and cook while the sauce thickens, approximately 2 minutes. Return the steak to the pan and simmer for the last 5 minutes. To serve, place the steak on a serving plate or divide it into individual plates. Pour the thick sauce over the meat and serve immediately.

Per serving: Kcal 270, Sodium 370 mg, Protein 25 g, Carbs 29 g, Fat 6 g

269. Fennel Lamb and Mushrooms

INGREDIENTS (Servings: 4)

8 white mushrooms, halved
1-pound lamb shoulder, boneless and cubed
2 tbsp. olive oil
2 garlic cloves, minced
1 yellow onion, chopped
1 cup low-sodium veggie stock
1½ tbsp. fennel powder
A bunch of scallions, chopped
black pepper to the taste

DIRECTIONS (Ready in about: 50 min)

Warm a pan with the oil over medium heat, add the onion and the garlic, toss and cook for 5 minutes. Add the meat and the mushrooms, toss and cook for 5 minutes more. Add the other ingredients, toss, bring to a simmer and cook over medium heat for 30 minutes. Divide the mix into bowls and serve.

Per serving: Kcal 290, Sodium 240 mg, Protein 14 g, Carbs 15 g, Fat 15.5 g

270. Garlic Pork Mix

INGREDIENTS (Servings: 8)

1 red onion, chopped
2 pounds pork meat, boneless and cubed
1 tbsp. olive oil
1 cup beef stock
3 garlic cloves, minced
2 tbsp. sweet paprika
1 tbsp. chives, chopped
Black pepper to the taste

DIRECTIONS (Ready in about: 55 min)

Warm a pan with the oil over medium heat, add the onion and the meat, toss, and brown for 5 minutes. Add the rest of the ingredients, toss, reduce heat to medium, cover and cook for 40 minutes. 3. Divide the mix between plates and serve.

Per serving: Kcal 407, Sodium 430 mg, Protein 15 g, Carbs 5 g, Fat 35 g

271. Grilled Pork Fajitas

INGREDIENTS (Servings: 8)

½ tsp. oregano
1 tsp. ground cumin
½ tsp. paprika
1 pound of pork tenderloin, cut into strips ½ inch wide and 2 inches long
¼ tsp. garlic powder
8 whole-wheat flour tortillas, about 8 inches in diameter, warmed in the microwave
1 small onion, sliced
¼ tsp. ground coriander
4 cups shredded lettuce
1 cup of salsa
4 medium tomatoes, diced (about 3 cups)
½ cup shredded sharp cheddar cheese

DIRECTIONS (Ready in about: 40 min)

Put on hot heat on a charcoal grill or heat a gas grill or grill over medium-high heat of 400°F. In a small bowl, combine the cumin, oregano, paprika, coriander, and garlic powder. Drain the pieces of pork in the seasonings, covering them completely. Put the pork strips and onions in a cast-iron skillet or grill basket. Broil or grill over medium-high heat, turning several times until golden brown on all sides, about 5 minutes. To serve, sprinkle an equal amount of pork and onion strips over each tortilla. Top each with 1 tbsp. of cheese, 2 tbsp. of tomatoes, ½ cup of shredded lettuce, and 2 tbsp. of salsa. Layer sides of tortilla over filling, then roll to seal.

Per serving: Kcal 180, Sodium 382 mg, Protein 17 g, Carbs 29 g, Fat 3 g

272. Lamb Chops with Kale

INGREDIENTS (Servings: 4)

1-pound lamb chops
1 cup kale, torn
½ cup low-sodium veggie stock
A pinch of black pepper
1 yellow onion, sliced
2 tbsp. low-sodium tomato paste
1 tbsp. olive oil

DIRECTIONS (Ready in about: 45 min)

Grease a roasting pan with the oil, arrange the lamb chops inside, also add the kale and the other ingredients, and toss gently. Bake everything at 390°F for 35 minutes, divide between plates and serve.

Per serving: Kcal 275, Sodium 420 mg, Protein 33.5 g, Carbs 7.5 g, Fat 12 g

273. Lamb Stir Fry

INGREDIENTS (Servings: 4)

1 tbsp. avocado oil
1-pound lamb meat, ground
1 red bell pepper, cut into strips
2 tomatoes, cubed
1 carrot, cubed
1 tbsp. cilantro, chopped
Black pepper to the taste
2 fennels bulbs, sliced
2 tbsp. balsamic vinegar
1 red onion, sliced

DIRECTIONS (Ready in about: 35 min)

Warm a pan with the oil over medium-high heat, add the onion and the meat, and brown for 5 minutes. Add the bell pepper and the other ingredients, toss, cook over medium heat for 20 minutes more, divide into bowls and serve immediately.

Per serving: Kcal 367, Sodium 314 mg, Protein 16 g, Carbs 15.5 g, Fat 14 g

274. Meatloaf

INGREDIENTS (Servings: 4)
¼ cup skim milk
2 small rolls (like brioche), torn into small pieces
2 tbsp. ketchup
1 large zucchini, shredded
2 tsp. Worcestershire sauce
1 large carrot, shredded
1 clove garlic, minced
1 large yellow squash, shredded
1-pound lean ground sirloin
½ tsp. kosher salt
1 large egg
½ tsp. freshly ground black pepper

DIRECTIONS (Ready in about: 1 h 15 min)
Preheat the oven to 350°F. Coat an 8 by 4-inch skillet with cooking spray. In an enormous bowl, mix the bread and the milk, and let sit for 5 minutes. Squash the milk from the bread and throw out the milk. Return the bread to the bowl, and add the ketchup, Worcestershire sauce, zucchini, carrot, squash, garlic, beef, egg, salt, and pepper. Uses spoon to mix the meat mixture well, but do not overmix. Transfer to the prepared pan. Bake until meatloaf is cooked through, 50 minutes to 1 hour. Serve.

Per serving: Kcal 239, Sodium 474 mg, Protein 29 g, Carbs 15 g, Fat 7 g

275. Mint Meatballs Spinach Sauté

INGREDIENTS (Servings: 4)
1 yellow onion, chopped
1-pound pork stew meat, ground
1 egg, whisked
Black pepper to the taste
1 tbsp. mint, chopped
2 garlic cloves, minced
½ cup low-sodium veggie stock
1 cup cherry tomatoes, halved
2 tbsp. olive oil
1 cup baby spinach

DIRECTIONS (Ready in about: 40 min)
In a portable bowl, combine the meat with the onion and the other ingredients except for the oil, cherry tomatoes, and spinach, stir well and shape medium meatballs out of this mix. Heat up a pan with the olive oil over medium-high heat, add the meatballs and cook them for 5 minutes on each side. Add the spinach, tomatoes and the stock, toss, simmer everything for 15 minutes. Serve.

Per serving: Kcal 320, Sodium 250 mg, Protein 12 g, Carbs 16 g, Fat 13.5 g

276. Nutmeg Pork Black Beans

INGREDIENTS (Servings: 8)
1 cup canned black beans, no-salt-added, drained
1 yellow onion, chopped
2 pounds pork stew meat, cubed
1 cup canned tomatoes, no-salt-added, chopped
2 garlic cloves, minced
½ tsp. nutmeg, ground
Black pepper to the taste
2 tbsp. olive oil

DIRECTIONS (Ready in about: 45 min)
Warm a pan with the oil over medium heat, add the onion and the garlic and sauté for 5 minutes. Add the meat, toss and cook for 5 minutes more. Add the rest of the ingredients, toss, bring to a simmer and cook over medium heat for 30 minutes. Divide the mix into bowls and serve.

Per serving: Kcal 365, Sodium 295 mg, Protein 39 g, Carbs 17.5 g, Fat 15 g

277. Paprika Pork with Carrots

INGREDIENTS (Servings: 4)
¼ cup low-sodium veggie stock
Black pepper to the taste
1 red onion, sliced
2 tbsp. olive oil
1-pound pork stew meat, cubed
2 carrots, peeled and sliced
2 tsp. sweet paprika

DIRECTIONS (Ready in about: 40 min)
Warm a pan with the oil over medium heat, add the onion, stir and sauté for 5 minutes. Add the meat, toss, and brown for 5 minutes more. Include the rest of the ingredients, bring to a simmer and cook over medium heat for 20 minutes. Divide the mix between plates and serve.

Per serving: Kcal 328, Sodium 320 mg, Protein 34 g, Carbs 6.5 g, Fat 18 g

278. Pork Chops with Black Currant

INGREDIENTS (Servings: 6)
¼ cup black currant jam
2 tbsp. Dijon mustard
6 center-cut pork loin chops, trimmed of all visible fat, each 4 oz.
6 orange slices
⅓ cup of wine vinegar
⅛ tsp. of fresh ground black pepper
2 tsp. olive oil

DIRECTIONS (Ready in about: 40 min)
In a portable bowl, combine the jam and mustard. In an enormous non-stick skillet, heat olive oil over medium-high heat. Add the pork chops in the hot oil and cook, turning once, until golden brown on both sides, about 5 minutes on one side. Top each pork chop with a tbsp. of the currant jam and mustard mixture. Cover and cook for another 2 minutes. Transfer the pork chops to the hotplates. Cool the pan to a warm, not hot, temperature. Pour the wine vinegar into the pan and stir to remove the pieces of pork and the jam. Over each pork chop, pour the vinegar sauce. Garnish with orange slices and sprinkle with pepper and serve immediately.
Per serving: Kcal 198, Sodium 188 mg, Protein 25 g, Carbs 11 g, Fat 6 g

279. Pork Medallions with Herbes

INGREDIENTS (Servings: 2)
8 oz. pork tenderloin, trimmed of visible fat and cut crosswise into 6 pieces
¼ cup dry white wine
½ tsp. herbes de Provence
Freshly ground black pepper, to taste

DIRECTIONS (Ready in about: 45 min)
Sprinkle with black pepper over the pieces of pork. Place the pork between waxed paper sheets. Pound with a mallet or roll until it is around ¼ inch thick with a rolling pin. In a large nonstick skillet, cook the pork over medium-high heat until the meat is golden brown, 2 to 3 minutes per side. Remove from the heat and sprinkle with Provencal herbs. Arrange the pork on individual plates and keep warm. Pour the wine into the saucepan. Cook until boiling. From the bottom of the plate, scrape out the brown bits. Over the meat, pour the wine sauce and serve immediately.
Per serving: Kcal 120, Sodium 62 mg, Protein 24 g, Carbs 1.5 g, Fat 2 g

280. Pork Tenderloin with Apples

INGREDIENTS (Servings: 4)
1 pound of pork tenderloin, trimmed of all visible fat
1 tbsp. olive oil
Black pepper, to taste
2 cups chopped apple
2 cups chopped onion
1½ tbsp. fresh rosemary, chopped
1½ tbsp. balsamic vinegar
1 cup low-sodium chicken broth

DIRECTIONS (Ready in about: 50 min)
Heat up the oven to 450°F. Lightly coat a baking sheet with cooking spray. In an enormous skillet, heat the olive oil over high heat. Include the pork and sprinkle with black pepper. Cook until steak is golden brown on all sides, about 3 minutes. Remove from the heat and place in the prepared pan. Grill the pork for about 15 minutes or until a food thermometer reads 165°F (medium). Meanwhile, including the onion, apple, and rosemary in the pan. Sauté over medium heat until onions and apples are tender, about 3 to 5 minutes. Add the broth and vinegar. Increase the heat and boil until the sauce has reduced by approximately 5 minutes. Place the pork in a large serving dish to serve. Cut diagonally and place on 4 hotplates. Add the onion and applesauce and serve immediately.
Per serving: Kcal 240, Sodium 83.5 mg, Protein 26 g, Carbs 17 g, Fat 6.5 g

281. Pork Tenderloin & Blue Cheese

INGREDIENTS (Servings: 4)
½ tsp. white pepper
1-pound pork tenderloin
2 tsp. black pepper
1 tsp. paprika
¼ tsp. cayenne pepper
2 tsp. canola oil
½ cup of white wine or ½ cup of unsweetened apple juice
2 apples, sliced
¼ cup (about 1 oz.) crumbled blue cheese

DIRECTIONS (Ready in about: 1 h 20 min)
Heat up the oven to 350°F. Cut the tenderloin of all the fatty and silvery membrane. Season with spices. In an enormous skillet over medium-high heat, add the oil and place the steak in the pan. Brown both sides using the tongs to turn the meat. Transfer the meat to a roasting pan and bake for 15 to 20 minutes, until the internal temperature reaches 155°F. Remove from the oven and transfer the steak to a saucepan. Cover with aluminum foil and let stand. Include the apples in the pan and sauté on the heat until they turn dark brown. Add wine (or juice) and simmer until liquid is reduced by half. Cut the pork into slices, place the apples on top and sprinkle with blue cheese.
Per serving: Kcal 235, Sodium 145 mg, Protein 26 g, Carbs 17.5 g, Fat 7 g

282. Pork Tenderloin with Fennel

INGREDIENTS (Servings: 4)

2 tbsp. olive oil
4 pork tenderloin fillets, each 4 oz.
Orange slices, for garnish
1 sweet onion thinly sliced
1 can (12 oz.) low-sodium chicken broth
½ cup dry white wine
Fennel fronds, for garnish
1 tsp. fennel seeds

DIRECTIONS (Ready in about: 1 h 20 min)

Place the pork between the sheets of waxed paper. Smash each one with a mallet or roll with a rolling pin until it is about ¼ inch thick. In a heavy-based non-stick skillet, heat oil over medium heat. Add the fennel seeds and mix until fragrant, about 3 minutes. Add and cook until it turns golden, about 3 minutes per side. To keep it warm, remove the pork from the pan and cover it. Add the onion slices and the fennel to the pan. Sauté until tender, about 5 minutes. Remove the vegetables from the pan and cover to keep them warm. Add wine and chicken broth to the pan. Cook over high heat until half the volume is depleted. Return the pork to the pan, cover, and simmer for 5 minutes. Remove the lid and add the fennel and onion mixture. Cover and cook for another 2 minutes. Serve on hot plates garnished with fennel leaves and orange slices.

Per serving: Kcal: 276, Sodium 122 mg, Protein 29 g, Carbs 13 g, Fat 12 g

283. Pork Tenderloin with Orange

INGREDIENTS (Servings: 6)

3 large fennel bulbs, trimmed of feathery stalks and chopped
4 oranges
½ cup coarsely chopped parsley
1½ tbsp. extra-virgin olive oil
2 tsp. canola oil
½ cup pitted black olives, coarsely chopped
½ tsp. kosher salt, divided
1 (1-pound) pork tenderloin
½ tsp. freshly ground black pepper, divided

DIRECTIONS (Ready in about: 40 min)

Preheat the oven to 400°F. Make the orange and fennel relish: supreme the oranges into a bowl. Add the fennel, parsley, and olives. Stir to combine, and drizzle with the olive oil. Season with ¼ tsp. of the salt and ¼ tsp. of the pepper and set aside. Season the pork tenderloin with the remaining ¼ tsp. salt and remaining ¼ tsp. pepper. Heat the canola oil in an ovenproof sauté pan or skillet over high heat. Sauté the pork on each side until golden brown, 2 to 3 minutes per side. Roast the pork in the oven until a meat thermometer registers 145°F, about 10 minutes. Take it away from the oven and let rest for 10 minutes. . Only slice the pork diagonally. Serve with the orange and fennel relish.

Per serving: Kcal 324, Sodium 552 mg, Protein 27 g, Carbs 31 g, Fat 12 g

284. Pork with Avocados

INGREDIENTS (Servings: 4)

1-pound pork steak, cut into strips
2 cups baby spinach
1 tbsp. olive oil
½ cup low-sodium veggie stock
2 avocados, peeled and cut into wedges
1 cup cherry tomatoes, halved
1 tbsp. balsamic vinegar

DIRECTIONS (Ready in about: 25 min)

Warm a pan with the oil over medium-high heat, add the meat, toss and cook for 10 minutes. Add the spinach and the other ingredients, toss, cook for 5 minutes more, divide into bowls and serve.

Per serving: Kcal 390, Sodium 340 mg, Protein 13.5 g, Carbs 17 g, Fat 12.5 g

285. Rosemary Pork Chops

INGREDIENTS (Servings: 4)

Olive oil in a pump sprayer
1 tbsp. finely chopped fresh rosemary
¼ cup balsamic vinegar
½ tsp. kosher salt
½ tsp. freshly ground black pepper
4 (4 oz.) boneless pork loin chops, about an inch thick

DIRECTIONS (Ready in about: 1 h 25 min)

Spray a large nonstick skillet with oil and heat over medium heat. Season the pork with rosemary, salt, and pepper. Add to the skillet and cook until the undersides are golden brown, about 3 minutes. Flip the pork and cook, adjusting the heat as needed, so the pork cooks steadily without burning until the other sides are browned, and the pork feels firm when pressed in the center with a fingertip, about 3 minutes more. Transfer each chop to a dinner plate.

Off heat, add the vinegar to the skillet. Using a wooden spoon, scrape up the browned bits in the bottom of the skillet. The residual heat of the skillet should be enough to evaporate the vinegar to about 2 tbsp. If necessary, return the skillet to medium heat to reduce the vinegar slightly. Drizzle the glaze over each chop and serve hot.

Per serving: Kcal 178, Sodium 579 mg, Protein 24 g, Carbs 3 g, Fat 6 g

286. Shepherd's Pie

INGREDIENTS (Servings: 6)

1 (1-pound) head cauliflower, chopped	½ (16 oz.) bag frozen green peas, thawed
½ kosher salt, divided	2 tsp. canola oil
1-pound lean ground lamb	2 cloves garlic, minced
	½ cup skim milk

DIRECTIONS (Ready in about: 1 h 30 min)

Preheat the oven to 350°F. Bring an enormous saucepan of salted water to a boil over high heat. Cook the cauliflower until tender, about 8 minutes, depending on the size of the cauliflower florets. Drain the cauliflower in a colander. Puree the cauliflower with the milk and ¼ tsp. of the salt in a food processor or blender, until smooth. Set aside. Heat the canola oil in a medium sauté pan or skillet over medium-high heat. Add the lamb and the remaining ¼ tsp. salt. Sauté, stirring occasionally to break up the meat, until browned, 5 to 7 minutes. Add the garlic and the peas, and cook 2 minutes longer, stirring constantly. Take it out from the heat, and drain any remaining oil from the lamb. Transfer the mixture to an ovenproof 9 x 13-inch casserole dish. Spread the cauliflower over the top. Bake, uncovered until the top is golden and the casserole is hot for 20 to 25 minutes. Serve.

Per serving: Kcal 280, Sodium 309 mg, Protein 17.5 g, Carbs 10 g, Fat 19 g

287. Sirloin

INGREDIENTS (Servings: 8)

1 tsp. curry powder	¼ cup smooth peanut butter
½ tsp. ground ginger	3 tbsp. light coconut milk
½ tsp. kosher salt	2 tsp. reduced-sodium soy sauce
½ tsp. granulated garlic	2 tsp. peeled and minced fresh ginger
½ tsp. freshly ground black pepper	1½ tsp. rice vinegar
1¾ pounds of sirloin steak, about 1-inch thick, excess fat trimmed	1 clove garlic, crushed through a press
Canola oil in a spray pump	2 tsp. curry powder
Peanut Dipping Sauce	Chopped fresh cilantro or mint for garnish
3 tbsp. brewed cold black tea	

DIRECTIONS (Ready in about: 60 min)

Mix the ground ginger, curry powder, granulated garlic, salt, and pepper in a small bowl to prepare the sirloin. Spray the oil with the curry mixture on both sides of the steak and season. Let the peanut sauce stand at room temperature when making it. To make Peanut Dipping Sauce: mix peanut butter, tea, coconut milk, ginger, soy sauce, vinegar, curry, and garlic in a medium dish. Spot a broiler rack about 4 inches from the heat source and preheat to high. Oil the rack for the broiler and add the steak. Broil, flipping the steak over after three minutes until browned on both sides and when pressed in the middle, the beef just feels slightly durable, around 6 minutes for medium-rare. Switch to a carving board and allow for 3 minutes to stand. Pour in the eight ramekins with the peanut sauce. Carve the steak into ½-inch-thick slices around the grain. Move to a dish and sprinkle the cilantro with it. Serve warm, with a sauce of peanuts.

Per serving: Kcal 198, Sodium 159 mg, Protein 4 g, Carbs 10 g, Fat 1 g

FISH AND SEAFOOD

288. Allspice Shrimps

INGREDIENTS (Servings: 4)
1 tsp. allspice, ground
2 tbsp. olive oil
1-pound shrimps, peeled

DIRECTIONS (Ready in about: 12 min)
Heat the olive oil in the pan. Combine allspice and shrimp in the bowl. Then transfer the shellfish to the hot oil and cook for 3 minutes per side or until the shrimp are bright pink. Serve immediately.
Per serving: Kcal 196, Sodium 277 mg, Protein 26 g, Carbs 2 g, Fat 9 g

289. Aromatic Salmon with Fennel

INGREDIENTS (Servings: 5)
4 medium salmon fillets, skinless and boneless
1 tbsp. fennel seeds
2 tbsp. olive oil
1 tbsp. lemon juice
1 tbsp. water

DIRECTIONS (Ready in about: 18 min)
Heat the olive oil in the pan. Add the fennel seeds and roast for 1 minute. Add the salmon fillets and sprinkle with lemon juice. Add water and grill the fish for 4 minutes per side over medium heat. Serve.
Per serving: Kcal 301, Sodium 81 mg, Protein 5 g, Carbs 19 g, Fat 18 g

290. Baked Cod

INGREDIENTS (Servings: 2)
10 oz. cod fillet
1 tsp. Italian seasonings
1 tbsp. margarine

DIRECTIONS (Ready in about: 40 min)
Rub the pan with margarine. Then chop the cod and sprinkle it with Italian seasonings. Put the fish in the pan and cover it with plastic wrap. Cook food 30 minutes at 375°F. Let the fish rest for 2-3 minutes and serve.
Per serving: Kcal 170, Sodium 155 mg, Protein 25 g, Carbs 0.5 g, Fat 7.5 g

291. Basil Halibut

INGREDIENTS (Servings: 4)
1-pound halibut, chopped
1 tbsp. dried basil
1 tsp. garlic powder
2 tbsp. olive oil

DIRECTIONS (Ready in about: 20 min)
Spurt the olive oil into the pan and heat it. Meanwhile, combine halibut, dried basil, and garlic powder. Put the fish in the hot oil and coot it for 3 minutes on each side. Dry oil and serve.
Per serving: Kcal 347, Sodium 123 mg, Protein 22 g, Carbs 0.5 g, Fat 28 g

292. Braised Seabass

INGREDIENTS (Servings: 2)
10 oz. seabass fillet
1 cup tomatoes, chopped
1 yellow onion, sliced
1 tbsp. avocado oil
1 tsp. ground black pepper

DIRECTIONS (Ready in about: 36 min)
Heat the olive oil in the pan. Add the seabass fillet and brown for 4 minutes on each side. Then remove take out the fish from the pan and add the chopped onion. Cook for 2 minutes. Then add the tomatoes and ground black pepper. Bring the mixture to a boil. Add the cooked seabass and close the lid. Cook for 15 minutes and serve.
Per serving: Kcal 285, Sodium 8 mg, Protein 27.5 g, Carbs 9.5 g, Fat 15 g

293. Broccoli and Cod Mash

INGREDIENTS (Servings: 4)
2 cups broccoli, chopped
4 cod fillets, boneless, chopped
1 white onion, chopped
2 tbsp. olive oil
1 cup of water
1 tbsp. low-fat cream cheese
½ tsp. ground black pepper

DIRECTIONS (Ready in about: 40 min)
Grill the cod in the pan with olive oil for 1 minute on each side. Then add up all the remaining ingredients except the cream cheese and boil the food for 18 minutes. Then drain the water, add the cream cheese and mix the meal well. Serve right away.

Per serving: Kcal 186, Sodium 105 mg, Protein 22.5 g, Carbs 6 g, Fat 2 g

294. Celery Crab Salad

INGREDIENTS (Servings: 4)

¼ tsp. dried rosemary
10 oz. crab meat, cooked, chopped
¼ tsp. white pepper
1 cup celery stalk, chopped
¼ cup low-fat yogurt

DIRECTIONS (Ready in about: 10 min)
Combine all the ingredients in the bowl. Refrigerate the salad for 5 to 10 minutes before serving.
Per serving: Kcal 79, Sodium 474 mg, Protein 10 g, Carbs 3.5 g, Fat 1.5 g

295. Clams Stew

INGREDIENTS (Servings: 5)

1-pound clams
1 tsp. dried thyme
1 tsp. ground paprika
½ cup light cream (low-fat)
1 tbsp. lemon juice

DIRECTIONS (Ready in about: 18 min)
Add the dried thyme, ground paprika, and cream. Bring the liquid to a boil. Then add the lemon juice and mix the mixture well. Add the clams and close the lid. Boil the clam stew for 5 minutes. Serve hot.
Per serving: Kcal: 94, Sodium 345 mg, Protein 0.6 g, Carbs 12 g, Fat 5.1 g

296. Cod in Orange Juice

INGREDIENTS (Servings: 4)

4 cod fillets, boneless
1 cup of orange juice
1 tbsp. chives, chopped
1 tbsp. olive oil
½ tsp. white pepper

DIRECTIONS (Ready in about: 20 min)
Heat up the pan with oil over medium heat. Sprinkle the fish with white pepper and season with hot oil. Add the orange juice and the chives. Cook the fish for 10 minutes. Serve right away.
Per serving: Kcal 149, Sodium 81 mg, Protein 20.5 g, Carbs 6.5 g, Fat 5 g

297. Cod in Tomatoes

INGREDIENTS (Servings: 4)

2 tbsp. avocado oil
½ tsp. minced garlic
½ cup of water
4 cod fillets, boneless
1 cup plum tomatoes, chopped
1 tsp. scallions, chopped

DIRECTIONS (Ready in about: 26 min)
Heat a pan with oil over medium-high heat, add the garlic and fish and cook for 3 minutes per side. Then top the fish with the remaining ingredients and cook for another 10 minutes. Serve immediately.
Per serving: Kcal 110, Sodium 87 mg, Protein 20.7 g, Carbs 2.9 g, Fat 2 g

298. Cod in Yogurt Sauce

INGREDIENTS (Servings: 2)

1 tsp. sesame oil
4 cod fillets, boneless and skinless
½ onion, diced
½ cup low-fat yogurt
1 tbsp. dried cilantro
½ tsp. minced garlic

DIRECTIONS (Ready in about: 36 min)
Rub the cod fillets with the dried cilantro, minced garlic, and sesame oil. Spot the fish in the pan and cook for 3 minutes per side. Add the onion and low-fat yogurt. Cook the food for another 12 minutes. Serve.
Per serving: Kcal 128, Sodium 102 mg, Protein 22 g, Carbs 3.5 g, Fat 2.5 g

299. Cod Relish

INGREDIENTS (Servings: 4)

2 cups broccoli, chopped
4 cod fillets, boneless, chopped
1 white onion, chopped
1 cup of water
1 tbsp. cream cheese
½ tsp. black pepper
2 tbsp. olive oil

DIRECTIONS (Ready in about: 15 min)
Grill the cod in the pan with olive oil for 1 minute on each side. Then add up all the remaining ingredients except the cream cheese and boil the food for 18 minutes. Then drain the water, add the cream cheese and mix the meal well. Serve right away.
Per serving: Kcal 223, Sodium 74 mg, Protein 22.5 g, Carbs 8 g, Fat 2.5 g

300. Cod with Grapefruit

INGREDIENTS (Servings: 4)

1 small fennel bulb
2 tbsp. fresh lemon juice
1 tbsp. olive oil
¼ tsp. kosher salt
1 ripe avocado, pitted, peeled, and cut
¼ tsp. black pepper
1 pink or red grapefruit, peel removed, cut between the membranes into segments Cod
2 tsp. olive oil
4 (5 oz.) cod fillets

DIRECTIONS (Ready in about: 25 min)
To make the salad: cut the fennel in half lengthwise. If the leaves are stuck, cut them off and set them aside. Cut out and remove the triangular core at the base of the bulb. Cut the fennel in half crosswise into thin crescents. Reserve the remaining half of the fennel and stems for another use. In a medium bowl, combine the lemon juice and oil and season with pepper and salt. Add the fennel, avocado, and grapefruit and mix gently. Set aside while the cod is being prepared. To prepare the cod: heat the oil in a large nonstick skillet over medium heat. Add the cod and cover. Cook until bases are golden, about 3 minutes. Flip and cook, uncovered, adjusting the heat if necessary, until the other side of each fillet is golden and the cod appears barely opaque when peeled on each fillet is golden browned, and the cod looks barely opaque when crumbled in the center with the tip of a knife, about 3 minutes longer. Divide the fennel salad among four dinner plates. Garnish each with a cod fillet and serve immediately.
Per serving: Kcal 270, Sodium 232 mg, Protein 27 g, Carbs 14.5 g, Fat 5 g

301. Cold Crab Mix

INGREDIENTS (Servings: 4)
3 cups watermelon, chopped
3 tbsp. apple cider vinegar
1 tbsp. sesame seeds
1 tbsp. avocado oil
1 cup crab meat, chopped
2 cups tomatoes, chopped

DIRECTIONS (Ready in about: 15 min)
Mix all the ingredients together in an enormous bowl and shake well. Chill the food for 10 minutes in the refrigerator.
Per serving: Kcal 111, Sodium 364 mg, Protein 5 g, Carbs 19.5 g, Fat 2 g

302. Crispy Mediterranean Tilapia

INGREDIENTS (Servings: 4)
1 tbsp. olive oil, plus more in a pump sprayer
1 medium yellow onion, chopped
2 cloves garlic, minced
1 zucchini, cut in half lengthwise and then into ½-inch slices
1 medium yellow squash, cut in half lengthwise and then into ½-inch-thick slices
4 plum tomatoes, seeded and cut into ½-inch dice
Freshly grated zest of 1 lemon
2 tbsp. fresh lemon juice
1 tbsp. chopped fresh oregano, or
1 tsp. dried oregano ¼ tsp. crushed hot red pepper
4 (5 oz.) tilapia fillets
3 tbsp. panko (Japanese-style bread crumbs), preferably whole-wheat panko

DIRECTIONS (Ready in about: 35 min)
Heat up the oven to 350°F. Heat 1 tbsp. of oil in a nonstick ovenproof skillet over medium heat. Add onion and garlic and cook, occasionally stirring, until just tender, about 3 minutes. Add the zucchini and yellow squash and cook until tender, about 3 minutes. Add the tomatoes, lemon zest & juice, oregano, and chilli. Remove from the heat. Arrange the tilapia fillets on the vegetables. Sprinkle with panko and drizzle with oil. Cook until tilapia is opaque when flattened in the thickest part with the tip of a knife, about 12 minutes. Serve hot.
Per serving: Kcal 240, Sodium 96 mg, Protein 32 g, Carbs 16 g, Fat 1 g

303. Crusted Salmon Horseradish

INGREDIENTS (Servings: 2)
2 cups broccoli, chopped
4 cod fillets, boneless, chopped
1 white onion, chopped
2 tbsp. olive oil
1 cup of water
1 tbsp. low-fat cream cheese
½ tsp. ground black pepper

DIRECTIONS (Ready in about: 23 min)
Grill the cod in the pan with olive oil for 1 minute on each side. Then add up all the remaining ingredients except the cream cheese and boil the food for 18 minutes. Then drain the water, add the cream cheese and mix the meal well. Serve right away.
Per serving: Kcal 220, Sodium 95 mg, Protein 22 g, Carbs 1.5 g, Fat 0.5 g

304. Cucumber and Seafood Bowl

INGREDIENTS (Servings: 3)
2 cucumbers, chopped
1 tsp. mustard
½ tsp. ground coriander
1 tsp. margarine
6 oz. shrimps, peeled
4 oz. salmon, chopped
1 tbsp. low-fat yogurt

DIRECTIONS (Ready in about: 25 min)
Heat the margarine in the pan. Add the chopped salmon and cook for 2 minutes per side.

Then add the shrimp and sprinkle the seafood with ground coriander. Close the lid and cook the ingredients for 10 minutes over low heat. Then transfer them to serving bowls. Add the cucumbers. Mix the yogurt and mustard. Sprinkle the food with the mustard mixture and serve.
Per serving: Kcal 168, Sodium 178 mg, Protein 22 g, Carbs 9.5 g, Fat 5 g

305. Curry Snapper

INGREDIENTS (Servings: 4)

1-pound snapper fillet, chopped	½ cup low-fat yogurt
1 cup celery stalk, chopped	¼ cup of water
	1 tbsp. olive oil
	1 tsp. curry powder

DIRECTIONS (Ready in about: 25 min)
Grill the snapper fillet in olive oil for 2 minutes on each side. Then add the celery stalk, curry powder, low-fat yogurt, and water. Stir the fish until you get a smooth consistency. Close the lid and simmer the fish for 10 minutes over medium heat. Serve immediately.
Per serving: Kcal 195, Sodium 105 mg, Protein 29.5 g, Carbs 3 g, Fat 6 g

306. Dill Steamed Salmon

INGREDIENTS (Servings: 4)

2 tbsp. dill, chopped	1-pound steamed salmon, chopped
1 tbsp. low-fat cream cheese	1 red onion, diced
1 tsp. chilli flakes	

DIRECTIONS (Ready in about: 25 min)
Mix up all ingredients in the bowl and carefully stir until homogenous.
Per serving: Kcal 174, Sodium 62 mg, Protein 23 g, Carbs 3.5 g, Fat 8 g

307. Fish Salsa

INGREDIENTS (Servings: 12)

1 cup tomatoes, chopped	1 cup watermelon, seedless and chopped
1-pound salmon, cooked, chopped	½ cup red onion, chopped
½ cup tomatillos, chopped	1 cup mango, chopped
3 tbsp. lemon juice	¼ cup cilantro, chopped
	2 tbsp. avocado oil

DIRECTIONS (Ready in about: 10 min)
Put all the ingredients in the bowl. Mix the salsa well and let it cool for at least 5 minutes.
Per serving: Kcal 67, Sodium 17.5 mg, Protein 7 g, Carbs 4 g, Fat 2.5 g

308. Fish Spread

INGREDIENTS (Servings: 8)

2-pounds trout, boiled	1 tbsp. fresh dill, chopped
2 tbsp. low-fat cream cheese	1 tsp. minced garlic
¼ cup low-fat yogurt	

DIRECTIONS (Ready in about: 10 min)
Put all the ingredients together in the food processor and mix until smooth. Transfer the fish spread to the bowl and flatten well. Refrigerate the spread for 5 to 10 minutes before serving.
Per serving: Kcal 231, Sodium 90 mg, Protein 31 g, Carbs 1 g, Fat 10.5 g

309. Five-Spices Sole

INGREDIENTS (Servings: 8)

3 sole fillets	1 tbsp. five-spice seasonings
1 tbsp. coconut oil	

DIRECTIONS (Ready in about: 22 min)
Rub the sole fillets with the seasonings. Then heat up the coconut oil in the pan for 2 minutes. Put the sole fillets in the boiling oil and cook for 4.5 minutes on each side.
Per serving: Kcal 204, Sodium 133 mg, Protein 32 g, Carbs 1 g, Fat 6.5 g

310. Greek Style Salmon

INGREDIENTS (Servings: 8)

4 medium salmon fillets, skinless and boneless	1 tsp. dried thyme
1 tbsp. lemon juice	¼ tsp. onion powder
1 tbsp. dried oregano	1 tbsp. olive oil

DIRECTIONS (Ready in about: 20 min)
Heat the olive oil in the pan. Sprinkle the salmon with dried oregano, thyme, onion powder, and lemon juice. Spot the fish in the pan and cook on each side for 4 minutes.
Per serving: Kcal 271, Sodium 80 mg, Protein 34.5 g, Carbs 1 g, Fat 14.5 g

311. Green Onion Salmon

INGREDIENTS (Servings: 4)

4 green olives, pitted, sliced
2 oz. green onions, blended
4 salmon fillets, skinless and boneless
½ tsp. chilli flakes
¼ tsp. ground black pepper
3 tbsp. avocado oil
1 oz. parsley, chopped

DIRECTIONS (Ready in about: 20 min)

Combine the green onions, red pepper flakes, ground black pepper, avocado oil, and parsley. Then rub the salmon fillets with the green onion mixture and transfer them to the preheated pan. Cook it for 4 minutes per side. Garnish the cooked fish with sliced olives and serve.

Per serving: Kcal: 272, Sodium 375 mg, Protein 35 g, Carbs 3 g, Fat 13.5 g

312. Grilled Tilapia

INGREDIENTS (Servings: 4)

1 tbsp. sesame oil
½ tsp. ground black pepper
½ tsp. garlic powder
4 medium tilapia fillets

DIRECTIONS (Ready in about: 25 min)

Sprinkle the fish with powdered garlic, ground black pepper, and sesame oil. Grill 3 minutes on each side on the grill preheated to 400°F. Serve right away.

Per serving: Kcal: 125, Sodium 40 mg, Protein 21 g, Carbs 0.5 g, Fat 4.5 g

313. Grouper with Tomato Sauce

INGREDIENTS (Servings: 8)

12 oz. grouper, chopped
2 cups grape tomatoes, chopped
1 chilli pepper, chopped
1 tbsp. margarine
1 tsp. ground coriander

DIRECTIONS (Ready in about: 25 min)

Put the margarine in the saucepan. Add the chopped grouper and sprinkle with ground coriander. Grill the fish for 2 minutes on each side. Then add the grape tomatoes and chilli. Mix the ingredients very well and close the lid. Cook the food for 10 minutes over low heat.

Per serving: Kcal 285, Sodium 166 mg, Protein 44 g, Carbs 7 g, Fat 8.5 g

314. Halibut with Radish Slices

INGREDIENTS (Servings: 4)

4 halibut fillets, boneless
1 cup radishes, sliced
1 tbsp. apple cider vinegar
¼ tsp. ground coriander
1 tbsp. olive oil
1 tsp. low-fat cream cheese

DIRECTIONS (Ready in about: 16 min)

Sprinkle the fish fillets with apple cider vinegar, ground cilantro, and olive oil. Then grill the halibut on the preheated 385°F grill for 3 minutes per side. Move the fish to the plates and garnish with the radish slices and cream cheese.

Per serving: Kcal 356, Sodium 170 mg, Protein 61 g, Carbs 1 g, Fat 10.5 g

315. Herbed Sole

INGREDIENTS (Servings: 3)

10 oz. sole fillet
2 tbsp. margarine
1 tbsp. dill weed
1 tsp. garlic powder
½ tsp. cumin seeds

DIRECTIONS (Ready in about: 20 min)

Put the margarine in the saucepan. Add the cumin seeds and dill weed. Melt the mixture and simmer for 30 seconds. Then cut the sole fillet into 2 portions and sprinkle with garlic powder. Place the fish fillets in the melted margarine mixture. Cook the fish for three minutes on each side.

Per serving: Kcal 185, Sodium 191 mg, Protein 23.5 g, Carbs 1.5 g, Fat 9 g

316. Horseradish Cod

INGREDIENTS (Servings: 4)

1 tbsp. avocado oil
12 oz. cod fillet
½ cup low-fat cream cheese
¼ tsp. ground black pepper
2 tbsp. dill, chopped
1 tbsp. horseradish

DIRECTIONS (Ready in about: 20 min)

Heat a pan with the oil over medium-high heat, add the cod, season with black pepper and cook for 5 minutes per side. In a portable bowl, mix the cream cheese with the dill and horseradish. Garnish the cooked cod with the horseradish mixture.

Per serving: Kcal 180, Sodium 154 mg, Protein 18 g, Carbs 2.5 g, Fat 11.5 g

317. Juicy Scallops

INGREDIENTS (Servings: 4)

12 oz. sea scallops
2 tbsp. olive oil
½ tsp. garlic powder
¼ cup low-fat yogurt

DIRECTIONS (Ready in about: 15 min)
Sprinkle the scallops with powdered garlic and olive oil and toss in the hot pan. Grill the scallops for 3 minutes per side or until golden brown. Add the yogurt and cook the seafood for another 2 minutes. Serve.
Per serving: Kcal 147, Sodium 148 mg, Protein 15 g, Carbs 3.5 g, Fat 8 g

318. Lemon Swordfish

INGREDIENTS (Servings: 8)

18 oz. swordfish fillets
1 tbsp. margarine
1 tsp. lemon zest
3 tbsp. lemon juice
1 tsp. ground black pepper
2 tbsp. olive oil
½ tsp. minced garlic

DIRECTIONS (Ready in about: 35 min)
Cut the fish into 4 portions. Then, in the bowl, combine the lemon zest, lemon juice, ground black pepper, and olive oil. Add the minced garlic. Rub the fish fillets with the lemon mixture. Grease the pan with margarine and arrange the swordfish fillets. Bake the fish for 25 minutes at 390°F and serve it right away.
Per serving: Kcal 288, Sodium 183 mg, Protein 32.5 g, Carbs 1 g, Fat 16.5 g

319. Lemon Zest Seabass

INGREDIENTS (Servings: 4)

1 tbsp. lemon zest, grated
¼ cup lemon juice
1 garlic clove, diced
1 tsp. margarine
2 tbsp. olive oil
1-pounds sea bass fillets, skinless and boneless

DIRECTIONS (Ready in about: 18 min)
Put the margarine in the saucepan. Add the chopped grouper and sprinkle with ground coriander. Grill the fish for 2 minutes on each side. Then add the grape tomatoes and chilli. Mix the ingredients very well and close the lid. Cook the food for 10 minutes over low heat.
Per serving: Kcal 215, Sodium 113 mg, Protein 27 g, Carbs 1 g, Fat 11 g

320. Lime Calamari

INGREDIENTS (Servings: 4)

1 tbsp. lime juice
1 tsp. lime zest, grated
1-pound calamari, sliced
¼ tsp. ground nutmeg
1 tbsp. olive oil
1 tsp. dried mint
¼ cup of water

DIRECTIONS (Ready in about: 15 min)
Combine lime juice, lime zest, calamari, nutmeg, and olive oil in the bowl. Add the dried mint and water. Stir the mixture and transfer it to the hot pan. Grill the squid for 5 minutes over medium heat. Add the seafood from time to time. Garnish with lime zest and serve.
Per serving: Kcal 139, Sodium 256 mg, Protein 8 g, Carbs 9 g, Fat 7.5 g

321. Limes and Shrimps Skewers

INGREDIENTS (Servings: 4)

1-pound shrimps, peeled
1 lime
1 tsp. lemon juice
½ tsp. white pepper

DIRECTIONS (Ready in about: 22 min)
Cut the lime into wedges. Then sprinkle the shrimp with lemon juice and white pepper. Place the lime and lime wedges one by one on the wooden skewers. Preheat the grill to 400°F. Spot the shrimp skewers on the grill and cook 3 minutes per side or until the shrimp turn light pink.
Per serving: Kcal 141, Sodium 277 mg, Protein 26 g, Carbs 3.5 g, Fat 2 g

322. Mint Cod

INGREDIENTS (Servings: 4)

1 tbsp. avocado oil
1 tbsp. lemon juice
1 tbsp. mint, chopped
1-pound cod fillet
2 tbsp. water

DIRECTIONS (Ready in about: 20 min)
Heat up the pan with the oil over medium heat, add the mint and the cod. Cook the fish for 3 minutes on each side. Then add the water and lemon juice. Cook the cod for another 2 minutes.
Per serving: Kcal 97, Sodium 72 mg, Protein 20.5 g, Carbs 0.5 g, Fat 1.5 g

323. Mustard Arctic Char

INGREDIENTS (Servings: 2)
1 tbsp. mustard
1 tbsp. olive oil
¼ tsp. dried rosemary
2 arctic char fillets

DIRECTIONS (Ready in about: 20 min)
Sprinkle the fish with rosemary, olive oil, and mustard. Then transfer the fish fillets into the pan and bake at 400°F for 10 minutes.
Per serving: Kcal 291, Sodium 27 mg, Protein 25.5 g, Carbs 2 g, Fat 10.5 g

324. Mustard Tuna Salad

INGREDIENTS (Servings: 2)
½ tsp. lemon juice
1 tbsp. mustard
¼ tsp. cayenne pepper
¼ cup chickpeas, cooked
5 oz. white tuna canned in water, drained
1 tsp. olive oil

DIRECTIONS (Ready in about: 10 min)
Combine olive oil, mustard, and lemon juice in a shallow bowl. Combine all the remaining ingredients in a bowl and top with the mustard mixture. Shake the salad very well.
Per serving: Kcal 291, Sodium 22 mg, Protein 25.5 g, Carbs 2 g, Fat 10.5 g

325. Onion Tilapia

INGREDIENTS (Servings: 4)
4 tilapia fillets, boneless
1 tbsp. apple cider vinegar
1 tbsp. olive oil
1 tsp. onion powder
1 white onion, sliced
½ tsp. ground black pepper

DIRECTIONS (Ready in about: 20 min)
Grill the onion with olive oil in a pan for 2 minutes. Meanwhile, sprinkle the tilapia with apple cider vinegar, ground black pepper, and onion powder. Add it to the onion and cook the meal for 4 minutes. Then turn the fish fillets over to the other side and cook for another 4 minutes. Serve immediately.
Per serving: Kcal 138, Sodium 42 mg, Protein 21.5 g, Carbs 3.5 g, Fat 5 g

326. Paprika Tilapia

INGREDIENTS (Servings: 2)
2 tilapia fillets
1 tsp. ground paprika
½ tsp. chilli powder
2 tbsp. avocado oil

DIRECTIONS (Ready in about: 17 min)
Sprinkle the tilapia fillets with ground paprika and chilli powder. Then heat the avocado oil in the pan for 2 minutes. Put the fish fillets in the hot oil and cook for 3 minutes on each side.
Per serving: Kcal 170, Sodium 47 mg, Protein 21.5 g, Carbs 1.5 g, Fat 3 g

327. Paprika Tuna

INGREDIENTS (Servings: 4)
1 tsp. avocado oil
4 tuna steaks, boneless
1 tsp. ground paprika

DIRECTIONS (Ready in about: 14 min)
Rub the fish with paprika and sprinkle with avocado oil. Then transfer the tuna steaks to the preheated 400°F grill and cook for 2 minutes per side. Serve warm.
Per serving: Kcal 159, Sodium 43 mg, Protein 25.5 g, Carbs 0.5 g, Fat 5.5 g

328. Parsley Trout

INGREDIENTS (Servings: 4)
1 tbsp. dried parsley
6 trout fillets
2 tbsp. margarine

DIRECTIONS (Ready in about: 20 min)
Rub the trout fillets with the parsley. Then pour the margarine into the saucepan and melt. Include the fish fillets and cook for 4 minutes per side. Serve warm.
Per serving: Kcal 152, Sodium 86 mg, Protein 16.5 g, Carbs 0 g, Fat 9 g

329. Rosemary Salmon

INGREDIENTS (Servings: 4)
1-pound salmon fillet
4 tsp. olive oil
4 tsp. lemon juice
1 tbsp. dried rosemary

DIRECTIONS (Ready in about: 22 min)
Cut the salmon fillet into 4 portions. Then rub the fillets with olive oil, lemon juice, and dried rosemary. Place the salmon on the baking sheet and bake for 12 minutes at 400°F. Serve immediately.
Per serving: Kcal 194, Sodium 51 mg, Protein 22 g, Carbs 0.5 g, Fat 11 g

330. Salmon and Corn Salad

INGREDIENTS (Servings: 4)

1-pound salmon, canned, shredded
1 tbsp. scallions, chopped
2 tbsp. canola oil
½ tsp. lemon juice
1 cup corn kernels, cooked

DIRECTIONS (Ready in about: 10 min)

Put all ingredients together in the bowl and mix up the salad.

Per serving: Kcal 246, Sodium 56 mg, Protein 23 g, Carbs 7.5 g, Fat 14.5 g

331. Salmon in Capers

INGREDIENTS (Servings: 4)

½ cup low-fat milk
1-pound salmon fillet, chopped
2 tbsp. avocado oil
1 tbsp. capers, drained

DIRECTIONS (Ready in about: 35 min)

Heat a pan with the oil over medium-high heat, add the salmon, and grill for 5 minutes. Add the capers and milk and sauté the flour for 10 minutes over medium heat.

Per serving: Kcal 173, Sodium 127 mg, Protein 24 g, Carbs 2 g, Fat 8 g

332. Salmon with Basil and Garlic

INGREDIENTS (Servings: 4)

2 tbsp. avocado oil
4 salmon fillets, skinless
1 tsp. dried basil
½ tsp. garlic powder

DIRECTIONS (Ready in about: 20 min)

Heat a pan with olive oil, add the fish and cook for 4 minutes on each side. Sprinkle cooked salmon with garlic powder and basil.

Per serving: Kcal 246, Sodium 79 mg, Protein 34.5 g, Carbs 0.5 g, Fat 12 g

333. Salmon with Grated Beets

INGREDIENTS (Servings: 5)

2 oz. beetroot, grated
½ tsp. minced garlic
1 tsp. olive oil
1-pound salmon fillet
1 tbsp. mustard
1 tbsp. margarine

DIRECTIONS (Ready in about: 20 min)

Spread the salmon with the mustard and put it in the pan. Add the margarine and grill the fish for 4 minutes on each side. Meanwhile, add the minced garlic, grated beetroot, and olive oil. Garnish the cooked salmon fillets with beetroot.

Per serving: Kcal 164, Sodium 75 mg, Protein 18.5 g, Carbs 2 g, Fat 9.5 g

334. Scallop Salad

INGREDIENTS (Servings: 6)

12 oz. sea scallops
4 tbsp. sesame oil
4 tsp. apple cider vinegar
1 cup quinoa, cooked
½ tsp. garlic powder
1 cup green peas, cooked
1 tbsp. dried cilantro

DIRECTIONS (Ready in about: 25 min)

In a bowl, combine the scallops apple cider vinegar, and sesame oil. Warm a pan over medium heat, add the scallops, toss and cook for 8 minutes (4 minutes per side). Add all the remaining ingredients, mix well. Cook the salad for 5 minutes over low heat.

Per serving: Kcal 164, Sodium 75 mg, Protein 18.5 g, Carbs 2 g, Fat 9.5 g

335. Shallot Tuna

INGREDIENTS (Servings: 4)

1-pound tuna fillet, chopped
1 tbsp. olive oil
½ cup shallot, chopped
2 tbsp. lime juice
½ cup of water

DIRECTIONS (Ready in about: 20 min)

Heat a pan with the oil over medium-high heat, add the shallot and sauté for 3 minutes. Add the fish and cook for 4 minutes on each side. Then sprinkle the fish with lemon juice and water. Close the lid and simmer the tuna for 3 minutes. Serve warm.

Per serving: Kcal 458, Sodium 5 mg, Protein 24.5 g, Carbs 4 g, Fat 39 g

336. Shrimp Putanesca

INGREDIENTS (Servings: 3)

5 oz. shrimps, peeled
1 tsp. chili flakes
½ onion, diced
1 tbsp. coconut oil
1 tsp. garlic, diced
1 cup tomatoes, chopped
¼ cup olives, sliced
¼ cup of water

DIRECTIONS (Ready in about: 25 min)

Heat the coconut oil in the pan. Add the shrimp and the chilli flakes. Cook the shrimp for 4 minutes. Mix well and add the chopped onion, garlic, tomatoes, olives, and water. Close the lid and brown the flour for 15 minutes.

Per serving: Kcal 128, Sodium 217 mg, Protein 11.5 g, Carbs 6 g, Fat 6.5 g

337. Spanish Style Mussels

INGREDIENTS (Servings: 8)

1 cup tomatoes, chopped
1 onion, diced
1 cup of water
½ cup fresh dill, chopped
3 tbsp. olive oil
2 pounds mussels, scrubbed
½ tsp. ground black pepper

DIRECTIONS (Ready in about: 30 min)

Heat a pan with the oil over medium-high heat, add the onion, stir and cook for 3 minutes. Add the water, tomatoes, and black pepper, mix, bring to a boil, and cook for 10 minutes. Add the mussels and parsley, mix, cover the pan and cook for another 7 minutes. Serve right away.

Per serving: Kcal 160, Sodium 333 mg, Protein 14.5 g, Carbs 8 g, Fat 8 g

338. Spiced Scallops

INGREDIENTS (Servings: 4)

1-pound scallops
1 tsp. Cajun seasonings
1 tbsp. olive oil

DIRECTIONS (Ready in about: 15 min)

Rub the scallops with the Cajun seasonings. Heat the olive oil in the pan. Add the scallops and cook for 2 minutes per side.

Per serving: Kcal 130, Sodium 195 mg, Protein 19 g, Carbs 2.5 g, Fat 4.5 g

339. Spicy Ginger Seabass

INGREDIENTS (Servings: 4)

1 tbsp. ginger, grated
2 tbsp. sesame oil
¼ tsp. chilli powder
4 sea bass fillets, boneless
1 tbsp. margarine

DIRECTIONS (Ready in about: 15 min)

Heat the sesame oil and margarine in the pan. Add the chilli powder and ginger. Then add the seabass and cook the fish for 3 minutes on each side. Then close the lid and cook the fish for 3 minutes over low heat.

Per serving: Kcal 216, Sodium 123 mg, Protein 24 g, Carbs 1 g, Fat 12.5 g

340. Spicy Shrimps

INGREDIENTS (Servings: 4)

1 tsp. lemon juice
1 tbsp. sesame oil
½ tsp. smoked paprika
1-pound shrimp, peeled
1 yellow onion, chopped
1 tsp. saffron powder

DIRECTIONS (Ready in about: 25 min)

Heat the sesame oil and add the onion. Cook for 2-3 minutes over medium heat. Meanwhile, combine the saffron powder, shrimp, lemon juice, and smoked paprika. Add up the shrimp to the pan and mix well. Cook the food for 10 min over medium heat and serve.

Per serving: Kcal 177, Sodium 278 mg, Protein 26 g, Carbs 4.5 g, Fat 5.5 g

341. Spinach Halibut

INGREDIENTS (Servings: 4)

4 halibut fillets
2 tbsp. spinach, blended
1 tsp. margarine

DIRECTIONS (Ready in about: 16 min)

In the pan, melt the margarine and add the fish fillets. Cook the halibut for 3 minutes on each side. Garnish the cooked halibut with spinach. Serve immediately.

Per serving: Kcal 327, Sodium 168 mg, Protein 60.5 g, Carbs 2g, Fat 7.5 g

342. Tilapia Veracruz

INGREDIENTS (Servings: 4)

1 cup tomatoes, chopped
1 tsp. dried oregano
½ cup bell pepper, chopped
¼ cup of water
1 tbsp. olive oil
4 tilapia fillets
1 onion, diced

DIRECTIONS (Ready in about: 30 min)

Heat the olive oil in the pan and add the tilapia fillets. Grill the fish on each side for four minutes. Remove the fish from the pan. Include the onion into the pan and cook for 2 minutes. Then add the peppers, oregano, and tomatoes. Mix the ingredients well and cook for 5 minutes. After that, add water and fish. Close the lid and cook the meal for another 5 minutes. Serve.

Per serving: Kcal 148, Sodium 181 mg, Protein 22 g, Carbs 5.5 g, Fat 5 g

343. Tomato Halibut Fillets

INGREDIENTS (Servings: 4)

1 cup cherry tomatoes
1 tsp. dried basil
2 tsp. sesame oil
4 halibut fillets, skinless

DIRECTIONS (Ready in about: 20 min)
Sprinkle the fish with basil and place it in the hot pan. Add the sesame oil and the cherry tomatoes. Grill food for 4 minutes, then mix well and cook for another 5 minutes. Serve hot.
Per serving: Kcal 346, Sodium 158 mg, Protein 70 g, Carbs 2.5 g, Fat 9 g

344. Tuna and Pineapple Kebob

INGREDIENTS (Servings: 4)
12 oz. tuna fillet
8 oz. pineapple, peeled
1 tsp. olive oil
¼ tsp. ground fennel
3 tbsp. olive oil
2 pounds mussels, scrubbed
½ tsp. ground black pepper

DIRECTIONS (Ready in about: 18 min)
Chop the tuna and pineapple into medium cubes and sprinkle with olive oil and ground fennel. Then put them on the skewers and place them on the grill preheated to 400°F. Cook the kebobs for 4 minutes per side. Serve.
Per serving: Kcal 347, Sodium 1 mg, Protein 18 g, Carbs 7.5 g, Fat 27.5 g

345. Tuna Stuffed Zucchini Boats

INGREDIENTS (Servings: 2)
1 zucchini, trimmed
2 oz. low-fat cheese, shredded
1 tsp. chilli flakes
1 tsp. olive oil
6 oz. tuna, canned

DIRECTIONS (Ready in about: 35 min)
Cut the zucchini in half and collect the zucchini flesh to get the zucchini boats. Fill the zucchini boats with tuna and grated cheese. Sprinkle the zucchini with olive oil and transfer to the oven. Cook food at 385°F for 20 minutes and serve right away.
Per serving: Kcal 308, Sodium 229 mg, Protein 31 g, Carbs 4 g, Fat 19 g

346. Turmeric Pate

INGREDIENTS (Servings: 6)
1-pound tuna, canned
3 tsp. lemon juice
¼ cup low-fat yogurt
1 tsp. ground cinnamon
½ tsp. ground

DIRECTIONS (Ready in about: 18 min)
Blend the ingredients together in the food processor. Mix the pâté until smooth and transfer to the bowl.

Per serving: Kcal 149, Sodium 46 mg, Protein 20.5 g, Carbs 1 g, Fat 6.5 g

347. Vinegar Trout

INGREDIENTS (Servings: 4)
4 trout fillets, boneless
1 tsp. ground coriander
2 tbsp. avocado oil
3 tbsp. apple cider vinegar

DIRECTIONS (Ready in about: 15 min)
Heat the pan with oil over medium heat, add the trout, sprinkle with apple cider vinegar, and ground coriander. Cook the fish for 4 minutes on each side. Serve warm.
Per serving: Kcal 129, Sodium 42 mg, Protein 16.5 g, Carbs 6 g, Fat 6 g

348. Yogurt Shrimps

INGREDIENTS (Servings: 5)
1-pound shrimp, peeled
1 tbsp. margarine
¼ cup low-fat yogurt
1 tsp. lemon zest, grated
1 chilli pepper, chopped

DIRECTIONS (Ready in about: 15 min)
Melt the margarine in the pan, add the red pepper and cook for 1 minute. Then add the shrimp and lemon zest and grill on both sides for 2 minutes. Then add the yogurt, mix the shrimp well and cook for 5 minutes. Serve.
Per serving: Kcal 137, Sodium 257 mg, Protein 21.5 g, Carbs 2.5 g, Fat 4 g

SIDE DISHES

349. Acorn Squash with Apples

INGREDIENTS (Servings: 2)

2 tbsp. brown sugar
1 small acorn squash, about 6 inches in diameter
2 tsp. trans-fat-free margarine
1 Granny Smith apple, peeled, cored, and sliced

DIRECTIONS (Ready in about: 1 h 15 min)
In a small bowl, combine the apple and brown sugar. Set aside. Punch the squash several times with a sharp knife to allow steam to escape during cooking. Microwave over high heat until tender, about 5 minutes. Turn the squash after 3 minutes to ensure even cooking. Place the squash on a cutting board and cut it in half. Scrape the seeds from the center of each half and discard them. Fill the pumpkin with the apple mixture. Return squash to microwave and cook until apples are tender about 2 minutes. Transfer the squash to a serving plate. Top each half with 1 tsp. of margarine and serve immediately.
Per serving: Kcal 204, Sodium 46 mg, Protein 2.5 g, Carbs 40 g, Fat 4 g

350. Asparagus with Hazelnut

INGREDIENTS (Servings: 4)

1-pound asparagus, tough ends removed, then peeled if the skin is thick
1 clove garlic, minced
1 tbsp. finely chopped toasted hazelnuts
2 tsp. fresh lemon juice
¼ tsp. finely grated lemon zest, plus extra for garnish
¼ tsp. salt
1 tbsp. chopped fresh flat-leaf (Italian) parsley, plus sprigs for garnish
1 tsp. olive oil

DIRECTIONS (Ready in about: 20 min)
In a big saucepan fitted with a steamer basket, bring about 1 inch of water to a boil. Add the asparagus, cover, and steam until tender, about 4 minutes. Remove from the pot. In a large bowl, combine the asparagus, garlic, chopped parsley, hazelnuts, ¼ tsp. lemon zest, lemon juice, olive oil, and salt. Stir well to mix and coat. Carefully arrange the asparagus in a serving dish and garnish it with parsley sprigs and lemon zest. Serve immediately.
Per serving: Kcal 50, Sodium 148 mg, Protein 3 g, Carbs 5 g, Fat 2 g

351. Baby Minted Carrots

INGREDIENTS (Servings: 4)

6 cups of water
1-pound baby carrots, rinsed (about 5 ½ cups)
¼ cup 100% apple juice
1 tbsp. cornstarch
½ tbsp. chopped fresh mint leaves
⅛ tsp. ground cinnamon

DIRECTIONS (Ready in about: 25 min)
Pour the water into a large saucepan. Include carrots and simmer until tender, about 10 minutes. Drain the carrots and set them aside in a serving bowl. In a small saucepan over medium heat, combine the apple juice and cornstarch. Stir until mixture thickens, about 5 minutes. Add the mint and cinnamon. Pour the mixture over the carrots. Serve immediately.
Per serving: Kcal 44, Sodium 51 mg, Protein 1 g, Carbs 10 g, Fat 0 g

352. Black Bean Cakes

INGREDIENTS (Servings: 8)

4 cups of water
2 cups of dried black beans, picked over and rinsed, soaked overnight, and drained
8 cloves garlic, chopped
½ tsp. salt
½ cup chopped fresh cilantro
2 tbsp. olive oil

DIRECTIONS (Ready in about: 2 h 20 min)
In a big size saucepan over high heat, mix the black beans and water. Bring to a boil. Reduce heat to low, partially cover, and simmer until beans are tender about 60 to 70 minutes. Drain well. In a big bowl, mash the beans and garlic. Add the cilantro and salt. Form 8 cakes with the mixture. Move to a plate and refrigerate for about 1 hour. In a large nonstick skillet, heat olive oil over medium heat. Add cakes and cook, turning once, until lukewarm and outside is slightly crisp, about 5 minutes. Serve immediately.
Per serving: Kcal 196, Sodium 156 mg, Protein 10.5 g, Carbs 30 g, Fat 4 g

353. Braised Kale

INGREDIENTS (Servings: 6)
4 garlic cloves, thinly sliced
1-pound kale, tough stems removed and leaves coarsely chopped
½ cup low-sodium vegetable stock or broth
1 cup cherry tomatoes, halved
1 tbsp. fresh lemon juice
¼ tsp. salt
⅛ tsp. freshly ground black pepper
2 tsp. olive oil

DIRECTIONS (Ready in about: 45 min)
In a big-size skillet, heat up the olive oil over medium heat. Add garlic and sauté until lightly browned for 1 to 2 minutes. Add the black cabbage and the vegetable broth. Cover, reduce heat to medium-low and cook until cabbage is wilted and some of the liquid has evaporated about 5 minutes. Include the tomatoes and cook, uncovered, until the cabbage is tender, another 5 to 7 minutes. Take it out from the heat and add the lemon juice, salt, and pepper. Serve immediately.

Per serving: Kcal 70, Sodium 133 mg, Protein 4 g, Carbs 9 g, Fat 4 g

354. Broccoli, Garlic, and Lemon

INGREDIENTS (Servings: 4)
1 tsp. olive oil
¼ tsp. ground black pepper
4 cups broccoli florets
1 tbsp. minced garlic
¼ tsp. kosher salt
1 tsp. lemon zest

DIRECTIONS (Ready in about: 20 min)
In a portable saucepan, bring one cup of water to a boil. Add up the broccoli to the boiling water and cook, 2 to 3 minutes or until just tender. Drain the broccoli. In a small pan, fry over medium-high heat. Add the garlic and sauté for 30 seconds. Add the broccoli, lemon zest, salt, and pepper. Mix well and serve.

Per serving: Kcal 45, Sodium 153 mg, Protein 3 g, Carbs 7 g, Fat 1 g

355. Brown Rice Pilaf

INGREDIENTS (Servings: 8)
1⅛ cups dark brown rice, rinsed and drained
2 cups of water
¾ tsp. salt, divided
¼ tsp. saffron threads or ground turmeric
¼ cup dried apricots, chopped
½ tsp. grated orange zest
3 tbsp. fresh orange juice
1½ tbsp. pistachio oil or canola oil
¼ cup chopped pistachio nuts

DIRECTIONS (Ready in about: 55 min)
In a big saucepan over high heat, combine the rice, water, ¼ tsp. of salt, and saffron. Bring to a boil. Reduce heat to low, cover, and simmer until water is absorbed and rice is tender, for about 45 minutes. Transfer to a large bowl and keep warm. In a portable bowl, mix the orange zest and juice, oil, and the remaining ½ tsp. of salt. Whisk to mix. Pour the orange mixture over the hot rice. Add the nuts and apricots and toss gently to combine and coat. Serve immediately.

Per serving: Kcal 153, Sodium 222 mg, Protein 3 g, Carbs 24 g, Fat 4 g

356. Brussels Sprouts with Shallots

INGREDIENTS (Servings: 4)
3 shallots, thinly sliced (about 3 tbsp.)
3 tsp. extra-virgin olive oil, divided
¼ tsp. salt, divided
½ cup no-salt-added vegetable stock or broth
1 pound of trimmed Brussels sprouts, cut into quarters
¼ tsp. finely grated lemon zest
¼ tsp. of black pepper
1 tbsp. fresh lemon juice

DIRECTIONS (Ready in about: 30 min)
In a big nonstick skillet, heat 2 tsp. of olive oil over medium heat. Add the shallot and sauté until tender and lightly browned, about 6 minutes. Stir in ⅛ tsp. of salt. Put it in a bowl and set it aside. In the same pan, heat the remaining 1 tsp. of olive oil over medium heat. Add the Brussels sprouts and sauté until just starting to brown for 3-4 minutes. Add the vegetable broth and bring to a boil. Cook, uncovered, until the Brussels sprouts are tender, 5 to 6 minutes. Return the shallots to the pan. Add lemon zest and juice, ⅛ tsp. of salt and pepper. Serve immediately.

Per serving: Kcal 104, Sodium 191 mg, Protein 5 g, Carbs 12 g, Fat 4 g

357. Buttermilk Mashed Potatoes

INGREDIENTS (Servings: 4)
½ tsp. kosher salt
2 pounds russet potatoes
2 tbsp. unsalted butter
2 tbsp. chopped chives, for garnish (optional)
¾ cup low-fat buttermilk

DIRECTIONS (Ready in about: 35 min)
Fill a large pot halfway with water. Chop the potatoes into medium pieces, as equal in size as possible. Add potatoes to the pot and add more water if needed to cover. Bring to a boil over high heat. Cook until the potatoes are tender (stick a knife into a potato to check), 12 to 15 minutes. Drain the potatoes, and transfer them to the pot. Add the salt, butter, and buttermilk. Mash the potatoes until smooth, adding more buttermilk for the desired consistency, if needed. Taste & season with extra salt if needed and garnish with chives if using.
Per serving: Kcal 241, Sodium 353 mg, Protein 6 g, Carbs 44 g, Fat 6 g

358. Cauliflower Mashed Potatoes

INGREDIENTS (Servings: 4)

1 head cauliflower	1 tbsp. soft-tub margarine, nonhydrogenated
1 clove garlic	
1 leek, white only, split into 4 pieces	Pepper to taste

DIRECTIONS (Ready in about: 40 min)
Break the cauliflower into small pieces. In a large saucepan, steam the cauliflower, garlic, and leeks in water until completely tender, about 20-30 minutes. Use a food processor to blend the vegetables until the consistency resembles mashed potatoes. Treat only a small portion at a time. If you prefer a softer texture, use a blender. Be sure to hold the blender lid firmly with a kitchen towel. Add a little hot water if the vegetables seem dry. Mix the margarine and pepper to taste and serve.
Per serving: Kcal 67, Sodium 60 mg, Protein 2 g, Carbs 40 g, Fat 1.5 g

359. Celery Root and Apple Puree

INGREDIENTS (Servings: 4)

2 pounds of peeled celery root, cut into 1-inch pieces	2 tbsp. unsalted butter
	¼ tsp. kosher salt
	2 red apples, peeled and sliced
½ cup low-fat milk	

DIRECTIONS (Ready in about: 40 min)
Add the celery root to a pot of salted water over high heat. When the water reaches a boil, add the apples and cook until the celery root is easily pierced with a knife, about 12 minutes. Reserving one cup of the cooking water, drain the celery root and apples and place them in a food processor. Add the butter, milk, and salt. Blend until smooth, scraping sides as needed. In case you want a smoother consistency, add the reserved cooking water as needed. Serve at once.
Per serving: Kcal 207, Sodium 348 mg, Protein 5 g, Carbs 35.5 g, Fat 7 g

360. Chinese-Style Asparagus

INGREDIENTS (Servings: 4)

1½ pounds fresh asparagus, woody ends removed and cut into 1 ½-inch length	½ cup water
	1 tsp. reduced-sodium soy sauce
	½ tsp. sugar

DIRECTIONS (Ready in about: 25 min)
In a big saucepan, heat up the water, sugar, and soy sauce over high heat. Cook to the boiling, then add the asparagus. Reduce heat and simmer until asparagus is crisp and tender about 3-4 minutes. Move to a serving plate and serve immediately.
Per serving: Kcal 24, Sodium 26 mg, Protein 2.5 g, Carbs 4 g, Fat 0 g

361. Cilantro Brown Rice

INGREDIENTS (Servings: 4)

1 bunch cilantro leaves, washed	2 scallions, coarsely chopped
1 cup of brown rice	1 clove garlic, crushed
1 avocado, chopped	1 tbsp. olive oil
Juice of 1 lime	½ tsp. kosher salt

DIRECTIONS (Ready in about: 45 min)
In a portable pot, cook the brown rice according to the package instructions. When the rice is almost done, puree the cilantro, avocado, scallions, lime juice, garlic, and salt in a food processor. Pour the olive oil through the feed tube and puree until smooth, 1 to 2 minutes. Drain when the rice is tender and return to the pot. Add the cilantro seasoning to the rice and stir to combine.
Per serving: Kcal 288, Sodium 300 mg, Protein 5 g, Carbs 42 g, Fat 12 g

362. Corn Pudding

INGREDIENTS (Servings: 8)

3 cups of water	⅛ tsp. nutmeg
3 cups skim milk	⅛ tsp. clove
2 cups coarse cornmeal	⅛ tsp. ginger

¼ cup maple syrup   ¼ tsp. cinnamon
½ cup raisins

DIRECTIONS (Ready in about: 55 min)
In a big saucepan, bring the water and milk to a boil. Add up the cornmeal and mix to remove lumps. Boil the water. Then lower the heat and cover, occasionally stirring for 10 to 15 minutes. Turn off the heat and add the other ingredients. Let it stand for about 10 to 15 minutes. Stir and serve.
Per serving: Kcal 213, Sodium 44 mg, Protein 6 g, Carbs 45.5 g, Fat 1 g

363. Couscous with Cranberries

INGREDIENTS (Servings: 4)
¼ cup pine nuts
2 tsp. canola oil
2 cups reduced-sodium vegetable stock
¼ tsp. freshly ground black pepper
½ tsp. kosher salt
1 cup couscous, preferably whole wheat
2 scallions, coarsely chopped
⅓ cup dried cranberries

DIRECTIONS (Ready in about: 30 min)
Heat up the canola oil in a medium saucepan over medium-high heat. Add pine nuts; cook until lightly browned, 2 to 3 minutes, stirring constantly. Add the vegetable broth, pepper, and salt. Bring to a boil and add the couscous and blueberries. Remove from heat, cover with a lid and let it stand for 10 minutes. Blow the couscous and add the scallion. Taste and adjust the dressing as needed.
Per serving: Kcal 283, Sodium 657 mg, Protein 7.5 g, Carbs 49 g, Fat 9 g

364. Creamed Swiss Chard

INGREDIENTS (Servings: 8)
2 tbsp. olive oil
1½ tbsp. unbleached all-purpose flour
3 garlic cloves, finely chopped
1¼ cups low-fat plain soy milk
2 pounds Swiss chard, washed, stemmed, and cut crosswise into strips ½ inch wide
½ tsp. freshly ground black pepper
1 tbsp. grated Parmesan

DIRECTIONS (Ready in about: 25 min)
In a big-size skillet, heat up the olive oil over medium heat. Incorporate the flour to obtain a homogeneous dough. Continue to beat and add the garlic; cook for another 30 seconds. Add the soy milk and cook until the mixture thickens a little. Add the chard and toss to coat them well. Cover the lid and cook until tender, about 2 minutes. Season with pepper. Sprinkle with Parmesan and serve hot.
Per serving: Kcal 80, Sodium 265 mg, Protein 3 g, Carbs 8 g, Fat 4 g

365. Creole-Style Black-Eyed Peas

INGREDIENTS (Servings: 8)
2 cups dried black-eyed peas
1 tsp. low-sodium vegetable-flavored bouillon granules
2 cups canned unsalted tomatoes, crushed
1 large onion, finely chopped
2 stalks celery, finely chopped
3 tsp. minced garlic
½ tsp. dry mustard
¼ tsp. ground ginger
¼ tsp. cayenne pepper
1 bay leaf
½ cup chopped parsley
3 cups of water

DIRECTIONS (Ready in about: 2 h 30 min)
In a portable saucepan over high heat, add 2 cups of water and the black-eyed peas. Bring to a boil for 2 minutes, cover, remove from heat and let it stand for an hour. Drain the water, leaving the black-eyed peas in the pot. Add the remaining 1 cup of water, the broth granules, tomatoes, onion, celery, garlic, mustard, ginger, cayenne pepper, and bay leaf. Stir and bring to a boil. Cover the lid and cook slowly for 2 hours over low heat, stirring occasionally. Add enough water to keep the peas covered in liquid. Remove the bay leaf, pour it into a bowl and garnish with parsley. Serve immediately.
Per serving: Kcal 168, Sodium 50 mg, Protein 11 g, Carbs 31 g, Fat 1.5 g

366. Curried Cauliflower

INGREDIENTS (Servings: 4)
2 tsp. curry powder
1 tbsp. unsalted butter
½ tsp. kosher salt
¼ cup dried cherries
⅓ cup water
1 head cauliflower, cut into bite-size pieces
¼ tsp. freshly ground black pepper

DIRECTIONS (Ready in about: 10 min)
Melt the butter in a large sauté pan or skillet over medium-high heat. Include the curry powder, salt, and pepper, and cook, stirring, until fragrant, 30 seconds. Add the cauliflower, and stir to combine with the butter and spices. Cook until slightly golden, 2 to 3 minutes. Add the water, and cover with a lid.

Cook until the cauliflower is tender and the water has evaporated, 3 to 4 minutes longer. Stir in the cherries. Taste and adjust the seasonings as needed.
Per serving: Kcal 84, Sodium 334 mg, Protein 3 g, Carbs 14 g, Fat 3 g

367. Fresh Fruit Kebabs

INGREDIENTS (Servings: 2)

6 oz. low-fat, sugar-free lemon yogurt	4 strawberries
1 tsp. fresh lime juice	½ banana, cut into 4½ inch chunks
4 pineapple chunks	4 wooden skewers
1 kiwi, peeled and quartered	4 red grapes
	1 tsp. lime zest

DIRECTIONS (Ready in about: 15 min)
In a portable bowl, combine yogurt, lime juice, and lime zest. Cover and refrigerate until you require it. Thread one of each fruit onto the skewer. Rehash with the other skewers until the fruit is gone. Serve with lemon-lime sauce.
Per serving: Kcal 190, Sodium 53 mg, Protein 4 g, Carbs 39 g, Fat 2 g

368. Garlic Mashed Potatoes

INGREDIENTS (Servings: 8)

3 pounds russet potatoes, peeled and cubed	1 tbsp. trans-fat-free margarine
6 garlic cloves, separated and peeled	Ground black pepper, to taste
½ cup fat-free milk	2 tbsp. chopped fresh parsley

DIRECTIONS (Ready in about: 50 min)
Cover the potatoes with water in an enormous saucepan. Just bring it to a boil. Reduce the pressure of the heat and simmer for approximately 15 minutes, until tender. Ensure to drain the potatoes very well and put them back into the pan. Cover the garlic with water in a shallow saucepan. Just bring it to a boil. Reduce the heat and simmer for about 10 minutes, until tender. Drain some garlic. Combine the garlic and milk in a food processor or blender. Blend until smooth. Add the garlic puree and the margarine to the potatoes. Mix until you get the desired consistency. Season with black pepper to taste. Garnish with parsley and serve immediately.
Per serving: Kcal 154, Sodium 36 mg, Protein 4 g, Carbs 30 g, Fat 2 g

369. Glazed Root Vegetables

INGREDIENTS (Servings: 4)

½ cup onions, cut into 1-inch pieces	1½ cups water
½ cup new potatoes, cut into 1-inch pieces	½ cup of carrots, cut into 1-inch pieces
2 tsp. of sugar	½ cup turnips, cut into 1-inch pieces
1 tsp. olive oil	

DIRECTIONS (Ready in about: 1 h 15 min)
In a saucepan, add the water, onion, carrots, turnips, and potatoes. Simmer and uncovered the mixture over medium heat for about 15 minutes until the vegetables are tender. Drain and sprinkle with sugar and olive oil. Increase the heat and continue cooking, shaking the pan until the vegetables are glazed and lightly browned. Move to a serving plate and serve immediately.
Per serving: Kcal 57, Sodium 24 mg, Protein 2 g, Carbs 10.5 g, Fat 1 g

370. Honey Sage Carrots

INGREDIENTS (Servings: 4)

1 tbsp. chopped fresh sage	2 cups sliced carrots
¼ tsp. ground black pepper	2 tsp. butter
	2 tbsp. honey
	⅛ tsp. salt

DIRECTIONS (Ready in about: 25 min)
Fill a portable saucepan with water and bring to a boil. Add the carrots and boil for about 5 minutes until the pork is tender. Drain and set aside. Preheat a medium pan and add the butter. When the pan is hot, and the butter has melted, add the carrots, honey, sage, pepper, and salt. Brown for about 3 minutes, stirring frequently. Remove from the heat and serve.
Per serving: Kcal 74, Sodium 112 mg, Protein 1 g, Carbs 15 g, Fat 2 g

371. Kasha with Spring Vegetables

INGREDIENTS (Servings: 4)

1 (9 oz.) bag fresh spinach	½ cup fiddleheads, or asparagus
1 medium zucchini, grated	¼ tsp. kosher salt
2 cups reduced-sodium vegetable broth	1 cup kasha
	¼ tsp. black pepper
	2 tsp. olive oil

DIRECTIONS (Ready in about: 15 min)
Warm the olive oil in a medium pot over medium-high heat. Add the spinach, in batches if necessary, and stir until wilted. Add the zucchini and the fiddleheads, sautéing until softened and combined with the spinach, 2 to 3 minutes. Add the broth, kasha, salt, and pepper. Heat up the mixture to the point of boiling, cover, and reduce the heat to low. Simmer until the kasha is tender, about 15 minutes. Remove from the heat and fluff the kasha with a fork. Taste and adjust the seasoning as needed.
Per serving: Kcal 204, Sodium 275 mg, Protein 8.5 g, Carbs 38 g, Fat 4.5 g

372. Low-Fat Creamed Spinach

INGREDIENTS (Servings: 6)

½ cup water	4 oz. reduced-fat cream cheese
2 (16 oz.) packages frozen chopped spinach, thawed	½ cup 2% Greek yogurt
4 cloves garlic, minced	¼ tsp. freshly ground black pepper
½ cup low-fat milk	¼ tsp. salt

DIRECTIONS (Ready in about: 30 min)
In an enormous pot over medium-high heat, cook the spinach in the water, stirring occasionally, until all the water evaporates, about 5 minutes. Stir in the garlic and cook for 1 minute. Reduce the heat to low, add the cream cheese and the milk, stirring and cooking until the cream cheese is melted, 5 to 7 minutes. Take it away from the heat and stir in the yogurt. Season with salt and pepper, and serve.
Per serving: Kcal 107, Sodium 311 mg, Protein 10 g, Carbs 10 g, Fat 4 g

373. Marinated Eggplant

INGREDIENTS (Servings: 4)

3 pounds russet potatoes, peeled and cubed	1 tbsp. trans-fat-free margarine
6 garlic cloves, separated and peeled	Ground black pepper, to taste
½ cup fat-free milk	2 tbsp. chopped fresh parsley

DIRECTIONS (Ready in about: 2 h 35 min)
Preheat the broiler. Line 1 or 2 baking tins lined with aluminum foil and add the eggplants. Drizzle with olive oil and season with salt and pepper. Broil the eggplant until slightly charred but still chewy, 3 to 4 minutes.

Turn the eggplant over and broil 3 to 4 minutes longer. Remove from the broiler and let cool. Repeat until all the eggplant has been broiled. When the eggplant has cooled, cut it into bite-size pieces. Move it into a bowl and combine with the mint and the olives. Drizzle with additional olive oil. Serve the marinated eggplant cold or at room temperature.
Per serving: Kcal 142, Sodium 246 mg, Protein 3 g, Carbs 17.5 g, Fat 9 g

374. Parmesan Roasted Cauliflower

INGREDIENTS (Servings: 6)

½ cup panko bread crumbs	1 tsp. finely chopped fresh basil
¼ cup finely grated Parmesan cheese	¼ tsp. paprika
2 tbsp. olive oil	¼ tsp. kosher salt
1 tsp. fresh lemon zest	3 cups small cauliflower florets

DIRECTIONS (Ready in about: 45 min)
Fill a normal size saucepan with water and bring to a boil. Heat the oven to 375°F. Lightly coat an 8 x 8-inch baking dish with cooking spray. In a small bowl, combine the breadcrumbs, cheese, oil, lemon zest, basil, paprika, and salt. Use your hands to mix the mixture evenly. Put the cauliflower in boiling water for 3 minutes; drain. Place the cauliflower in the pan and sprinkle the breadcrumb mixture evenly. Bake for about 15 minutes or until the crust is lightly golden.
Per serving: Kcal 84, Sodium 163 mg, Protein 3 g, Carbs 6 g, Fat 6.5 g

375. Pesto-Stuffed Tomatoes

INGREDIENTS (Servings: 4)

⅓ cup panko bread crumbs	2 tbsp. grated Parmesan cheese
4 small to medium tomatoes, hulled	1 tbsp. prepared pesto

DIRECTIONS (Ready in about: 45 min)
Preheat the oven to 400°F. Combine the cheese and bread crumbs in a small bowl. Add the pesto, and stir to combine with the dry ingredients. Fill each tomato's cavity with the bread crumb mixture. Spot the tomatoes in an ovenproof dish and bake until the tomatoes and the filling are hot, and the tops are browned for about 15 minutes.
Per serving: Kcal 284, Sodium 140 mg, Protein 3g, Carbs 11 g, Fat 2 g

376. Polenta with Mushrooms

INGREDIENTS (Servings: 4)
1½ cups hot water
½ oz. dried black trumpet mushrooms
2 cups low-fat milk
1½ tbsp. unsalted butter
½ tsp. dried thyme
½ cup coarse cornmeal
¼ tsp. kosher salt

DIRECTIONS (Ready in about: 1 h 30 min)
For 15 minutes, soak the dried mushrooms in water. Drain the mushrooms through a ne-mesh sieve set over a 2-cup measure and reserve the soaking liquid. Rinse the mushrooms, chop them, and reserve. Pour 1 cup of the soaking liquid into a medium pot through the strainer again to make sure there's no dirt left. Add the milk, thyme, and salt, and bring to a boil over high heat. Add the cornmeal, whisking constantly. Turn down the heat and let simmer until the polenta is as thick as you want it, 5 to 10 minutes. Stir in the butter. Taste and adjust the seasonings if necessary.
Per serving: Kcal 145, Sodium 205 mg, Protein 5 g, Carbs 18.5 g, Fat 6 g

377. Quick-Sautéed Cucumbers

INGREDIENTS (Servings: 4)
2 tsp. dried red pepper flakes
1 tbsp. reduced-sodium soy sauce
2 tbsp. extra-virgin olive oil
2 cloves garlic, minced
3 English cucumbers, peeled, cut in half lengthwise, and cut into 1-inch pieces
1-inch piece fresh ginger, grated

DIRECTIONS (Ready in about: 20 min)
Warm the olive oil in a large sauté pan or skillet over high heat. Add the pepper flakes, garlic, and ginger, and cook, stirring constantly, until fragrant, 15 to 30 seconds. Add the cucumber, stirring constantly to cook and combine with the other ingredients, about 1 minute. Add the soy sauce, and continue stirring for 1 more minute, scraping up any bits that have stuck to the bottom, and serve.
Per serving: Kcal 82, Sodium 137 mg, Protein 1.5 g, Carbs 4.5 g, Fat 7 g

378. Roasted Asparagus

INGREDIENTS (Servings: 4)
1-pound asparagus, cut into 1-inch pieces
2 cups morel or other mushrooms, cut into quarters
1 tsp. olive oil
2 tbsp. balsamic vinegar
Zest of one lemon
1 tsp. black pepper

DIRECTIONS (Ready in about: 1 h 20 min)
Combine the ingredients together in a glass container or a large, zipped food bag. Toss to coat. Allow it to marinate for about 1-2 hours in the refrigerator. Place in a nonstick skillet. Lift the grill. Cook, 2 to 3 minutes, turning the vegetables once or more until lightly browned. Serve immediately.
Per serving: Kcal 57, Sodium 11 mg, Protein 4 g, Carbs 8 g, Fat 0.5 g

379. Roasted Asparagus & Orange

INGREDIENTS (Servings: 4)
Grated zest and juice of 1 orange
½ tsp. freshly ground black pepper
¼ tsp. kosher salt
1½ tbsp. extra-virgin olive oil
2 bunches of asparagus, trimmed

DIRECTIONS (Ready in about: 30 min)
Preheat the oven to 400°F. Line a rimmed baking sheet with foil and spread the asparagus in rows. Sprinkle with olive oil and orange juice. Sprinkle with salt and pepper. Roast until the asparagus is tender, about 20 minutes. Garnish with the orange zest and serve.
Per serving: Kcal 99, Sodium 150 mg, Protein 5 g, Carbs 11 g, Fat 5 g

380. Roasted Brussels Sprouts

INGREDIENTS (Servings: 4)
1 tbsp. freshly squeezed lemon juice
¼ tsp. freshly ground black pepper
¼ tsp. kosher salt
1½ tsp. mustard seeds
2½ tbsp. extra-virgin olive oil, divided
1¼ pounds Brussels sprouts end trimmed and halved lengthwise

DIRECTIONS (Ready in about: 60 min)
Preheat the oven to 400°F. Line a rimmed baking sheet with foil. Spread the Brussels sprouts on the sheet and cover with 1½ tbsp. of the olive oil and the lemon juice, salt, and pepper. Toss to combine.

Roast the sprouts until the outer leaves are crisped, about 45 minutes, rotating the baking sheet once midway through. Remove from the oven and add the remaining 1 tbsp. olive oil and mustard seeds. Toss to combine with the sprouts. Taste and adjust the seasonings as needed.
Per serving: Kcal 154, Sodium 188 mg, Protein 6 g, Carbs 16.5 g, Fat 9.5 g

381. Roasted Green Beans
INGREDIENTS (Servings: 4)
2 cups green beans, cleaned and trimmed	1 tsp. dried basil
1 cup cherry tomatoes (about 20)	1 tsp. dried oregano
	1 tsp. onion powder
1 tbsp. minced garlic	½ tsp. salt
2 tsp. olive oil	½ tsp. pepper

DIRECTIONS (Ready in about: 30 min)
Heat up the oven to 400°F. Lightly grease a baking sheet. In a medium bowl, combine the chopped green beans, tomatoes, garlic, oil, basil, oregano, onion powder, salt, and pepper; Stir until beans are evenly coated with olive oil and seasoning. Place the green beans on the baking sheet, making sure they are evenly distributed. Bake for 10 to 15 minutes, stirring after 10 minutes. Serve hot.
Per serving: Kcal 59, Sodium 132 mg, Protein 2.5 g, Carbs 9 g, Fat 3 g

382. Roasted Potatoes
INGREDIENTS (Servings: 4)
1 pound of large red or white potatoes with skins, cut into wedges ¼-inch thick	1 tbsp. olive oil
	1 tsp. Rosemary or oregano

DIRECTIONS (Ready in about: 1 h 35 min)
Heat up the oven to 400°F. Coat a baking sheet lightly with cooking spray. Soak the potato slices in ice water for 5 minutes. Drain the potatoes and rinse them well in cold water. Press between the paper towels to dry. Move the potatoes to a large bowl, pour the olive oil over the potatoes and toss to coat. Spot the potatoes in a single layer on the prepared baking sheet. Bake for 15 minutes. Flip the potatoes and cook for another 5 minutes. Sprinkle with the herbs. Return the potatoes to the oven and cook until golden brown and crisp, about 5 minutes. Serve immediately.
Per serving: Kcal 116, Sodium 18 mg, Protein 2 g, Carbs 18.5 g, Fat 4 g

383. Roasted Winter Squash
INGREDIENTS (Servings: 8)
2 tsp. canola oil, divided	¼ cup walnuts, chopped
4 cups of peeled and diced (½-inch pieces) winter squash	Black pepper to taste
	½ tbsp. chopped Italian parsley
1 cup diced onion	1 small orange, peeled and segmented
4 cups cooked wild rice	
1 cup fresh cranberries	¼ tsp. thyme

DIRECTIONS (Ready in about: 1 h 15 min)
Heat up the oven to 400°F. Place the squash in the pan and season with 1 tsp of oil. Bake for 40 minutes or until golden brown. In a hot skillet, brown the onions with the remaining oil. Add the cranberries and sauté for 1 minute. Add remaining ingredients and sauté for 4 to 5 minutes or until heated through. Serve.
Per serving: Kcal 184, Sodium 6 mg, Protein 5.5 g, Carbs 32 g, Fat 4 g

384. Sauteed Zucchini Coins
INGREDIENTS (Servings: 4)
1 tbsp. olive oil	1 tsp. dill weed
2 cups thinly sliced yellow zucchini	2 tbsp. fresh cilantro
	2 scallions, chopped
2 cups thinly sliced green zucchini	2 tbsp. lemon juice

DIRECTIONS (Ready in about: 15 min)
In a large nonstick skillet, heat oil over medium heat. Add the zucchini slices and sauté until their color intensifies, about 5 minutes. Add the dill, cilantro, and shallot and mix until smooth. Transfer to a serving bowl. Sprinkle with lemon juice and serve immediately.
Per serving: Kcal 64, Sodium 9 mg, Protein 2 g, Carbs 5.5 g, Fat 4 g

385. Seared Endive
INGREDIENTS (Servings: 4)
8 heads of Belgian endive, washed and halved	Ground black pepper, if desired
	2 tbsp. chopped fresh parsley
Juice from 1 lemon	
¼ tsp. salt	1 tbsp. water

DIRECTIONS (Ready in about: 30 min)
In a large skillet, heat the water over medium heat. Add the endives, cut sides down. Cover the lid and cook for several minutes until the outer leaves become translucent. Remove from the heat and uncover. Squeeze the lemon juice over the endive and season with pepper. Transfer to a serving platter and garnish with parsley. Serve immediately.
Per serving: Kcal 24, Sodium 150 mg, Protein 1 g, Carbs 5 g, Fat 0 g

386. Shrimp Ceviche

INGREDIENTS (Servings: 8)
½ pound raw shrimp, cut in ¼-inch pieces
2 lemons, zest, and juice
2 limes, zest, and juice
2 tbsp. olive oil
2 tsp. cumin
½ cup diced red onion
1 cup diced tomato
¼ cup chopped cilantro
2 tbsp. minced garlic
1 cup black beans, cooked
¼ cup diced serrano chilli pepper and seeds removed
1 cup diced cucumber, peeled and seeded

DIRECTIONS (Ready in about: 3 h 15 min)
Place the shrimp in a shallow pan and cover with the lemon and lime juice, reserving the zest. Refrigerate for at least 3 hours or until shrimp are firm and white. Combine the remaining ingredients in another bowl and set aside while the shrimp is cold cooking. When ready to serve, mix the shrimp and citrus juice with the rest of the ingredients. Serve with baked tortilla chips.
Per serving: Kcal 98, Sodium 167 mg, Protein 7.5 g, Carbs 10 g, Fat 4.5 g

387. Smashed "Fried" Potatoes

INGREDIENTS (Servings: 6)
2 tbsp. olive oil
¼ tsp. freshly ground black pepper
8 medium red potatoes (about 1½ pounds)
½ tsp. kosher salt

DIRECTIONS (Ready in about: 1 h 20 min)
Add up the potatoes to a large pot and fill three-quarters full with water, making sure to cover the potatoes. Bring the mixture to a boil over warm heat and cook the potatoes until almost tender, about 30 minutes. Drain and let cool. Preheat the oven to 450°F. Line a rimmed baking sheet with foil. When the potato is cool, cut them in half lengthwise. Place the potato halves cut side up on the prepared baking sheet. Press down on the potatoes gently with the potato masher to flatten them. Season with olive oil, salt, and pepper. Roast the potatoes until slightly browned and crispy on top, about 30 minutes.
Per serving: Kcal 258, Sodium 211 mg, Protein 6 g, Carbs 52.5 g, Fat 5 g

388. Spicy Red Cabbage

INGREDIENTS (Servings: 6)
1½ pounds red cabbage, cored, quartered, and shredded (about 10 cups)
2 medium onions, chopped (about 1½ cups)
1 tart apple, cored, peeled, and chopped (about 1 cup)
1 cup pitted prunes, chopped
1 garlic clove, crushed
1 tsp. ground cinnamon
¼ tsp. ground cloves
1 tsp. cumin seed
1 tsp. coriander seed
2 tbsp. red wine vinegar
Ground nutmeg, to taste
½ cup water

DIRECTIONS (Ready in about: 50 min)
In a big saucepan, add up all the ingredients. Stir to mix well. Cover and cook, frequently stirring, over medium heat until vegetables are tender, about 1 hour. Add enough water to prevent the cabbage from drying out. Transfer to a bowl and either serve hot or cold.
Per serving: Kcal 148, Sodium 35 mg, Protein 3 g, Carbs 34 g, Fat 0.5 g

389. Sweet Carrots

INGREDIENTS (Servings: 4)
½ cup water
¼ tsp. salt
2 cups shredded carrots
1 tsp. trans-free margarine
The sugar substitute, to taste
1 tsp. lemon juice
4 tbsp. fresh parsley, chopped

DIRECTIONS (Ready in about: 25 min)
In a portable saucepan, bring the water to a boil. Add salt and chopped carrots. Cover the lid and cook until the water has evaporated for about 5 minutes. Remove the carrots from the heat. Add the margarine, sugar substitute, lemon juice, and parsley. Serve immediately.
Per serving: Kcal 148, Sodium 35 mg, Protein 3 g, Carbs 34 g, Fat 0.5 g

390. Tangy Green Beans

INGREDIENTS (Servings: 10)

1½ pounds green beans, fresh, frozen or canned
⅓ cup diced sweet red bell peppers
4½ tsp. olive oil or canola oil
4½ tsp. water
1½ tsp. vinegar
1½ tsp. mustard
¼ tsp. salt
¼ tsp. pepper
⅛ tsp. garlic powder

DIRECTIONS (Ready in about: 30 min)

Cook the beans and red peppers in a steamer basket over water until tender. Beat all remaining ingredients in a small bowl. Transfer the beans to a serving bowl. Add dressing and toss to coat.

Per serving: Kcal 42, Sodium 72 mg, Protein 1 g, Carbs 5 g, Fat 2 g

391. Thyme Roasted Beets

INGREDIENTS (Servings: 4)

1 tbsp. olive oil
2 medium golden or red beets, washed and trimmed
1 tsp. fresh thyme
¼ tsp. ground black pepper
¼ tsp. salt

DIRECTIONS (Ready in about: 55 min)

Heat up the oven to 400°F. Wrap beets in foil and bake for 40 minutes or until tender. Cool slightly and set it aside. Peel and cut the beets into medium pieces. In a medium bowl, combine the cooked beets, oil, thyme, salt, and pepper. Place on a baking sheet and bake for an additional 5 to 10 minutes until heated through.

Per serving: Kcal 59, Sodium 176 mg, Protein 1g, Carbs 7 g, Fat 3 g

392. Lentil Ragout

INGREDIENTS (Servings: 6)

1 tsp. olive oil
1 cup chopped onions
6 medium tomatoes, chopped
5 cups of water
1 cup raw red lentils
1 tbsp. chopped fresh thyme
4 cloves garlic, minced
1 tsp. kosher salt
¼ tsp. ground black pepper

DIRECTIONS (Ready in about: 45 min)

In a big saucepan, add up all the ingredients. Stir to mix well. Cover and cook, frequently stirring, over medium heat until vegetables are tender, about 1 hour. Add enough water to prevent the cabbage from drying out. Transfer to a bowl and either serve hot or cold.

Per serving: Kcal 152, Sodium 179 mg, Protein 10 g, Carbs 27 g, Fat 1 g

DISHES WITH SAUCES

393. Asian-Style Lettuce Wraps

INGREDIENTS (Servings: 4)

4 cups low-sodium vegetable broth
2 cups uncooked red quinoa
8 large butter lettuce leaves
1 cup bean sprouts
1 cup chopped snow peas (in thirds)
½ cup chopped red bell pepper
4 tsp. sesame seeds
½ cup shredded carrot

For the Peanut Sauce:
1¼ cup low-sodium vegetable broth
1 cup and 6 tbsp. crunchy peanut butter
Juice of ½ lime
½ tsp. low-sodium soy sauce
½ tsp. sesame oil
2 tbsp. chopped green onion, white end discarded
¼ tsp. ground ginger

DIRECTIONS (Ready in about: 20 min)
Rinse the quinoa. In a large, covered pot, bring the quinoa and vegetable broth to a boil over high heat. Reduce heat and simmer for 10 to 15 minutes or until liquid is almost completely absorbed. The cooked quinoa should be slightly al dente; it's ready when most of the nuclei have unfolded, and you can see the germ unfolding. Leave the quinoa to sit for about five minutes in a covered jar. Stir gently with a fork. Place ½ cup cooked quinoa on each lettuce leaf. In a medium bowl, combine the peas, bean sprouts, bell pepper, and carrots. In a small saucepan, combine all the ingredients for the peanut sauce. Heat to the point of boiling and stir until the peanut butter is melted. Pour the sauce into the bowl with the chopped vegetables. Toss well and spoon evenly on top of the quinoa in each lettuce leaf. Sprinkle the sesame seeds over the vegetables and serve.
Per serving: Kcal 486, Sodium 77 mg, Protein 17.5 g, Carbs 73 g, Fat 2 g

394. Chicken and Garlic Sauce

INGREDIENTS (Servings: 4)

1 tbsp. olive oil
1 yellow onion, chopped
A pinch of black pepper
1 tbsp. basil, chopped
1 cup low-sodium chicken stock
2 cups coconut cream
Add the mustard and the rest of the ingredients, mix gently, bring to a boil and cook over medium heat
1-pound chicken breasts, skinless, boneless, and cubed
1 tbsp. chives, chopped
4 garlic cloves, minced

DIRECTIONS (Ready in about: 25 min)
Heat a pan with the oil over medium-high heat, add the garlic, onion, and meat, mix and sauté for 5 minutes. Add the broth and the rest of the ingredients and bring to a boil and cook over medium heat for 15 minutes. Divide the mixture between the plates and serve.
Per serving: Kcal 157, Sodium 550 mg, Protein 34.5 g, Carbs 21 g, Fat 16.5 g

395. Chicken and Ginger Sauce

INGREDIENTS (Servings: 4)

1-pound chicken breast, skinless, boneless, and cubed
1 tbsp. ginger, grated
1 tbsp. olive oil
2 shallots, chopped
1 tbsp. balsamic vinegar
A pinch of black pepper
¾ cup low-sodium chicken stock
1 tbsp. basil, chopped

DIRECTIONS (Ready in about: 25 min)
Warm a pan with the oil over medium heat, add the shallot and ginger, stir and sauté for 5 minutes. Include the rest of the ingredients except the chicken, mix, bring to a boil and cook for another 5 minutes. Add the chicken, mix, simmer everything for 25 minutes, divide into plates, and serve.
Per serving: Kcal 294, Sodium 558 mg, Protein 15.5 g, Carbs 16 g, Fat 15.5 g

396. Chicken and Mustard Sauce

INGREDIENTS (Servings: 4)

1-pound chicken thighs, boneless and skinless
1 tbsp. avocado oil
2 tbsp. mustard
1 shallot, chopped
½ tsp. basil, dried
1 cup low-sodium chicken stock
⅛ tsp. of salt and black pepper
3 garlic cloves, minced

DIRECTIONS (Ready in about: 25 min)
Warm a pan with the oil over medium heat, add the shallots, garlic, and chicken and sauté for 5 minutes.

for 30 minutes. Divide everything between the plates and serve hot.
Per serving: Kcal 299, Sodium 380 mg, Protein 12.5 g, Carbs 30 g, Fat 15.5 g

397. Chicken Fajitas

INGREDIENTS (Servings: 4)
For the Sauce:
½ cup low-fat plain Greek yogurt
1 big avocado, pitted, peeled, and cut in fourths
¼ cup water
⅛ tsp. cracked black pepper
½ small serrano chile pepper
Juice of ½ lemon
⅛ tsp. sea salt
For the Fajitas:
1 large white onion, cut into ½-inch slivers
2 large cloves garlic, minced
8 corn tortillas
3 tbsp. olive oil
2 large yellow bell peppers, cut into ½-inch-thick strips
¼ tsp. ground cumin
2 big green bell peppers, cut into ½-inch-thick strips
2 large red bell peppers, cut into ½-inch-thick strips
1 tsp. dried oregano, divided
⅛ tsp. cracked black pepper
⅛ tsp. sea salt
4 (4 oz.) boneless, skinless chicken breasts, cut into ½-inch- thick strips

DIRECTIONS (Ready in about: 20 min)
For the sauce, put all the ingredients in a blender and whisk until smooth. Set aside. For the fajitas, season the chicken with salt, pepper, cumin, and half of the oregano. Warm the oil in a large saucepan over medium-high heat. Once the oil is hot, add the chicken and cook for 4-5 minutes. Add the peppers, onion, garlic, and remaining dried oregano. Season with pepper and salt to taste and cook for a few more minutes, until the vegetables are soft. Heat the tortillas in a skillet over low heat. Pour the chicken and veggie mixture over each tortilla and drizzle with avocado sauce. Fold the tortilla and serve.
Per serving: Kcal 453, Sodium 415 mg, Protein 32 g, Carbs 46 g, Fat 20.5 g

398. Chipotle Aioli Dip

INGREDIENTS (Servings: 8)
2 whole chipotle peppers in adobo sauce, reserving
1 tbsp. adobo sauce
1 pinch smoked paprika
6 stalks celery, cut into 3-inch lengths
¾ cup raw cashews
½ cup almond milk
2 tbsp. lemon juice
½ tsp. coconut aminos
1 packet stevia

DIRECTIONS (Ready in about: 25 min)
In a bowl, put the cashews and cover them with boiling water. Leave to stand for an hour, then drain thoroughly. Place the drained cashews in a blender and add the rest of the ingredients. Blend until smooth and creamy. Serve with separate celery sticks.
Per serving: Kcal 52, Sodium 22 mg, Protein 1.5 g, Fat 3 g, Carbs 5 g

399. Cod and White Sauce

INGREDIENTS (Servings: 4)
2 tbsp. olive oil
4 cod fillets, boneless and skinless
1 shallot, chopped
½ cup coconut cream
3 tbsp. nonfat yogurt
2 tbsp. dill, chopped
A pinch of black pepper
1 garlic clove minced

DIRECTIONS (Ready in about: 25 min)
Warm a pan with the oil over medium heat; add the shallots and sauté for 5 minutes. Add the fish and other ingredients and cook for another 10 minutes. Divide everything between the plates and serve.
Per serving: Kcal 252, Sodium 194 mg, Protein 22 g, Carbs 4.5 g, Fat 15.5 g

400. Dash Apple Sauce French Toast

INGREDIENTS (Servings: 6)
¾ cup milk
2 eggs
6 slices bread
1 tsp. ground cinnamon
¼ cup applesauce
2 tbsp. white sugar

DIRECTIONS (Ready in about: 20 min)
In an enormous bowl, combine the eggs, milk, cinnamon, sugar, and applesauce; mix well. Steep the bread one slice at a time until it is saturated with liquid. Prepare in a lightly greased skillet or griddle over medium/high heat until lightly browned on both sides. Serve hot.
Per serving: Kcal 127, Sodium 206 mg, Protein 5.5 g, Carbs 19 g Fat 3.5 g

401. Grapes with Sour Cream

INGREDIENTS (Servings: 6)
3 tbsp. chopped walnuts
1½ cups green seedless grapes
1½ cups red seedless grapes
⅛ tsp. vanilla extract
½ tsp. lemon juice
½ tsp. lemon zest
2 tbsp. powdered sugar
½ cup fat-free sour cream

DIRECTIONS (Ready in about: 20 min)
Put the powdered sugar, sour cream, vanilla, lemon juice, and lemon zest in a bowl. Beat until just combined. Cover the bowl and let it cool for at least 4 hours. Place the grapes in 6 dessert bowls or glasses. Pour over the sauce and add half a tbsp. of chopped walnuts to each cup. Serve immediately.
Per serving: Kcal 106, Sodium 132 mg, Protein 0.5 g, Carbs 22 g, Fat 2 g

402. Grilled Chicken Skewers

INGREDIENTS (Servings: 6)
4 (4 oz.) chicken breasts, cut into 1-inch cubes
3 large red bell peppers, cut into 1-inch pieces
2 large white onions, cut into 1-inch pieces
6 apricots, pitted and cut into 1-inch pieces
Marinade:
1 heaping tbsp. reduced-sugar apricot marmalade
½ tsp. sesame oil
1 ½ tsp. finely chopped fresh ginger or ¾ tsp. ground ginger
1 tbsp. Dijon mustard or brown mustard
4 tbsp. apple cider vinegar
¼ cup extra virgin olive oil
1 large clove garlic, chopped

DIRECTIONS (Ready in about: 20 min)
In a big tub, combine all the marinade ingredients together. Place the diced chicken in a large, zipped bag, pour in the marinade, squeeze the air out of the bag, and seal tightly. Work the mixture into the chicken by hand by moving the bag and contents around. Refrigerate for at least 2 hours. Dip 12 large wooden skewers in the water, then cut the peppers, onions, and apricots into pieces of similar size. Prick the chicken, pepper, onion, and apricot pieces, alternating the ingredients. Grill the skewers on a grill or in a hot pan, 4 to 5 minutes per side, or until the chicken is no longer pink in the center. If using a charcoal or gas grill, close the grill lid, so the chicken does not dry out. Serve right away.
Per serving: Kcal 314, Sodium 357 mg, Protein 25 g, Carbs 21 g, Fat 2 g

403. Grilled Salmon with Lemon

INGREDIENTS (Servings: 4)
Marinade:
1 tbsp. chopped fresh dill weed
1 tbsp. canola or olive oil
1 tsp. grated lemon peel
2 tbsp. honey
1 lb. salmon fillets, cut into 4 pieces (4 oz. each)
3 tbsp. lemon juice
½ tsp. garlic-pepper blend
Lemon-Dill Sauce:
1 tbsp. Chopped fresh dill weed or 1 tsp. dried dill
1 container (6 oz.) Greek Fat-Free plain yogurt
½ tsp. grated lemon peel
⅛ tsp. pepper
1 tbsp. lemon

DIRECTIONS (Ready in about: 20 min)
Heat up your gas or charcoal grill. Blend all the marinade ingredients in a small bowl except the salmon. In an 8-inch (2 quarts) square glass baking dish, arrange the salmon pieces skin-side up in a single layer. Pour the marinade over the salmon; turn to stick. Cover with plastic wrap; refrigerate for 20 minutes. Heat up your gas or charcoal grill. Brush the grill with oil. Remove the salmon from the marinade; throw in the marinade. Place the skin side down on the grill over medium heat. Cover the grill; cook for 10 to 15 minutes or until salmon flakes easily with a fork. Meanwhile, in a small bowl, combine the ingredients for the sauce. Serve with the salmon.
Per serving: Kcal 250, Sodium 140 mg, Protein 27 g, Carbs 12 g, Fat 10 g

404. Meatballs and Coconut Sauce

INGREDIENTS (Servings: 4)
2 pounds pork, ground
Black pepper to the taste
¾ cup almond flour
2 eggs, whisked
1 tbsp. parsley, chopped
2 red onions, chopped
2 tbsp. olive oil
½ cup coconut cream
Black pepper to the taste

DIRECTIONS (Ready in about: 30 min)
In a tub, mix the pork with the almond flour and the other ingredients except for the onion, oil, and cream, mix well and form medium meatballs with this mixture. Warm a pan with the oil over medium heat, add the onions, mix and sauté for 5 minutes. Include the meatballs and cook for another 5 minutes. Add the coconut cream, bring to a boil, cook for another 10 minutes, divide between bowls and serve.

405. Pork Chops Mushroom Sauce

INGREDIENTS (Servings: 4)

¼ tsp. paprika
1-pound boneless pork chops
½ pinch kosher salt and ground black pepper to taste
½ tsp. Dijon mustard
½ (8 oz.) package sliced fresh mushrooms
2 tbsp. butter, divided
1 cup beef broth
2 cloves garlic, minced
1 tbsp. all-purpose flour

DIRECTIONS (Ready in about: 30 min)

Season the pork chops with paprika, pepper, and salt on both sides. Heat a large skillet over medium-high heat; add 2 tbsp. of butter. Brown the pork chops until golden brown and no longer pink in the center, 2 to 4 minutes per side. Remove the pork chops from the pan and set them aside. Dissolve the remaining butter over medium-high heat in the same skillet. Add the mushrooms and cook until golden brown and excess moisture evaporates about 5 minutes. Add the garlic and mustard; cook until garlic is fragrant, about 1 minute. Add flour to skillet, stirring to remove lumps. Slowly add the beef broth, stirring until just incorporated. Add salt and pepper. Reduce the heat to medium and simmer, frequently stirring, until the sauce thickens about 5 minutes. Check the seasoning again. Return the pork chops to the pan and cook until heated for about 1 minute. Serve hot.

Per serving: Kcal: 199, Sodium 332 mg, Protein 16 g, Carbs 3 g, Fat 13.5 g

406. Pork Chops with Mushroom

INGREDIENTS (Servings: 6)

6 pork loin chops
2 tbsp. tapioca, crushed
1 yellow onion, chopped
10 oz. low-sodium cream of mushroom soup
½ cup apple juice
2 tsp. thyme, chopped
1½ cups mushrooms, sliced
¼ tsp. garlic powder
1 tbsp. olive oil

DIRECTIONS (Ready in about: 9 h 10 min)

Bring the saucepan to medium-high heat, add the pork chops, sauté 4 minutes per side and transfer to a slow cooker. Add the tapioca puree, onion, cream of mushroom soup, apple juice, thyme, mushrooms, and garlic powder, mix, cover, and simmer for 9 hours. Divide the pork ribs with the mushroom sauce between the plates and serve.

Per serving: Kcal 229, Sodium 610 mg, Protein 17.5 g, Carbs 11.5 g, Fat 4 g

407. Pork with Cilantro Sauce

INGREDIENTS (Servings: 4)

2 pounds pork stew meat, roughly cubed
1 cup cilantro leaves
4 tbsp. olive oil
1 tbsp. pine nuts
1 tbsp. fat-free Parmesan, grated
1 tbsp. lemon juice
1 tsp. chili powder
Black pepper to the taste

DIRECTIONS (Ready in about: 30 min)

Mix the cilantro in a blender with the pine nuts, 3 tbsp. of oil, Parmesan, and lemon juice and mix well. Heat a skillet with the remaining oil over medium heat, add the meat, chili powder, and black pepper, stir and sauté for 5 minutes. Add the cilantro sauce and cook over medium heat for another 15 minutes, stirring occasionally. Divide the pork between plates and serve immediately.

Per serving: Kcal 270, Sodium 450 mg, Protein 22.5 g, Fat 6.5 g

408. Shrimp with Lemon Sauce

INGREDIENTS (Servings: 4)

1-pound shrimp, peeled and deveined
2 tbsp. olive oil
Zest of 1 lemon, grated
Juice of ½ lemon
1 tbsp. chives, chopped

DIRECTIONS (Ready in about: 15 min)

Heat a pan with the oil over medium-high heat, add the lemon zest, lemon juice, and cilantro, mix and cook for 2 minutes. Add the shrimp, cook for another 6 minutes, divide between plates and serve.

Per serving: Kcal 195, Sodium 127 mg, Protein 26 g, Fat 9 g

409. Spiced Applesauce

INGREDIENTS (Servings: 4)

5 large apples, peeled
¼ cup water
1 cinnamon stick
3 cloves
Zest of ½ lemon
½ tsp. ground ginger

DIRECTIONS (Ready in about: 20 min)
Cut the peeled apples into quarters and discard the cores. Place the apples, water, and spices in a large pot. Cover and boil for about 20 minutes or until the liquid is absorbed by the apples and is frothy to the touch. Remove the cinnamon stick and cloves and mash the apples with a potato masher or fork to the desired consistency. For super smooth applesauce, transfer the mixture to a blender and mix in small batches.
Per serving: Kcal 157, Sodium 2 mg, Protein 3 g, Carbs 5 g, Fat 0.5 g

410. Tzatziki Greek Yogurt Sauce

INGREDIENTS (Servings: 8)

2 large cloves garlic, very finely chopped	1¾ cups low-fat plain Greek yogurt
¼ cup finely diced Persian or English cucumber	Juice of ½ lemon
	1 tbsp. extra virgin olive oil
¼ cup chopped fresh mint leaves	¼ tsp. cracked black pepper
⅛ tsp. sea salt	

DIRECTIONS (Ready in about: 60 min)
In a big tub, combine all the chopped ingredients together with the yogurt, lemon juice, and oil. Mix well and add salt and pepper. Before serving, let the mixture sit for about 30 minutes to an hour for the flavors to blend.
Per serving: Kcal 51, Sodium 57 mg, Protein 3.5 g, Carbs 4 g, Fat 3 g

411. Vegetarian Spaghetti Sauce

INGREDIENTS (Servings: 4)

2 small onions, chopped	1 tbsp. basil, dried
2 tbsp. olive oil	1 6 oz. can tomato paste
3 cloves garlic, chopped	1 8 oz. can tomato sauce
1 tbsp. oregano, dried	
1¼ cups zucchini, sliced	2 medium tomatoes, chopped
1 cup of water	

DIRECTIONS (Ready in about: 50 min)
In a medium skillet, heat the oil. Sauté the onion, garlic, and zucchini in oil for 5 minutes over medium heat. Add the remaining ingredients and cook for 45 minutes, covered, until set. Serve over spaghetti.
Per serving: Kcal 105, Sodium 479 mg, Protein 3 g, Carbs 15.5 g, Fat 5 g

412. Whole-Wheat Spaghetti Ragu

INGREDIENTS (Servings: 8)

1 box whole-wheat spaghetti	1 tsp. basil
	1 tsp. marjoram
1 tbsp. extra-virgin olive oil	1-pound lean ground beef
1 medium onion, chopped fine	1 28 oz. can crushed tomatoes, unsalted
1 large carrot, chopped fine	½ tsp. salt
	¼ cup flat-leaf parsley, chopped
1 stalk celery, chopped fine	½ cup grated Parmesan cheese
4 cloves garlic, minced	
1 tsp. oregano	

DIRECTIONS (Ready in about: 30 min)
Cook spaghetti according to package directions. Drain. While the pasta cooks heat the oil in a large skillet over medium heat. Add onion, carrot, and celery and cook, occasionally stirring, until onion becomes translucent about 5 minutes. Include the garlic and seasonings and cook for another 30 seconds. Add the beef and cook, stirring, until the beef is golden brown and no longer pink, about 4-5 minutes. Add the tomato puree and continue cooking, occasionally stirring, until the sauce thickens about 5 minutes. Season with salt and add the parsley. To serve top with sauce and sprinkle with Parmesan cheese.
Per serving: Kcal 385, Sodium 415 mg, Protein 28.5 g, Carbs 52 g, Fat 9 g

SNACKS

413. Arugula and Salami

INGREDIENTS (Servings: 10)

3 to 4 tbsp. low-fat cream cheese
10 Peppadew peppers, drained
1 tsp. canola oil
1 (5 oz.) package arugula
3 tbsp. chopped

DIRECTIONS (Ready in about: 30 min)
Arrange the peppers on a plate. Fill each pepper with about 1 tsp. cream cheese. Heat up the canola oil in a portable nonstick sauté pan or skillet over medium-high heat. Add the salami and cook, stirring constantly, for 1 to 2 minutes. Add the arugula and cook, stirring constantly, until wilted, 2 to 4 minutes. Remove from the heat. Fill each pepper with an equal portion of the salami arugula mixture. Serve.
Per serving: Kcal 143, Sodium 461 mg, Protein 5 g, Carbs 1 g, Fat 4 g

414. Asian Asparagus Dish

INGREDIENTS (Servings: 6)

1 tsp. reduced-sodium soy sauce
½ cup water
½ tsp. sugar
1½ pounds fresh asparagus (ends removed and cut into strips)

DIRECTIONS (Ready in about: 30 min)
Heat the soy sauce, sugar, and water in a pan over a high flame. Bring to a boil. Stir in asparagus and turn heat to low. Simmer for 4 minutes.
Per serving: Kcal 24, Sodium 26 mg, Protein 3 g, Carbs 15 g, Fat 2 g

415. Black-Eyed Pea Dip

INGREDIENTS (Servings: 4)

1-pint grape tomatoes, halved
½ small red onion, coarsely chopped
1 tbsp. olive oil
1 jalapeño chile, seeded and chopped
1 roasted red bell pepper, chopped
Multi-grain tortilla chips
1 (15 oz.) can of black-eyed peas, rinsed and drained
1 tbsp. chopped cilantro
¼ tsp. kosher salt
¼ tsp. freshly ground black pepper
1 tbsp. lemon juice

DIRECTIONS (Ready in about: 30 min)
Preheat the broiler. Line the baking sheet with foil and add the tomatoes and onion. Drizzle the olive oil over top the vegetables, tossing to coat. Broil until semi-charred, 4 to 5 minutes, watching closely to prevent burning. Meanwhile, combine the jalapeño, bell pepper, black-eyed peas, lemon juice, cilantro, salt, and pepper in a medium bowl. Add the tomatoes and onions to the bowl and stir to combine. Serve with chips.
Per serving: Kcal 187, Sodium 405 mg, Protein 8 g, Carbs 31 g, Fat 9 g

416. Black Bean Cakes

INGREDIENTS (Servings: 8)

2 tbsp. olive oil
½ tsp. salt
½ cup chopped fresh cilantro
8 garlic cloves (chopped)
2 cups water
2 cups dried black beans (picked over, washed, soaked overnight, and drained)

DIRECTIONS (Ready in about: 1 h 30 min)
Put water and black beans in a pan over a high flame. Bring to a boil. Turn heat to low and simmer for 70 minutes while partially covered. Drain the liquid. Put garlic and beans in a bowl. Mash as you mix. Add salt and cilantro. Mix well. Use your hands to form 8 cakes from the mixture. Arrange on a plate and keep in the fridge for an hour. Heat the oil in a pan over medium flame. Cook the cakes for 5 minutes or until crisp. Serve at once.
Per serving: Kcal 196, Sodium 156 mg, Protein 9.5 g, Carbs 31 g, Fat 7 g

417. Braised Celery Root

INGREDIENTS (Servings: 6)

¼ tsp. freshly ground black pepper
2 tsp. fresh thyme leaves
¼ tsp. salt
¼ cup sour cream
1 cup vegetable stock (or broth)
1 tsp. Dijon mustard
1 celery root (peeled and diced)

DIRECTIONS (Ready in about: 55 min)
Pour stock in a pan over a high flame. Bring to a boil. Add celery root. Turn heat to low and cover the pan. Simmer for 12 minutes while occasionally stirring. Scoop out celery root to a bowl. Loosely cover with foil to keep warm. Turn the heat of the stove to high and bring the cooking liquid to a boil. Remove from heat. Add pepper, salt, mustard, and sour cream. Whisk until combined. Turn on heat to medium. Add thyme and celery root. Cook until warmed.
Per serving: Kcal 54, Sodium 206 mg, Protein 1.5 g, Carbs 4.5 g, Fat 6 g

418. Braised Kale

INGREDIENTS (Servings: 6)
- ¼ tsp. salt
- ⅛ tsp. freshly ground black pepper
- 1 tbsp. fresh lemon juice
- ½ cup of low-sodium vegetable stock (or broth)
- 2 tsp. olive oil
- 1 cup of cherry tomatoes (halved)
- 4 garlic cloves (thinly sliced)
- 1-pound kale (remove tough stems and coarsely chop the leaves)

DIRECTIONS (Ready in about: 1 h 10 min)
Heat up the oil in a pan over a medium flame. Add garlic and cook for a minute or until lightly golden. Add stock and kale. Cover the pan and lower the heat. Cook for 5 minutes. Remove the cover and add tomatoes. Continue cooking for 7 minutes. Turn off the heat and add pepper, salt, and lemon juice.
Per serving: Kcal 70, Sodium 133 mg, Protein 11 g, Carbs 24 g, Fat 16 g

419. Broccoli with Lemon

INGREDIENTS (Servings: 4)
- ¼ tsp. kosher salt
- ¼ tsp. black pepper
- 1 tsp. lemon zest
- 4 cups broccoli florets
- 1 tsp. olive oil
- 1 tbsp. minced garlic

DIRECTIONS (Ready in about: 30 min)
Spurt a cup of water into a saucepan over medium-high flame. Bring to a boil. Add the broccoli and cook until tender. This will take about 3 minutes. Drain the water. Heat up the oil in a pan over medium-high flame. Add garlic and cook for 30 seconds while stirring. Add pepper, salt, lemon zest, and broccoli. Transfer to a serving platter and serve.
Per serving: Kcal 45, Sodium 153 mg, Protein 7 g, Carbs 7 g, Fat 2 g

420. Brown Rice Pilaf

INGREDIENTS (Servings: 8)
- ¼ tsp. saffron threads or ground turmeric
- 2 cups water
- ¼ cup dried apricots (chopped)
- 1⅛ cups dark brown rice (rinsed and drained)
- ½ tsp. grated orange zest
- ¼ cup chopped pistachio nuts
- 3 tbsp. fresh orange juice
- 1½ tbsp. pistachio oil or canola oil
- ¾ tsp. salt

DIRECTIONS (Ready in about: 55 min)
Put water, saffron, ¼ tsp. of salt, and rice in a saucepan over a high flame. Bring to a boil. Turn heat to low and cover the pan. Simmer for 45 minutes. Transfer to a bowl and loosely cover with foil to keep warm. Put the rest of the salt, oil, and orange zest, and juice in a bowl. Whisk until combined. Pour over the rice. Add apricots and nuts. Toss until coated.
Per serving: Kcal 153, Sodium 222 mg, Protein 5 g, Carbs 50 g, Fat 9 g

421. Buffalo Chicken Dip

INGREDIENTS (Servings: 8)
- ½ cup cottage cheese, fat-free
- 1-piece chicken breast half, sliced into strips
- 1 tbsp. ranch dressing
- 6 stalks celery, cut into 4-inch lengths
- ¼ cup low-fat cheddar cheese
- 2 tbsp. hot sauce

DIRECTIONS (Ready in about: 55 min)
Place a frying pan on medium fire and pan-fry chicken pieces until cooked, around 8 minutes. Stir in ranch dressing, hot sauce, and cheddar cheese until melted. Turn off fire and transfer to a bowl. Mix in cottage cheese and stir well. Serve with celery sticks on the side.
Per serving: Kcal 71, Sodium 290 mg, Protein 8.5 g, Carbs 1.5 g, Fat 3 g

422. Caramelized Onion Dip

INGREDIENTS (Servings: 4)
- 4 cups chopped yellow onions
- 1½ tbsp. canola oil
- ¼ tsp. kosher salt
- 3 tbsp. crème fraîche
- 2 tsp. freshly squeezed lemon juice
- 2½ tbsp. low-fat mayonnaise

DIRECTIONS (Ready in about: 55 min)
Whole-grain chips or crackers, to serve Heat the canola oil in a large pan or skillet and sautè over medium-high heat. Add the onions and salt, coating in the oil. Decrease the heat to medium-low, and cook the onions, stirring every couple of minutes. Monitor the onions to ensure they caramelize but do not burn. If the onions are cooking too quickly, decrease the heat. Let the onions cook for about 25 minutes. Remove from heat and stir in the mayo, crème fraîche, and lemon juice. Taste the dip and adjust the ingredients as needed. Transfer to a bowl, cover, and refrigerate for several hours. Serve with chips or crackers.
Per serving: Kcal 169, Sodium 222 mg, Protein 2 g, Carbs 15 g, Fat 2 g

423. Cheese Log with Apple Slices

INGREDIENTS (Servings: 4)
1½ oz. reduced fat cream cheese
4 oz. reduced-fat sharp cheddar cheese, coarsely chopped
1 scallion, coarsely chopped
½ cup unsalted walnuts, chopped, divided
2 tsp. Worcestershire sauce
Sliced apples such as Granny Smith, Gala, or Red Delicious, as needed

DIRECTIONS (Ready in about: 1 h 25 min)
Add the cheddar cheese, cream cheese, scallion, Worcestershire sauce, and ¼ cup of walnuts to a food processor. Pulse until smooth, approximately 1 to 2 minutes, stopping once to scrape down the mixture. Transfer the cheese mixture to waxed paper, and mold it into a log shape. Sprinkle on the remaining ¼ cup walnuts. Wrap the entire log in waxed paper and refrigerate for a few hours. Serve with apple slices.
Per serving: Kcal 169, Sodium 249 mg, Protein 10 g, Carbs 4 g, Fat 13 g

424. Corn Pudding

INGREDIENTS (Servings: 8)
⅛ tsp. ginger
½ cup raisins
⅛ tsp. clove
¼ tsp. cinnamon
⅛ tsp. nutmeg
¼ cup maple syrup
3 cups skim milk
2 cups coarse cornmeal
3 cups of water

DIRECTIONS (Ready in about: 55 min)
Put milk and water in a saucepan over medium-high flame. Bring to a boil. Add cornmeal. Mix to free it from lumps. Bring to another boil. Lower the heat, cover, and simmer for 15 minutes while occasionally stirring. Remove pan from the stove. Add the rest of the ingredients. Mix well and leave for 15 minutes.
Per serving: Kcal 213, Sodium 44 mg, Protein 5 g, Carbs 25 g, Fat 2 g

425. Cornbread with Southern Twist

INGREDIENTS (Servings: 8)
1¼ cups skim milk
1 tbsp. olive oil
¼ cup egg substitute
½ cup flour
4 tbsp. sodium-free baking powder
1½ cups cornmeal

DIRECTIONS (Ready in about: 30 min)
Prepare an 8 x 8-inch baking dish or a black iron skillet then add shortening. Put the baking dish or skillet inside the oven on 425°F and leave it there for 10 minutes. In a bowl, add milk and egg then mix well. Take out the skillet and add the heated oil into the batter and stir well. Pour the mixture into a pan once all the ingredients are combined. Then cook for 15 to 20 minutes in the oven until golden brown.
Per serving: Kcal 206, Sodium 40 mg, Protein 5 g, Carbs 38 g, Fat 4 g

426. Crab Stuffed Mushrooms

INGREDIENTS (Servings: 6)
1 cup cooked crabmeat, chopped finely
2 tbsp. minced green onion
1 tsp. lemon juice
¼ cup Monterey Jack cheese, shredded, low fat
1 lb. fresh button mushrooms
½ tsp. dill

DIRECTIONS (Ready in about: 1 h 25 min)
Wash and drain well mushrooms stems. Chop mushroom stems. Preheat the oven to 400°F and lightly grease a baking pan with cooking spray. In a small bowl, whisk well green onion, crabmeat, lemon juice, dill, and chopped mushroom stems. Evenly spread mushrooms on prepared pan with cap sides up. Evenly spoon crabmeat mixture on top of mushroom caps. Pop in the oven and bake for 20 minutes. Remove from oven and sprinkle cheese on top. Take it back to the oven and broil for 3 minutes. Serve and enjoy.
Per serving: Kcal 58, Sodium 128 mg, Protein 8 g, Carbs 4 g, Fat 1 g

427. Crunchy Garbanzo Bean

INGREDIENTS (Servings: 8)
- 2 cans unsalted garbanzo beans
- 1 tsp. crushed garlic
- 1 tsp. fresh dill
- 1 tsp. fresh parsley

DIRECTIONS (Ready in about: 50 min)
Preheat the oven to 350°F. Make a baking tray with cooking spray in a mixing bowl, put the drained beans, and toss with fresh dill, crushed garlic, onion powder, salt, parsley, and pepper. Give the mixture a good toss, then pour it into the baking tray. Place the baking tray in the oven and cook for 35 to 40 minutes. The beans should be crisp and bloated. Spurt them into a bowl and allow them to cool. Serve and eat as or when needed.

Per serving: Kcal 56, Sodium 56 mg, Protein 3 g, Carbs 10 g, Fat 1 g

428. Deviled Eggs Guac Style

INGREDIENTS (Servings: 12)
- 6 medium eggs, hard-boiled and peeled
- ½ jalapeno chili pepper
- 1 tbsp. Lime
- 1 tbsp. light sour cream
- 1 tbsp. green onion, chopped
- 1 ripe avocado
- 1 tbsp. Cilantro

DIRECTIONS (Ready in about: 30 min)
In a medium bowl, mash avocado. Mix in green onion, cilantro, lime, pepper, and sour cream. Mix well. Slice hard-boiled eggs in half lengthwise. Scoop out yolk and place in a bowl of avocadoes. Mix well. Scoop out avocado yolk mixture and spoon into egg white holes. Serve and enjoy or refrigerate for future use.

Per serving: Kcal 60, Sodium 34 mg, Protein 3 g, Carbs 2 g, Fat 5

429. Fish Tacos

INGREDIENTS (Servings: 6)
- 1 cup chopped fresh cilantro
- 2 medium limes (cut into wedges)
- 2 cups red cabbage (chopped)
- 6 mahi-mahi fillets
- 12 corn tortillas
- Hot pepper sauce
- 1 tsp. pepper
- Salsa verde (optional)
- 1 tsp. salt
- ¼ cup olive oil
- 1 tsp. ground cardamom
- 1 tsp. paprika

DIRECTIONS (Ready in about: 1 h 30 min)
Put olive oil, paprika, ground cardamom, salt, and pepper in a bowl. Mix until combined. Arrange fillets on a baking dish. Cover with the seasoning mixture. Leave the mixture covered in the refrigerator for 30 minutes. Drain liquid from the fillets. Place on an oiled grill rack over medium-high heat. Cover and grill for 5 minutes. Transfer to a plate. Warm the tortillas on the grill for 45 seconds. Put fish inside each tortilla. Add cilantro and red cabbage. Squeeze a bit of hot pepper sauce and lime juice. You can also add salsa verde if preferred. Fold the sides of the tortilla. Add more pepper sauce if you want and serve with lime wedges.

Per serving: Kcal 284, Sodium 273 mg, Protein 8 g, Carbs 15 g, Fat 2 g

430. Forbidden Rice with Mangoes

INGREDIENTS (Servings: 4)
- 1 cup forbidden black rice
- 1¾ cups water
- 2 tbsp. sugar
- ⅛ tsp. of salt
- ½ cup light coconut milk
- 3 mangoes, sliced
- ¼ cup unsweetened dried coconut

DIRECTIONS (Ready in about: 60 min)
Add the rice, water, sugar, and salt to a medium, heavy pot. Bring to a boil over high warmth, cover with a lid, and reduce the heat to low. Simmer until the water is absorbed, 30 to 35 minutes. Add the coconut milk, and let the rice sit for 10 minutes. Stir to combine. To serve, scoop the rice into bowls, and garnish with the mango and coconut.

Per serving: Kcal 247, Sodium 66 mg, Protein 5 g, Carbs 49 g, Fat 5 g

431. Grilled Shrimp with Lime

INGREDIENTS (Servings: 4)
- 1 cup cooked crabmeat, chopped finely
- 2 tbsp. minced green onion
- 1 tsp. lemon juice
- ¼ cup Monterey Jack cheese, shredded, low fat
- 1 lb. fresh button mushrooms
- ½ tsp. dill

DIRECTIONS (Ready in about: 35 min)
Put shrimp in a bowl. Include the rest of the ingredients, except the lime slices, and toss until combined. Leave for 15 minutes. Thread lime slices and seasoned shrimp on 4 metal skewers. Put on a grill rack over medium heat. Cover and grill each side for 4 minutes.

Per serving: Kcal 167, Sodium 284 mg, Protein 15.5 g, Carbs 3 g, Fat 8 g

432. Guacamole with Pomegranate
INGREDIENTS (Servings: 4)
2 tbsp. chopped cilantro
2 ripe avocados, diced
1 scallion, chopped
Multigrain tortilla chips, to serve
¼ tsp. kosher salt
Juice of ½ lime
¼ cup pomegranate seeds

DIRECTIONS (Ready in about: 20 min)
In a portable bowl, mash the avocado using a fork. Add the cilantro, scallion, lime juice, salt, and half the pomegranate seeds and mix. Top with the remaining pomegranate seeds and serve with tortilla chips.

Per serving: Kcal 173, Sodium 154 mg, Protein 2 g, Carbs 11 g, Fat 7 g

433. Honey Orange Sauce
INGREDIENTS (Servings: 4)
2 tbsp. lemon juice
⅓ cup unsweetened orange juice
1½ tbsp. honey
1 dash nutmeg
¼ tsp. ground ginger

DIRECTIONS (Ready in about: 25 min)
Prepare the fruit. Combine all ingredients for sauce and mix. Pour honey–orange sauce over fruit.

Per serving: Kcal 96, Sodium 4 mg, Protein 1 g, Carbs 24 g, Fat 1 g

434. Hummus Dip
INGREDIENTS (Servings: 4)
½ cup of extra-virgin olive oil, or more as needed, plus more for garnish
2 (15 oz.) cans chickpeas, drained and rinsed
½ lemon, juiced
2 cloves garlic, peeled
¼ cup water
2 tbsp. roughly chopped fresh parsley leaves, plus more for garnish
1½ tsp. salt
Paprika, for garnish
½ to 1 tsp. ground cumin 12 to 15 grinds black pepper
½ tsp. dark Asian sesame oil

DIRECTIONS (Ready in about: 20 min)
Blend together everything but parsley and paprika. Blend until smooth on a low setting. Add garnish and allow it to cool.

Per serving: Kcal 57, Sodium 96 mg, Protein 1 g, Carbs 5 g, Fat 0.5 g

435. Hummus with Carrot
INGREDIENTS (Servings: 2)
4 medium celery sticks
1 medium carrot
1 large lemon
⅓ cup sesame seeds
1 can chickpeas, unsalted
1 tsp. crushed red chili pepper
2 tbsp. olive oil
½ tsp. crushed garlic
½ tsp. salt

DIRECTIONS (Ready in about: 1 h 25 min)
Preheat the oven to 350°F. Prepare a roasting dish and place the sesame seeds on it. Cut the lemon in half and squeeze the juice. Roast the sesame seeds for around 10 to 12 minutes. Take them out when they are done and put them aside to cool. Wash and peel the carrot, then cut into sticks. Wash and cut the celery into sticks. In a blender, puree the chickpeas, chilis, and sesame seeds. Add garlic, olive oil, and freshly squeezed lemon juice. Mix until the mixture is firm and takes form into a paste. Cover the mixture and let stand for at least 1 hour. Serve with carrot and celery sticks.

Per serving: Kcal 250, Sodium 317 mg, Protein 10 g, Carbs 32 g, Fat 10 g

436. Hummus with Cucumber Slices
INGREDIENTS (Servings: 4)
1 (15 oz.) can of chickpeas, rinsed and drained, 1 tbsp. liquid reserved
2 cloves garlic
Grated zest and juice of 1 lemon
¼ tsp. kosher salt
1 tsp. sweet paprika
¼ tsp. black pepper
Fresh parsley, for garnish
¼ cup of extra-virgin olive oil
2 cucumbers, sliced, to serve (optional)
2 whole-grain pita bread, quartered, to serve (optional)
1-pint cherry tomatoes, to serve

DIRECTIONS (Ready in about: 20 min)
In a food processor, puree the garlic, chickpeas, reserved chickpea liquid, lemon zest, lemon juice, paprika, salt, and pepper. Spurt the olive oil through the feed tube while the food processor is still running, and process until emulated. Taste the hummus, and adjust the salt and lemon juice, if needed. Include an additional drizzle of olive oil to the tip, a sprinkle of paprika, and parsley, if using. Serve with cucumber slices, tomatoes, and pita, if desired.

Per serving: Kcal 249, Sodium 360 mg, Protein 5 g, Carbs 25 g, Fat 15 g

437. Lemon Rice

INGREDIENTS (Servings: 8)

2 tsp. lemon zest
1¾ cup unsalted chicken broth
½ cup slivered almonds (coarsely chopped)
1 cup uncooked brown rice
1 tbsp. trans-free margarine
½ tsp. ground cinnamon
¼ tsp. ground nutmeg
¼ cup chopped onions
⅓ cup water
½ cup frozen peas
2 tbsp. honey
½ cup golden raisins
3 tbsp. lemon juice

DIRECTIONS (Ready in about: 1 h 30 min)

Put almonds in a baking tray. Preheated oven at 325°F and bake for 10 minutes while stirring every 2 minutes. Leave to cool. Heat the broth in a saucepan over medium flame. Add margarine, nutmeg, cinnamon, onion, lemon zest and juice, and rice. Mix well. Cover the pan and simmer for 30 minutes while occasionally stirring. Put raisins and water in a saucepan over medium flame. Cover and simmer for 5 minutes. Stir in the pea and simmer for a minute. Add mixture to the rice. Simmer for 20 more minutes. Fluff the cooked rice and transfer to a bowl. Add honey and toasted almonds on top.

Per serving: Kcal 201, Sodium 44 mg, Protein 6 g, Carbs 53 g, Fat 8 g

438. Mashed Cauliflower

INGREDIENTS (Servings: 4)

1 leek (white part, cut into 4)
1 head cauliflower
1 garlic clove
1 tbsp. non-hydrogenated soft-tub margarine
Pepper to taste

DIRECTIONS (Ready in about: 35 min)

Cut cauliflower into florets. Steam along with leeks and garlic for 30 minutes. Transfer to a food processor. Process until the consistency is similar to mashed potatoes. Add pepper and margarine before serving.

Per serving: Kcal 201, Sodium 44 mg, Protein 6 g, Carbs 53 g, Fat 8 g

439. Mediterranean Hummus Dip

INGREDIENTS (Servings: 12)

1 cup crumbled feta cheese
Baked pita chips
1 large English cucumber (chopped)
½ cup Greek olives
¼ cup red onion (finely chopped)
2 medium tomatoes (seeded and chopped)
1 10 oz. carton hummus

DIRECTIONS (Ready in about: 30 min)

Put hummus in a round dish. Spread all over. Add cheese, cucumber, tomatoes, olives, and onion. Leave it in the refrigerator until ready to serve. You can use this as dipping for crackers, sliced veggies, or chips.

Per serving: Kcal 88, Sodium 273 mg, Protein 7 g, Carbs 20 g, Fat 8.5 g

440. Nilla, Pecan, and Pretzel Mix

INGREDIENTS (Servings: 15)

3 cups Nilla wafers
1 cup pecan halves
1 cup unsalted pretzels
¼ tsp. salt
3 tbsp. butter
1 cup yogurt covered raisins
2 tbsp. brown sugar

DIRECTIONS (Ready in about: 2 h 35 min)

Preheat the oven to 350°F. Pour the Nilla wafers, pecan halves, and unsalted pretzels into a mixing bowl. Melt the butter on the stove and add sugar, as well as salt. Pour the melted butter mixture over the Nilla mixture and toss to ensure all the ingredients in the bowl are coated. Place the Nillas mixture into a greased baking tray and put it in the oven. Bake for approximately 10 to 15 minutes or until the ingredients start to darken and brown. Take the mixture out and let it cool. Once it has cooled down, add the yogurt-covered raisins and mix them in. Sprinkle cinnamon over the mixture, once again giving it a good toss to ensure the cinnamon coats all the ingredients. They are now ready to serve or pack for an on-the-go snack.

Per serving: Kcal 152, Sodium 108 mg, Protein 1.5 g, Carbs 14 g, Fat 10.5 g

441. Pita Chips

INGREDIENTS (Servings: 4)

1 tbsp. Italian seasoning
2 6-inch whole-wheat pita wraps
¼ tsp. salt
Cooking spray
¼ tsp. garlic powder
½ tsp. virgin olive oil

DIRECTIONS (Ready in about: 35 min)

Cut cauliflower into florets. Steam along with leeks and garlic for 30 minutes. Transfer to a food processor. Process until the consistency is similar to mashed potatoes. Add pepper and margarine before serving.

Per serving: Kcal 81, Sodium 263 mg, Protein 2.5 g, Carbs 14.5 g, Fat 4.5 g

442. Potato Casserole

INGREDIENTS (Servings: 10)
¼ tsp. black pepper
1 tsp. dried dill weed
¼ cup green onions, chopped
16 small new potatoes, around 5 cups
2 tbsp. olive oil

DIRECTIONS (Ready in about: 30 min)
Using water and vegetable brush clean all potatoes. For about 20 minutes, boil potatoes then drain and cool them for 20 minutes. Mix spices, onions, and olive oil. Then cut potatoes into quarters and combine with the mixture. Refrigerate and enjoy!
Per serving: Kcal 237, Sodium 22.5 mg, Protein 6 g, Carbs 47 g, Fat 3 g

443. Pumpkin Walnut Cookie

INGREDIENTS (Servings: 24)
½ tsp. salt
1 tbsp. baking powder
1½ tsp. pumpkin pie spice mix
1½ cups flour
1¼ cups whole wheat flour
½ cup vegetable oil
1 cup brown sugar
2 eggs
1 cup raisin
3 packets Stevia
1 cup walnuts or hazelnuts, chopped
1¾ cups pumpkin, cooked and pureed (15 oz. can)

DIRECTIONS (Ready in about: 45 min)
Ensure to grease the cookie sheet with cooking spray and preheat the oven to 400°F. In a medium bowl mix baking powder, salt, pumpkin pie spice mix, whole wheat flour, and flour. In a large bowl beat eggs and oil thoroughly. Add in brown sugar and stevia beat for at least 3 minutes. Mix in pumpkin puree and beat well. Slowly add the dry ingredients beating well after each addition. Fold in nuts and raisins. Using a 1 tbsp. measuring spoon, get two salt spoonfuls of the dough, and place them on a sheet at least an inch apart. With the bottom of a spoon, flatten the cookie. Pop into the oven and bake until golden brown, around 10 minutes. 1Once done, remove from oven, serve and enjoy or store in tightly lidded containers for up to a week.
Per serving: Kcal 230, Sodium 82 mg, Protein 6 g, Carbs 22 g, Fat 13.5 g

444. Ricotta Bruschetta

INGREDIENTS (Servings: 12)
1 cup Low Fat Ricotta Cheese
6 slice Whole Grain Nut Bread
½ tsp. Grated lemon zest
2 tsp. Thyme, Fresh
½ cup Pomegranate Arils

DIRECTIONS (Ready in about: 20 min)
Toast bread until lightly browned. Meanwhile, in a small bowl whisk well cheese and lemon zest. Slice the toasted bread in half. Slather top with cottage cheese. Top with thyme and pomegranate. Serve and enjoy.
Per serving: Kcal 69, Sodium 123 mg, Protein 4 g, Carbs 11 g, Fat 1 g

445. Roasted Bananas and Potatoes

INGREDIENTS (Servings: 6)
¼ tsp. ground nutmeg
3 tbsp. brown sugar
¼ tsp. ground cardamom
Chopped parsley for garnish
1½ pounds sweet potatoes (rinsed)
½ tsp. ground cinnamon
Red pepper flakes to taste
2 medium bananas (peeled and halved)
2 tbsp. orange juice

DIRECTIONS (Ready in about: 1 h 25 min)
Poke sweet potatoes using a fork to create several holes. Place in a greased baking dish and bake in a preheated oven at 375°F for an hour. Leave to cool before removing the peel. Arrange the banana halves in the greased baking dish. Bake for 15 minutes. Transfer to a bowl. Add orange juice and mash the bananas as you mix. Add brown sugar, spices, and sweet potatoes. Blend using an electric mixer until smooth. Transfer to a heatproof bowl. Bake until warmed. Top with chopped parsley before serving.
Per serving: Kcal 156, Sodium 64 mg, Protein 10 g, Carbs 77 g, Fat 12 g

446. Roasted Tomato Bruschetta

INGREDIENTS (Servings: 6)
2 pints cherry tomatoes, halved1 loaf whole-wheat French bread, thinly sliced
4 cloves garlic, peeled
2 tbsp. chopped basil
¼ tsp. kosher salt
1 tbsp. olive oil
¼ tsp. freshly ground black pepper

DIRECTIONS (Ready in about: 60 min)
Preheat the oven to 375°F. Unfurl the bread slices on a baking sheet, lightly brush the tops with olive oil, and bake until toasted, about 10 minutes. Remove the bread slices from the oven and raise the temperature to 425°F. Line a rimmed baking sheet with foil. Spread the tomatoes and the garlic on the prepared baking sheet. Dredge with salt and pepper and top with olive oil. Toss to coat with olive oil and seasonings. Roast until the tomatoes are crinkly and collapsed, 30 to 35 minutes, turning the baking sheet once halfway through cooking. Set aside to cool. Use your hands to combine the tomatoes and the garlic. Taste the spread and adjust the seasoning, if needed. To serve, spread the tomato mixture onto each crostini and garnish with the basil.
Per serving: Kcal 210, Sodium 441 mg, Protein 9 g, Carbs 6 g, Fat 1 g

447. Root Veggies with Glaze

INGREDIENTS (Servings: 4)
½ cup of onions (cut into 1-inch pieces)
1½ cups water
½ cup of carrots (cut into 1-inch pieces)
½ cup turnips (chopped)
1 tsp. olive oil
½ cup new potatoes (cubed)
2 tsp. sugar

DIRECTIONS (Ready in about: 55 min)
Put water in a pan over medium flame. Add potatoes, turnips, carrots, and onions. Simmer for 15 minutes. Drain cooking liquid and add olive oil and a sprinkle of sugar. Turn heat to medium-high, stir the veggies and cook until golden.
Per serving: Kcal 57, Sodium 24 mg, Protein 1 g, Carbs 21 g, Fat 2 g

448. Shrimp with Spicy Cocktail

INGREDIENTS (Servings: 4)
1½ tbsp. prepared horseradish
1 cup ketchup, preferably low salt
1 tbsp. lemon juice
1-pound frozen peeled, cooked shrimp, thawed
2 tsp. hot sauce, like Sriracha
1 tsp. grated lemon zest

DIRECTIONS (Ready in about: 15 min)
Combine the ketchup, horseradish, lemon zest, lemon juice, and hot sauce in a medium bowl. Taste the sauce and change the ingredients if necessary. Serve with the cold-cooked shrimp.
Per serving: Kcal 175, Sodium 340 mg, Protein 25 g, Carbs 17 g, Fat 1 g

449. Sour Cream Carrot Sticks

INGREDIENTS (Servings: 8)
½ cup sour cream
2 cups carrot sticks
4 stalks celery, cut into 3-inch lengths
1 sweet onion, peeled and minced
2 tbsp. low-fat mayonnaise

DIRECTIONS (Ready in about: 1 h 15 min)
In a bowl, whisk well sour cream and mayonnaise until thoroughly combined. Stir in onion and mix well. Let it sit for an hour in the fridge and serve with carrot and celery sticks on the side.
Per serving: Kcal 60, Sodium 38 mg, Protein 1.6 g, Carbs 7 g, Fat 3 g

450. Spiced Carrot Raisin Bread

INGREDIENTS (Servings: 18)
½ tsp. baking soda
1½ cup whole-wheat pastry flour
1½ tsp. baking powder
1 tbsp. cinnamon
½ tsp. salt
½ tsp. nutmeg
¼ tsp. paprika or cayenne
¼ tsp. cloves
1 tbsp. grated lemon zest
2 eggs
¼ cup ground flaxseed
½ cup brown sugar
½ cup unsweetened applesauce ¼ cup olive oil
¼ cup honey
¾ tsp. almond extract
⅔ cup raisins
2 cups shredded carrots (

DIRECTIONS (Ready in about: 1 h 25 min)
Combine dry ingredients. In a different bowl, combine wet ingredients. Add carrots and raisins. Mix wet to dry ingredients until moist. Pour into a greased bread pan. Bake at 375°F for about an hour.
Per serving: Kcal 136, Sodium 196 mg, Protein 3 g, Carbs 36 g, Fat 4 g

451. Spring Rolls

INGREDIENTS (Servings: 10)
1 medium carrot
½ English cucumber, peeled
6 radishes
1 (10.5 oz.) package spring roll wrappers
2 scallions, chopped
2 tbsp. hoisin sauce, plus more to serve
1 avocado, sliced
12 basil leaves

DIRECTIONS (Ready in about: 40 min)
Position a box grater in a medium bowl. Grate the cucumber, carrot, and radishes into the bowl and add the scallions. Stir together the vegetables, then blot with paper towels to absorb excess moisture. Fill another medium bowl with cold water. Individually soak each spring roll wrapper in the cold water for 15 to 30 seconds until pliable. Spot the wrapper on a flat work surface. Spread ½ tsp. hoisin sauce in a line down the center of the wrapper. Fill with 1 basil leaf, 1 slice of avocado, and 1½ tbsp. - filling. Roll the wrapper over the mixture once, then fold in the sides and roll to close. Repeat for the remaining wrappers. Serve with additional hoisin sauce.
Per serving: Kcal 130, Sodium 232 mg, Protein 4 g, Carbs 2 g, Fat 0.5 g

452. Sunflower, Dill 'n Garlic Dip

INGREDIENTS (Servings: 10)

4 carrots, peeled and sliced into sticks	6 cloves garlic, peeled
½ cup lemon juice	1½ cups raw sunflower seeds
1 tbsp. olive oil	1 tsp. coconut aminos
½ cup fresh dill	⅓ cup tahini
½ cup water	

DIRECTIONS (Ready in about: 2 h 20 min)
Soak sunflower seeds in water overnight or for at least 2 hours. In a blender, add soaked sunflower seeds and peeled garlic. Add remaining ingredients except for water and ¼ cup dill. Puree until smooth and creamy. Add water slowly until desired consistency is reached. Chop the remaining dill and stir in to mix well. Serve with sliced fresh veggies. The mixture can be stored for a week in a lidded jar in the fridge.
Per serving: Kcal 188, Sodium 13 mg, Protein 6 g, Carbs 7.5 g, Fat 16.5 g

453. Sweet and Spicy Snack Mix

INGREDIENTS (Servings: 12)

2 cups Wheat Chex cereal	2 tbsp. honey
2 can of (15 oz. each) garbanzos, rinsed, drained, and patted dry	1 cup raisins
	2 tbsp. reduced-sodium Worcestershire sauce
	1 tsp. garlic powder
1 cup dried pineapple chunks	½ tsp. chili powder

DIRECTIONS (Ready in about: 1 h 20 min)
Turn on the oven to 350°F. Grease a large baking sheet with low-fat oil or cooking spray. Put garbanzo beans in a pan and cook until brown or for about 10 minutes. Put beans on the cooking sheet. Add cooking spray. Bake until crisp or for about twenty minutes. Spray roasting pan with cooking spray. Add cereal, raisins, and pineapple. Add beans and stir. In a large glass bowl add honey, spices, and Worcestershire sauce. Mix. Back an additional 15 minutes. Remove and cool.
Per serving: Kcal 109, Sodium 203 mg, Protein 2 g, Carbs 19 g, Fat 3 g

454. Tasty Turkey Burgers

INGREDIENTS (Servings: 4)

½ tsp. baking soda	2 eggs
1½ cup whole-wheat pastry flour	¼ cup ground flaxseed
	½ cup brown sugar
1½ tsp. baking powder	½ cup unsweetened applesauce
1 tbsp. cinnamon	¼ cup olive oil
½ tsp. salt	
½ tsp. nutmeg	¼ cup honey
¼ tsp. paprika or cayenne	¾ tsp. almond extract
¼ tsp. cloves	⅔ cup raisins
1 tbsp. grated lemon zest	2 cups shredded carrots

DIRECTIONS (Ready in about: 20 min)
Put pepper, garlic salt, oats, barbecue sauce, and basil in a bowl. Mix well. Add turkey and gently mix until combined. Divide mixture into 4 and shape each into a patty with ½-inch thickness. Place patties on a greased grill rack over medium heat. Cover and grill each side for 7 minutes. Slice and grill the buns for 30 seconds. Put the burgers in the buns and add your preferred toppings.
Per serving: Kcal 315, Sodium 482 mg, Protein 21 g, Carbs 1 g, Fat 3 g

455. Tasty Zucchini

INGREDIENTS (Servings: 4)

2 scallions (chopped)	1 tbsp. olive oil
2 tbsp. lemon juice	1 tsp. dill weed
2 tbsp. fresh cilantro	2 cups thinly sliced yellow zucchini
2 cups thinly sliced green zucchini	

DIRECTIONS (Ready in about: 20 min)
Heat up the oil in a pan over medium flame. Add zucchini and cook for 5 minutes while constantly stirring. Stir in scallions, cilantro, and dill. Transfer to a bowl. Add lemon juice before serving.

Per serving: Kcal 264, Sodium 9 mg, Protein 1 g, Carbs 3 g, Fat 1 g

456. Tea Cookies Flavored

INGREDIENTS (Servings: 40)

⅔ cup brown sugar
2 cups all-purpose flour
¼ tsp. baking soda
1 large egg
¼ tsp. salt
½ tsp. ground cardamom
1 cup butter

DIRECTIONS (Ready in about: 1 h 25 min)

Prepare a baking dish or baking sheet. In an enormous mixing bowl, sift together all the dry ingredients, except for the sugar. In a medium mixing bowl, cream together butter and sugar. Add the egg to the butter and sugar mix and whisk it until it is creamy. Add the egg mixture to the dry ingredients and mix it together until it becomes a non-sticky dough. Shape it into a ball, cover with wrap, and let it stand for 30 minutes at room temperature. Heat the oven to 350°F. After 30 minutes, break the dough into small balls and shape it into small cookies, place on a baking sheet and bake for 10 to 15 minutes or until the cookies are golden brown. After taken it out of the oven, let it cool down before serving.

Per serving: Kcal 72, Sodium 52 mg, Protein 1 g, Carbs 8 g, Fat 4.5 g

457. Trail Mix

INGREDIENTS (Servings: 4)

¼ cup unsalted dry-roasted peanuts
¼ cup whole shelled (unpeeled) almonds
¼ cup dried cranberries
2 oz. dried apricots, or other dried fruit
¼ cup chopped pitted dates

DIRECTIONS (Ready in about: 15 min)

Mix all the ingredients together and enjoy.

Per serving: Kcal 156, Sodium 76 mg, Protein 4 g, Carbs 21 g, Fat 7 g

458. Tuna Kabobs

INGREDIENTS (Servings: 4)

2 large sweet red peppers (chopped)
1 medium mango (peeled and cubed)
1 tsp. pepper (coarsely ground)
1-pound tuna steaks (cut into 1-inch cubes)
½ cup frozen corn (thawed)
2 tbsp. fresh parsley (coarsely chopped)
4 green onions (chopped)
1 jalapeno pepper (seeded and chopped)
2 tbsp. lime juice

DIRECTIONS (Ready in about: 1 h 35 min)

Prepare the salsa. Put corn, lime juice, parsley, jalapeno, and onions in a bowl. Mix until combined. Set aside. Season the tuna with pepper. Thread mango, tuna, and red peppers in an alternate fashion on 4 metal skewers. Put on a lightly greased grill rack over medium heat. Cover and grill for 12 minutes. Serve kabobs along with the prepared salsa.

Per serving: Kcal 205, Sodium 273 mg, Protein 29 g, Carbs 8 g, Fat 3 g

DESSERTS

459. Apples with Dip

INGREDIENTS (Servings: 8)

- 4 medium or 8 small apples, cored and sliced
- 2 tbsp. chopped unsalted peanuts
- ½ cup orange juice
- 2 tbsp. brown sugar
- 8 oz. fat-free cream cheese
- 1½ tsp. vanilla

DIRECTIONS (Ready in about: 10 min)

Take the cream cheese out of the refrigerator to soften it, about 5 minutes. Combine the brown sugar, vanilla, and cream cheese in a small bowl. Blend until smooth. Add the chopped peanuts. Place the sliced apples in another bowl. Pour the orange juice over the apples to prevent them from turning brown. Drain the sliced apples and serve with the dip.

Per serving: Kcal 118, Sodium 202 mg, Protein 6 g, Carbs 19 g, Fat 2 g

460. Apricot and Almond Crisp

INGREDIENTS (Servings: 6)

- 1-pound apricots, halved with pits removed
- 1 tsp. anise seeds
- 2 tbsp. honey
- 1 tsp. olive oil
- ½ cup almonds, chopped
- 1 tbsp. oats (certified gluten-free)

DIRECTIONS (Ready in about: 60 min)

Heat the oven to 350°F. Brush olive oil in a 9-inch glass cake pan. Chop the apricots and place them in the pan. Sprinkle with almonds, oat, and anise seed. Season with honey. Cook for 25 minutes until the almond filling is golden brown, and the apricots are bubbling. Serve hot.

Per serving: Kcal 134, Sodium 1 mg, Protein 3 g, Carbs 17 g, Fat 6 g

461. Baked Apples Stuffed

INGREDIENTS (Servings: 4)

- 4 large green apples
- ¼ cup dried apricots
- ¼ flaked coconut
- 2 tbsp. brown sugar
- 2 tsp. orange zest
- ½ cup unsweetened orange juice

DIRECTIONS (Ready in about: 45 min)

Peel only the top of the apple and remove the core. Place the apples on a microwavable plate. In a mixing bowl, mix the apricots with the coconut and orange zest. Spoon the coconut mixture into the center of each apple. In a bowl, mix the sugar with the orange juice and put it over each apple. Cover the bowl and place the apples in the microwave for 6 to 8 minutes. When the apples are soft in the center, they are done. Dish onto serving plates and serve.

Per serving: Kcal 96, Sodium 9 mg, Protein 2 g, Carbs 43.5 g, Fat 9 g

462. Banana Bread

INGREDIENTS (Servings: 4)

- 3 ripe bananas
- 2 tbsp. unsalted butter, melted
- 1 large egg
- ½ cup low-fat buttermilk
- ⅓ cup maple syrup
- 1 tsp. vanilla extract
- ⅛ tsp. of salt
- 1½ tsp. baking soda
- 1¼ cups whole wheat flour
- ½ cup coarsely chopped walnuts (optional)

DIRECTIONS (Ready in about: 1 h 30 min)

Preheat the oven to 325°F. Coat an 8 by 4-inch loaf pan with cooking spray. Add the bananas to a large bowl and use a fork to mash the bananas into a paste-like consistency. Add the butter, egg, buttermilk, and vanilla; stir to combine. Sprinkle the salt and the baking soda over the mixture and stir to combine. Include the flour, and use a wooden spoon to combine it with the other ingredients. Stir in the walnuts, if using. Pour the batter into the prepared loaf pan. Bake until a toothpick inserted into the center of the bread comes out clean, 50 minutes to 1 hour. Slice and serve.

Per serving: Kcal 208, Sodium 74 mg, Protein 7 g, Carbs 36 g, Fat 6 g

463. Berries Marinated

INGREDIENTS (Servings: 2)

- 2 tbsp. brown sugar
- ¼ cup balsamic vinegar
- 1 tsp. vanilla extract
- 2 shortbread biscuits
- ½ cup blueberries
- ½ cup sliced strawberries
- ½ cup raspberries

DIRECTIONS (Ready in about: 45 min)
In a small bowl, combine the brown sugar, vanilla, and balsamic vinegar. In another bowl, add the blueberries, raspberries, and strawberries. Pour the balsamic vinegar mixture over the berries. Allow the fruit to marinate for 10-15 minutes. Drain the marinade. Refrigerate or right away. To serve, divide the berries among two serving plates. Set the shortbread cookie on one side of the bowl.
Per serving: Kcal 176, Sodium 56 mg, Protein 2 g, Carbs 33.5 g, Fat 4 g

464. Black and Blueberry Yogurt

INGREDIENTS (Servings: 2)

½ cup frozen blackberries	1 cup low-fat Greek-style yogurt
½ cup frozen blueberries	2 tsp. honey
½ cup frozen raspberries	4 fresh mint leaves

DIRECTIONS (Ready in about: 15 min)
In a mixing bowl, add berries and pour the yogurt over them. Gently mix them all together and dish them up into 2 pudding dishes. Drizzle honey over the top and add a few mint leaves, then serve.
Per serving: Kcal 160, Sodium 112 mg, Protein 4 g, Carbs 34.5 g, Fat 2 g

465. Broiled Plums

INGREDIENTS (Servings: 4)

8 ripe plums, halved and pitted	2½ tsp. sugar
½ cup all-natural vanilla ice cream	1½ tsp. ground cardamom

DIRECTIONS (Ready in about: 30 min)
Heat up the broiler and line a rimmed baking sheet with foil. Combine the sugar and the cardamom in a small bowl. Add the plum halves to the prepared baking sheet, cut side up, and sprinkle with the sugar mixture. Broil until the edges are slightly charred, 6 to 8 minutes. Let the plums cool slightly. Scoop little balls of ice cream into the center of each cooled plum and serve.
Per serving: Kcal 105, Sodium 13 mg, Protein 2 g, Carbs 2 g, Fat 2 g

466. Chocolate Pudding

INGREDIENTS (Servings: 4)

2 tbsp. unsweetened cocoa powder	½ cup of chocolate chips

DIRECTIONS (Ready in about: 30 min)
In a portable saucepan, mix together the cocoa powder, sugar, salt, and cornstarch. Heat the ingredients on medium heat. While it is heating up, whisk in the milk and stir the mixture regularly. At the point when the mixture begins to bubble, remove it from the stove. Add the vanilla and chocolate chips, giving it a good whisk to ensure the chocolate chips melt. When the pudding is smooth, dish into 4 pudding bowls and serve.
Per serving: Kcal 537, Sodium 91 mg, Protein 6.5 g, Carbs 109 g, Fat 4.5 g

467. Cookies and Cream Shake

INGREDIENTS (Servings: 3)

3 cups vanilla ice cream	1⅓ cups vanilla soy milk (soya milk), chilled
6 chocolate wafer cookies, crushed	

DIRECTIONS (Ready in about: 10 min)
In a blender, combine soy milk and ice cream. Mix until the mixture is light and fluffy. Add the cookies and toss several times to combine. Pour into tall, chilled glasses and serve immediately.
Per serving: Kcal 270, Sodium 224 mg, Protein 9 g, Carbs 52 g, Fat 3 g

468. Creamy Fruit Dessert

INGREDIENTS (Servings: 4)

½ cup plain fat-free yogurt	4 tbsp. shredded coconut, toasted
4 oz. fat-free cream cheese softened	1 can (8 oz.) water-packed pineapple chunks, drained
1 can (15 oz.) mandarin oranges, drained	1 tsp. sugar

DIRECTIONS (Ready in about: 25 min)
Combine the cream cheese, yogurt, sugar, and vanilla in a small bowl. Beat the mixture until it becomes smooth, using an electric mixer at high speed. Get the canned fruit to drain. Combine the peaches, oranges, and pineapple in a separate bowl. Attach a mixture of cream cheese and roll it up. Cover and refrigerate until chilled. Transfer to a serving bowl or individual bowls. Garnish with grated coconut and serve immediately.

Per serving: Kcal 206, Sodium 241 mg, Protein 6 g, Carbs 41 g, Fat 0.5 g

469. Fig Bars

INGREDIENTS (Servings: 36)

16 oz. dried figs
½ cup walnuts
1½ cups all-purpose flour
1¼ cup old fashioned organic rolled oats
1⅓ cup brown sugar
½ cup butter
4 cup orange juice
2 tbsp. hot water
cooking spray
½ tsp. baking soda

DIRECTIONS (Ready in about: 45 min)

Prepare an oven dish by spraying it with non-stick cooking spray. Preheat the oven to 350°F. In a mixing bowl, mix the figs, orange juice, hot water, walnuts, and ⅓ cup sugar. In another mixing bowl, mix 1 cup of sugar and butter until light and fluffy. Add the egg to the sugar mixture and whisk it until it is smooth. In an enormous mixing bowl, sift together the baking soda and flour. Add the egg mixture to the flour and mix it into a soft dough. Take one cup of the dough and put it aside. Press the rest of the dough into the bottom of the prepared baking tray. Pour and spread the fig mixture evenly over the top of the pressed dough in the baking tray. Crumble the remaining dough over the top of the fig mixture. Place the fig mixture into the oven and bake for 25 to 30 minutes until the crust is golden brown. When the fig bars are done, take them out of the oven and let them cool. When the fig bar has cooled down, cut it into equal squares, and serve.

Per serving: Kcal 92, Sodium 18 mg, Protein 2 g, Carbs 18 g, Fat 1.5 g

470. Fruit and Nut Bar

INGREDIENTS (Servings: 24)

½ cup quinoa flour
¼ cup flaxseed flour
¼ cup chopped almonds
¼ cup wheat germ
¼ cup chopped dried apricots
2 tbsp. cornstarch
¼ cup honey
¼ cup chopped dried figs
¼ cup chopped dried pineapple
½ cup oats

DIRECTIONS (Ready in about: 50 min)

Line a baking sheet with parchment paper. Combine all the ingredients, mix well. Press the mixture into the skillet until it is ½ inch thick. Bake at 300°F for 20 minutes. Let it cool completely and cut into 24 pieces.

Per serving: Kcal 70, Sodium 4 mg, Protein 2 g, Carbs 11 g, Fat 2 g

471. Fruit Compote a la Mode

INGREDIENTS (Servings: 4)

½ cup unsweetened orange juice
1¼ cups water
1 12 oz. package mixed dried fruit (dice larger pieces of fruit)
4 cups fat-free vanilla frozen yogurt
¼ tsp. ground nutmeg
1 tsp. ground cinnamon
¼ tsp. ground ginger

DIRECTIONS (Ready in about: 30 min)

Combine the water, orange juice, dried fruits, cinnamon, nutmeg, and ginger in a saucepan over medium heat. Stir gently and simmer for 10 minutes, covered. Remove the lid and continue cooking over very low heat for another 10 minutes or until the fruit is tender. Serve hot or cold in bowls with vanilla frozen yogurt.

Per serving: Kcal 208, Sodium 68 mg, Protein 5 g, Carbs 47 g, Fat 1 g

472. Fruitcake

INGREDIENTS (Servings: 12)

½ cup plain fat-free yogurt
4 oz. fat-free cream cheese softened
1 tsp. sugar
1 can (15 oz.) mandarin oranges, drained
½ tsp. vanilla extract
1 can (14.5 oz.) water-packed sliced peaches, drained
4 tbsp. shredded coconut, toasted
1 can (8 oz.) water-packed pineapple chunks, drained

DIRECTIONS (Ready in about: 2 h 40 min)

Combine the cream cheese, yogurt, sugar, and vanilla in a small bowl. Beat the mixture until it becomes smooth, using an electric mixer at high speed. Get the canned fruit to drain. Combine the peaches, oranges, and pineapple in a separate bowl. Attach a mixture of cream cheese and roll it up. Cover and refrigerate until chilled. Transfer to a serving bowl or individual bowls. Garnish with grated coconut and serve immediately.

Per serving: Kcal 206, Sodium 241 mg, Protein 6 g, Carbs 41 g, Fat 0.5 g

473. Grapes with Sour Cream

INGREDIENTS (Servings: 6)
2 tbsp. powdered sugar
½ cup fat-free sour cream
½ tsp. lemon zest
1½ cups green seedless grapes
½ tsp. lemon juice
1½ cups red seedless grapes
⅛ tsp. vanilla extract
3 tbsp. chopped walnuts

DIRECTIONS (Ready in about: 2 h 30 min)
In a small bowl, mix sour cream, powdered sugar, lemon zest, lemon juice, and vanilla. Beat to mix evenly. Cover and refrigerate for several hours. Divide the grapes evenly among 6 dessert glasses or steamless bowls. Add a tbsp. of sauce to each plate and garnish with ½ tbsp. of chopped walnuts. Serve immediately.
Per serving: Kcal 106, Sodium 32 mg, Protein 2.5 g, Carbs 208 g, Fat 2 g

474. Lemon Cheesecake

INGREDIENTS (Servings: 8)
1 envelope unflavored gelatin
2 tbsp. cold water
2 tbsp. lemon juice
Egg substitute equivalent to 1 egg or 2 egg whites
½ cup of skim milk, heated almost to boiling
Lemon zest
¼ cup sugar
2 cups low-fat cottage cheese
1 tsp. vanilla

DIRECTIONS (Ready in about: 2 h 30 min)
Mix the water, gelatin, and lemon juice in the bowl of the blender. Work on low speed for 1 to 2 minutes to soften the gelatin. Add the hot milk, processing until the gelatin is dissolved. Include egg substitute, sugar, vanilla, and cheese in the bowl of the blender. High-speed process until smooth. Pour into a 9-inch cake pan or round flat plate. Refrigerate for 2 to 3 hours. If desired, add lemon zest just before serving.
Per serving: Kcal 80, Sodium 252 mg, Protein 9 g, Carbs 9 g, Fat 1 g

475. Lemon Pudding Cakes

INGREDIENTS (Servings: 6)
¼ tsp. salt
2 eggs
¾ cup sugar
⅓ cup freshly squeezed lemon juice
1 cup skim milk
3 tbsp. all-purpose flour
1 tbsp. melted butter
1 tbsp. finely grated lemon peel

Preheat the oven to 350°F. Coat 6 cups of custard (6 oz.) with cooking spray. Set the eggs and put the whites in a bowl; put the egg yolks in another bowl. Using a high-speed mixer or electric mixer, beat the whites and salt. Gradually add ¼ cup of sugar; beat until sugar is completely dissolved and stiff peaks form. Beat the egg yolks with a whisk and ½ cup of the sugar until smooth; Add the milk, lemon juice, flour, lemon peel, and butter. Blend until smooth, 2 to 3 minutes. Using a rubber spatula, gently mix the egg whites with the egg yolk mixture until well blended. Put ½ cup of the mixture in each cup of custard. Place custard cups in a 13 x 9-inch skillet; Put in the oven. Fill the pot with boiling water until the water reaches the middle of the sides of the custard cups. Bake for 45 - 50 minutes until the top of the pudding is golden and firm. Remove from the oven and baking sheet and let the custard cups cool on a wire rack.
Per serving: Kcal 174, Sodium 124 mg, Protein 4 g, Carbs 34 g, Fat 4 g

476. Mixed Berry Pie

INGREDIENTS (Servings: 6)
¾ cup of sliced strawberries (about 12 to 15 medium strawberries)
½ cup of fat-free, sugar-free instant vanilla pudding made with fat-free milk
¾ cup raspberries
6 tbsp. light whipped topping
6 single-serve (tart-size) graham cracker pie crusts
6 mint leaves, for garnish

DIRECTIONS (Ready in about: 1h 30 min)
Prepare the pudding as per the package instructions. In a portable bowl, combine the strawberries and raspberries. Divide the pudding among the pies (about 4 tsp. each). Add about 2 tbsp. of the berry mixture to each cake. Top each with 1 tbsp. of whipped topping. Garnish with mint leaves. Serve immediately or refrigerate until ready to serve.
Per serving: Kcal 133, Sodium 169 mg, Protein 2.5 g, Carbs 20 g, Fat 5.5 g

477. Mixed Berry Coffeecake

INGREDIENTS (Servings: 8)
1 tbsp. vinegar
½ cup skim milk
2 tbsp. canola oil
1 egg
¼ cup low-fat granola, slightly crushed
1 cup whole-wheat pastry flour

1 tsp. vanilla
⅓ cup packed brown sugar
½ tsp. baking soda
½ tsp. ground cinnamon
1 cup frozen mixed berries
⅛ tsp. salt

DIRECTIONS (Ready in about: 50 min)
Warm the oven to 350°F. Spray an 8-inch round cake pan with cooking spray and coat with flour. In a large bowl, whisk together milk, vinegar, oil, vanilla, egg, and brown sugar until smooth. Add the flour, baking soda, cinnamon, and salt until moist. Gently fold half of the berries into the dough. Pour into the prepared pan. Sprinkle with remaining berries and garnish with granola. Bake for 30 - 35 minutes or until golden brown and top springs back when touched in the center. Let cool in a pan on the grill for 10 minutes. Serve hot.

Per serving: Kcal 165, Sodium 153 mg, Protein 4 g, Carbs 26 g, Fat 5 g

478. Mixed Fruit Smoothie

INGREDIENTS (Servings: 3)
1¼ cups low-fat plain Greek yogurt
1½ cups frozen strawberries
1 tbsp. agave nectar or honey
¾ cup freshly squeezed orange juice
1 banana, cut into pieces

DIRECTIONS (Ready in about: 10 min)
In a blender or food processor, add the yogurt, strawberries, orange juice, banana, and agave nectar. Puree until the strawberries are broken up, and the smoothie is thoroughly blended, 30 seconds to 1 minute.

Per serving: Kcal 272, Sodium 51 mg, Protein 16.5 g, Carbs 48 g, Fat 3 g

479. Orange Dream Smoothie

INGREDIENTS (Servings: 4)
1 cup light vanilla soy milk, chilled
1½ cups orange juice, chilled
⅓ cup silken or soft tofu
1 tsp. grated orange zest
1 tbsp. dark honey
½ tsp. vanilla extract
4 peeled orange segments
5 ice cubes

DIRECTIONS (Ready in about: 10 min)
Mix the orange juice, soy milk, tofu, honey, orange zest, vanilla, and ice cubes in a blender. Blend until fluffy and bright, for about 30 seconds.

Pour in large, chilled glasses and add an orange slice to each bottle.

Per serving: Kcal 106, Sodium 32 mg, Protein 2 g, Carbs 208 g, Fat 2 g

480. Peach Crumble

INGREDIENTS (Servings: 8)
Juice from 1 lemon (about 3 tbsp.)
8 ripe peaches, peeled, pitted, and sliced
⅓ tsp. ground cinnamon
½ cup whole-wheat flour
¼ tsp. ground nutmeg
¼ cup packed dark brown sugar
¼ cup quick-cooking oats (uncooked)
2 tbsp. trans-free margarine, cut into thin slices

DIRECTIONS (Ready in about: 1h 10 min)
Preheat oven to 375°F. Lightly coats 9-inch cake pan with cooking spray. Place the peach slices in the prepared pie pan. Sprinkle with lemon juice, cinnamon, and nutmeg. In a small bowl, combine the flour and brown sugar. Using your fingers, crumble the margarine into the flour and sugar mixture. Add the raw oat and toss to combine evenly. Sprinkle the flour mixture over the peaches. Cook for 35 minutes until the peaches are soft and the topping is golden. Cut into 8 equal slices and serve hot.

Per serving: Kcal 152, Sodium 41 mg, Protein 3 g, Carbs 26 g, Fat 1.5 g

481. Peach Floats

INGREDIENTS (Servings: 4)
32 oz. club soda or seltzer water
Ground nutmeg, to taste
½ cup reduced-fat whipped topping
4 cups vanilla ice milk
1 can (15 oz.) of peaches, drained, except for ½ cup juice

DIRECTIONS (Ready in about: 60 min)
In a portable bowl, mash the peaches with a fork. Divide the peach puree among 4 glasses (12 oz. each). Add 2 tbsp. of peach juice and 1 cup of ice milk to each glass. Pour 1 cup of soda or seltzer into the glasses. Garnish each drink with 2 tbsp. of whipped topping and a pinch of nutmeg. Serve immediately.

Per serving: Kcal 233, Sodium 189 mg, Protein 7 g, Carbs 49 g, Fat 1 g

482. Pineapple Pops

INGREDIENTS (Servings: 4)

4 cups chopped fresh pineapple
2 tbsp. sugar, plus more as needed
1 cup water
1½ tbsp. freshly squeezed lime juice, plus more as needed

DIRECTIONS (Ready in about: 30 min)

Pulse the pineapple, sugar, water, and lime juice in a food processor until pureed, about 15 one-second pulses. Adjust the flavor with additional lime juice and sugar as needed. Fill 6 ice pop molds according to the manufacturer's directions and freeze at least overnight. Run the pops to clear them under warm water and serve immediately.

Per serving: Kcal 72, Sodium 1 mg, Protein 1 g, Carbs 19 g, Fat 0.5 g

483. Poached Pears

INGREDIENTS (Servings: 4)

¼ cup apple juice
1 cup of orange juice
1 tsp. ground cinnamon
2 tbsp. orange zest
4 whole pears
1 tsp. ground nutmeg
½ cup fresh raspberries

DIRECTIONS (Ready in about: 45 min)

In a small bowl, combine the juice, cinnamon, and nutmeg. Stir to blend uniformly. Peel the pears and put the stems away. Withdraw the core from the bottom of the pear. Put in a shallow pot. Add the mixture of juice to the pot and heat over medium heat. Cook over low heat for about 30 minutes, turning the pears frequently. Do not boil. Transfer the pears to individual plates. Top with raspberries and orange zest and serve immediately.

Per serving: Kcal 140, Sodium 9 mg, Protein 1 g, Carbs 34 g, Fat 0.5 g

484. Poached Pears with Yogurt

INGREDIENTS (Servings: 4)

4 large pears
2 cups water
⅓ cup sugar
1½ cups freshly squeezed orange juice
1 tbsp. vanilla extract
2 tsp. ground ginger
1 tsp. ground cinnamon
¼ cup low-fat plain Greek yogurt
Grated zest of ½ lemon

DIRECTIONS (Ready in about: 60 min)

Peel and core the pears, then trim the bottoms slightly, so they sit flat. Add the water, sugar, orange juice, vanilla, ginger, and cinnamon to a large, heavy pot. Bring to a boil and stir to combine the ingredients. Add the pears to the liquid, cover the pan with a lid, and reduce the heat to low. Simmer the pears until tender, about 30 minutes. Remove from the heat, and let the pears cool in the syrup before removing. In a small bowl, combine the yogurt and the lemon zest. To serve, stand each cooled pear upright and spoon an equal amount of the lemon yogurt over the top.

Per serving: Kcal 222, Sodium 9 mg, Protein 3 g, Carbs 54 g, Fat 1 g

485. Pumpkin Cream Cheese Dip

INGREDIENTS (Servings: 12)

¾ cup of unsweetened and unsalted canned pumpkin
8 oz. low-fat cream cheese (room temperature)
3 tbsp. sugar
¼ tsp. nutmeg
½ tsp. cinnamon
¼ tsp. ground cloves
6 apples, sliced
½ tsp. vanilla

DIRECTIONS (Ready in about: 10 min)

Combine all the cream ingredients in a bowl by hand or with an electric mixer (medium speed). Serve with apple slices for dipping.

Per serving: Kcal 99, Sodium 69 mg, Protein 2 g, Carbs 10 g, Fat 3 g

486. Pumpkin Pie

INGREDIENTS (Servings: 8)

16 oz. can of organic pumpkin
1 cup reduced-fat ginger snaps
½ cup brown sugar
½ cup butter
2 large eggs
12 oz. can non-fat evaporated milk
2 tsp. pumpkin spice
cooking spray

DIRECTIONS (Ready in about: 65 min)

Preheat the oven to 350°F. Crush the ginger snaps into crumbs in a food processor or sealed plastic bag. Place them into a mixing bowl when they have been crumbed. Melt the butter in a saucepan on the stove. Pour butter over the gingersnap crumbs and mix it in until the crumbs have been coated with the butter. Spray a 9" pie pan or bowl with cooking spray to completely coat it. Press the ginger snaps into a pie crust shape into the pie dish.

In a clean mixing bowl, combine the organic pumpkin, brown sugar, 2 large eggs, and the evaporated milk. Pour the pumpkin mixture into the pie crust. Place it in the oven and bake for around 45 minutes. The pie is done when you can stick a skewer or knife in the center, and it comes out clean. Once the pie is done, leave it to cool and then serve.
Per serving: Kcal 121, Sodium 87 mg, Protein 5.5 g, Carbs 21 g, Fat 2 g

487. Rainbow Ice Pops

INGREDIENTS (Servings: 6)
½ cup blueberries
1½ cups diced strawberries, watermelon, and cantaloupe
2 cups 100% apple juice
6 craft sticks
6 paper cups (6-8 oz. each)

DIRECTIONS (Ready in about: 2 h)
Mix the fruits together and distribute them evenly among the paper cups. For each paper cup, pour in ⅓ cup of juice. Place the cups in the freezer on a flat surface. Freeze until partially frozen, about 1 hour. Insert a stick in the center of each cup. Freeze until firm.
Per serving: Kcal 60, Sodium 6 mg, Protein 0.5 g, Carbs 14 g, Fat 0.5 g

488. Red, White, and Blue Parfait

INGREDIENTS (Servings: 4)
1½ cups fresh blueberries
1-pint fresh strawberries, sliced
1 tsp. honey
Creamy filling
¼ cup fat-free cream cheese softened
1 cup low-fat, artificially sweetened vanilla yogurt

DIRECTIONS (Ready in about: 30 min)
Make a creamy filling by placing yogurt, cream cheese, and honey in the bowl and whisking until fluffy. Assemble parfait glasses by putting in each parfait glass ⅓ cup of strawberries. Top each with a creamy filling of 3 tbsp., followed by ¼ cup blueberries. Decorate each one by dividing the rest of the filling. Allow it to cool until ready to serve.
Per serving: Kcal 129, Sodium 144 mg, Protein 6 g, Carbs 24 g, Fat 1 g

489. Seasonal Fruit Palette

INGREDIENTS (Servings: 4)
¼ tsp. sugar
¼ tsp. ground cinnamon
2 cups frozen strawberries,
1-star fruit, sliced
1 kiwi, peeled and sliced
½ cup powdered sugar
1 peach, pitted and sliced
Fresh mint leaves, for garnish
1 plum, pitted and sliced
1 pear, pitted and sliced

DIRECTIONS (Ready in about: 30 min)
In a small tub, combine the sugar and cinnamon. Set aside. Combine the strawberries and powdered sugar in a blender or food processor. Blend until smooth. Pour into cold-rimmed dessert plates. Place the sliced fruit on top. Sprinkle with a mixture of cinnamon and sugar. Garnish with fresh mint and serve immediately.
Per serving: Kcal 152, Sodium 3 mg, Protein 2 g, Carbs 36 g, Fat 1.5 g

490. Soft Chocolate Cake

INGREDIENTS (Servings: 16)
1¾ cups all-purpose flour
2 cups of sugar
¾ cup cocoa powder
2 tsp. baking powder
2 tsp. baking soda
1 tsp. salt
1½ tsp. vanilla extract
1½ cups plain yogurt
1 cup hot coffee
2 eggs

DIRECTIONS (Ready in about: 50 min)
Heat up the oven to 350°F. In a medium bowl, sift together sugar, flour, cocoa powder, baking soda, baking powder, and salt. In a bowl, add the yogurt. Turn the mixer on low speed and alternately add the dry ingredients and the eggs to the bowl. Slowly add coffee and vanilla to the mixture. Until you have a smooth paste, keep stirring. Coat two 8-inch round cake pans with nonstick spray and pours equal amounts of batter into each pan. Bake for about 30 to 35 minutes until a toothpick comes out clean when placed in the center of the cakes.
Per serving: Kcal 157, Sodium 34 mg, Protein 2 g, Carbs 38 g, Fat 1 g

491. Strawberries and Cream

INGREDIENTS (Servings: 16)
½ cup brown sugar
1-quart fresh strawberries, hulled and halved
1½ cups fat-free sour cream
2 tbsp. amaretto liqueur

In a small bowl, combine fat-free sour cream, brown sugar, and liqueur. In a large bowl, add the halved strawberries and sour cream mixture. Stir gently to combine. Cover and refrigerate for about 60 minutes, until chilled. Place the strawberries in 6 colored bowls or cooled sherbet glasses. Garnish with whole strawberries and serve immediately.
Per serving: Kcal 136, Sodium 95 mg, Protein 3 g, Carbs 31 g, Fat 2 g

492. Strawberries Crepes

INGREDIENTS (Servings: 4)

2 tbsp. sifted powdered sugar	8 strawberries, hulled and sliced
4 tbsp. cream cheese softened	2 prepackaged crepes, each about 8 inches in diameter
2 tsp. vanilla extract	
2 tbsp. caramel sauce, warmed	1 tsp. powdered sugar for garnish

DIRECTIONS (Ready in about: 60 min)
Heat up the oven to 325°F. Lightly coat a baking sheet with cooking spray. In a bowl, combine the cream cheese until smooth with an electric mixer. Add the icing sugar and vanilla. Mix well. Spread half of the cream cheese mixture over each pancake, leaving ½ inch around the edge. Garnish with 2 tbsp. of strawberries. Roll up and place the seam down on the prepared baking sheet. Cook until lightly browned, about 10 minutes. Cut the crepes in half. Transfer to four individual serving plates. Sprinkle each with powdered sugar and top with ½ tbsp. of the caramel sauce. Serve immediately.
Per serving: Kcal 143, Sodium 161 mg, Protein 3 g, Carbs 17 g, Fat 7 g

493. Sweet Potato and Squash Pie

INGREDIENTS (Servings: 8)

1 buttercup squash peeled, seeded, cooked	½ tsp. each clove, cinnamon, nutmeg, and vanilla extract
1 sweet potato (about ¼ pound), peeled, cooked	1 tsp. orange zest
½ cup silken tofu	1 frozen pre-made 9-inch pie shell
¼ cup egg whites	
½ cup soy milk	3 tbsp. honey
1 tsp. freshly grated ginger	¼ cup rye flour

DIRECTIONS (Ready in about: 1 h 10 min)
Heat the oven to 300°F. Mashed sweet potatoes and pumpkin in a food processor. Put them in a large bowl. Add the rest of the ingredients and mix until smooth and well combined. Place the pie shell on the baking sheet. Spurt the mixture into the pie shell and bake for 45 to 55 minutes or until internal temperature is 180°F.
Per serving: Kcal 210, Sodium 109 mg, Protein 5 g, Carbs 34 g, Fat 6 g

494. Tofu Chocolate Pudding

INGREDIENTS (Servings: 4)

1½ cups dark chocolate chips	1 (14 oz.) package silken tofu, drained
2 tsp. pure vanilla extract	¼ tsp. salt

DIRECTIONS (Ready in about: 2 h 20 min)
In a microwave-safe dish, melt the chocolate chips in 45-second increments, stirring at each break, until the chocolate is fully melted, 2 to 3 minutes. Puree the chocolate, tofu, salt, and vanilla in a food processor until smooth, just 30 seconds to 1 minute. Transfer the pudding to a container and refrigerate for 2 hours to set.
Per serving: Kcal 160, Sodium 184 mg, Protein 6 g, Carbs 15 g, Fat 11 g

495. Two-Ingredients Ice Cream

INGREDIENTS (Servings: 4)

3 to 4 ripe bananas, cut into 1-inch pieces	2 tbsp. raspberry preserves

DIRECTIONS (Ready in about: 2 h 15 min)
Place the bananas in a shallow container, and leave in the freezer until frozen, about 2 hours minimum. Transfer to a food processor and add the preserves. Puree until smooth and the consistency of ice cream, 1 to 2 minutes. Serve at once.
Per serving: Kcal 228, Sodium 2 mg, Protein 2 g, Carbs 5 g, Fat 1 g

496. Vanilla Poached Peaches

INGREDIENTS (Servings: 4)

½ cup sugar	1 cup of water
Mint leaves or cinnamon, for garnish	1 vanilla bean, split and scraped

DIRECTIONS (Ready in about: 40 min)
Put the water, sugar, vanilla bean, and scrapings in a saucepan. Mix the blend over low heat until the sugar has dissolved. Continue to simmer until the mixture thickens, about 10 minutes. Add the sliced fruit. Cook over low heat for about 5 minutes. Transfer the peaches and sauce to small decorative bowls. Garnish with mint leaves or a pinch of cinnamon. Serve immediately.
Per serving: Kcal 156, Sodium 2 mg, Protein 1 g, Carbs 38 g, Fat 3 g

497. Watermelon-Cranberry

INGREDIENTS (Servings: 6)
1 cup fruit-sweetened cranberry juice (sometimes called cranberry nectar)
1 lime, cut into 6 slices
2½ pounds seedless watermelon, rind removed and diced (about 7 cups)
¼ cup fresh lime juice

DIRECTIONS (Ready in about: 60 min)
Put the melon in a blender or food processor. Blend until smooth. Pass the mash through a fine-mesh strainer placed over a bowl to remove the pulp and clarify the juice. Pour the juice into a large pitcher. Add the cranberry and lime juice and mix well. Refrigerate until very cold. Pour into tall, chilled glasses and garnish each with a lemon wedge.
Per serving: Kcal 84, Sodium 9 mg, Protein 1 g, Carbs 20 g, Fat 2.5 g

498. White Chocolate Pie

INGREDIENTS (Servings: 4)
1 large ripe banana
2 cups graham crackers
4 oz. white Swiss chocolate
¼ cup brown sugar
⅓ cup sour cream
½ cup heavy cream
1 tsp. vanilla extract
½ cup low-fat plain cream cheese

DIRECTIONS (Ready in about: 2 h 15 min)
Melt the chocolate in a small pot set inside a large saucepan of boiling water on the stove. In a mixing bowl, mix the sugar, vanilla, and cream cheese. Whisk the melted chocolate into the cream cheese mix. Whisk in the sour cream. Whisk the heavy cream until it forms peaks and is firm. Fold the heavy cream into the chocolate cream cheese mixture. Crush the graham crackers in a sealed plastic bag and transfer the crushed crackers into a mixing bowl. Heat the ½ cup butter and pour it over the crushed graham crackers, then stir it in until the crackers are moist. In a pie dish, press the graham cracker crust. Scoop the cream cheese filling on top of the graham cracker pie crust. Put it in the refrigerator and let it sit for around 2 hours. When the pie has been set cut, into eight servings and serve.
Per serving: Kcal 237, Sodium 167 mg, Protein 2 g, Carbs 36 g, Fat 10 g

499. Whole-Grain Banana Bread

INGREDIENTS (Servings: 14)
½ cup amaranth flour
½ cup brown rice flour
½ cup tapioca flour
½ cup quinoa flour
½ cup millet flour
1 tsp. baking soda
⅛ tsp. salt
½ tsp. baking powder
¾ cup egg substitute (or use egg whites)
2 cups mashed banana
½ cup raw sugar
2 tbsp. grapeseed oil

DIRECTIONS (Ready in about: 1 h 30 min)
Heat oven to 350°F. Prepares 5 x 9-inch loaf pan by lightly spraying with cooking spray. Sprinkle with a little flour. Set aside. In a large bowl, combine all the dry ingredients except the sugar. In another bowl, combine the egg, oil, sugar, and mashed bananas. Mix well. Mix the dry ingredients into the wet mixture and blend well. Pour into the pan. Bake for 50 to 60 minutes. Check that it is cooked with a toothpick; When the toothpick is removed, there should be no sticky mass. Remove the bread from the oven, let cool, slice, and serve.
Per serving: Kcal 163, Sodium 146 mg, Protein 4 g, Carbs 30 g, Fat 3 g

500. Yogurt Berry Burst Popsicles

INGREDIENTS (Servings: 8)
1 cup blueberries
1 cup blackberries
1 cup raspberries
1 cup low-fat Greek-style yogurt
1¼ cup nonfat milk

DIRECTIONS (Ready in about: 45 min)
You can use either hand mix or blend all the ingredients in a blender. Pour the mixture equally into ice cream-pop molds. The size of each popsicle will depend on the size of the molds that are being used. For the standard ice-cream stick molds, it will make around 8 popsicles. Place the pops in the freezer. They take approximately 30 to 40 minutes to freeze.
Per serving: Kcal 50, Sodium 48 mg, Protein 2.5 g, Carbs 9 g, Fat 0.5 g

21-DAY MEAL PLAN

Caloric Intake on the DASH Diet:

The DASH diet is centered on the inclusion of a wide variety of food groups. These food groups and their recommended serving sizes are determined by personal characteristics: age, gender, and activity level. In order to determine your own personal DASH diet guidelines, you have to estimate your calorie needs.

Please consult the charts below, which you can then use with the **Daily Serving Recommendations Table** (p.128) to determine your approximate serving recommendations for each food group.

ESTIMATED DAILY CALORIE FOR WOMEN

AGE (YEARS)	SEDENTARY		MODERATELY ACTIVE		ACTIVE	
	DAILY NEEDS	TO LOSE WEIGHT	DAILY NEEDS	TO LOSE WEIGHT	DAILY NEEDS	TO LOSE WEIGHT
19-30	2.000	1.500-1.750	2.100	1.600-1.850	2.400	1.900-2.150
31-50	1.800	1.300-1.550	2.000	1.500-1.750	2.200	1.700-1.950
51+	1.600	1.100-1.350	1.800	1.300-1.550	2.100	1.600-1.850

ESTIMATED DAILY CALORIE FOR MEN

AGE (YEARS)	SEDENTARY		MODERATELY ACTIVE		ACTIVE	
	DAILY NEEDS	TO LOSE WEIGHT	DAILY NEEDS	TO LOSE WEIGHT	DAILY NEEDS	TO LOSE WEIGHT
19-30	2.400	1.900-2.150	2.700	2.200-2.450	3.000	2.500-2.750
31-50	2.200	1.700-1.950	2.500	2.000-2.250	2.900	2.400-2.650
51+	2.000	1.500-1.750	2.300	1.800-2.050	2.600	2.100-2.350

Once you have determined your daily caloric needs, consult the sample 21-day Meal Plan above (p.129). This meal plan is intended to be a general idea on how you can organize your DASH menu, follow it according to your needs and tastes. As you'll go deeper into the DASH diet, you'll be able to build your menus using charts and recipes contained in this book.

DAILY SERVINGS RECOMMENDATIONS TABLE

Food group	Servings per day 1600 Kcal	Servings per day 2000 Kcal	Servings per day 2600 Kcal	Serving sizes	Examples and notes	Benefits of each food group to the DASH eating plan
Grains	6	6-8	10-11	1 slice bread 1 oz. Dry cereal ½ cup cooked rice, pasta, or cereal	Whole wheat bread and rolls, whole wheat pasta, English muffin, pita bread, bagel, cereals, oatmeal, brown rice	Major sources of energy and fiber
Vegetables	3-4	4-5	5-6	1 cup raw leafy vegetable ½ cup cut-up raw or cooked vegetable ½ cup fruit juice	Broccoli, carrots, green beans, green peas, kale, potatoes, spinach, squash, sweet potatoes, tomatoes	Rich sources of potassium, magnesium, and fiber
Fruits	4	4-5	5-6	1 medium fruit ¼ cup dried fruit ½ cup fresh, frozen, or canned fruit ½ cup fruit juice	Apples, apricots, bananas, dates, grapes, oranges, grapefruit, mangoes, melons, peaches, pineapples, raisins, strawberries, tangerines	Rich sources of potassium, magnesium, and fiber
Low-fat (or fat-free) milk and milk products	2-3	2-3	3	1 cup milk or yogurt 1½ oz. cheese	Low-fat (2%) milk or buttermilk, low-fat cheese, low-fat yogurt	Major sources of calcium and protein
Lean meats, poultry, and fish	3-6	6 or fewer	6	1 oz. Cooked meats, poultry, or fish 1 egg	Only lean meats, trim away visible fat; broil or roast, remove the skin from poultry	Rich sources of protein and magnesium
Nuts, seeds, and legumes	3 per week	4-6	1	⅓ cup or 1½ oz. Nuts 2 tbsp. peanut butter 2 tbsp. or ½ oz. Seeds ½ cup cooked legumes (dry beans and peas)	Almonds, hazelnuts mixed nuts, peanuts, sunflower seeds, peanut butter, lentils	Rich sources of energy, magnesium, protein, and fiber
Fats and oils	2	2-3	3	1 tsp. soft margarine 1 tsp. vegetable oil 1 tbsp. mayonnaise 2 tbsp. salad dressing	Vegetable oil, low-fat mayonnaise, light salad dressing	DASH diet had 27% of calorie as fat, including fat in or added to foods
Sweets and added sugars	0	5 or fewer per week	1-2	1 tbsp. sugar 1 tbsp. jelly or jam ½ cup sorbet, gelatin 1 cup lemonade	Fruit-flavored gelatin, hard candy, jelly, maple syrup, sorbet and ices, sugar	Sweets should be low in fat

N.B.
- Whole grains are recommended for most grain servings as a good source of fibers and nutrients.
- Serving sizes vary between ½ cup and 1½ cups, depending on the cereal type. Check the product's nutrition facts label.
- Fat content changes serving amount for fats and oils. (1 tbsp. of regular salad dressing = 1 serving; 1 tbsp. of low-fat dressing ½ serving; 1 tbsp. of fat-free dressing = 0 servings).
- Eggs are high in cholesterol, so limit gg yolk intake to no more than 4 every week.

	Day 1	**Day 2**	**Day 3**
Breakfast (1 serving)	Egg Muffins (p.19)	Greek-Style Breakfast Scramble (p.20)	Swiss Chard Omelet (p.24)
Snack A.M.	1 medium banana	1 cup grapes	1 cup raspberries
Lunch (1 serving)	Mac Stuffed Sweet Potatoes (p.57) Apple, Blue Cheese Salad (p.39)	Bean Salad with Vinaigrette (p.40) Brown Rice Pilaf (p.94)	Cod with Grapefruit (p.84) 1 medium banana
Snack P.M.	1 cup raspberries	1 clementine	1 medium pear, sliced topped with cinnamon
Dinner (1 serving)	Cod and White Sauce (p.104) Celery Root and Apple Puree (p.95)	Shrimp with Lemon Sauce (p.106) Arugula, Peach Almond Salad (p.40)	Classic Chicken Salad (p.42) Eggplant Croquettes (p.55)
Tot Nutritions	Kcal: 1119 Sodium: 991 mg Protein: 52.5 g Carbs: 87 g Fat: 36.5 g	Kcal: 1087 Sodium: 835 mg Protein: 59 g Carbs: 93 g Fat: 35 g	Kcal: 1186 Sodium: 490 mg Protein: 47 g Carbs: 62 g Fat: 37 g
To make it 1500 Kcal add:	¼ cup unsalted dry-roasted almonds to breakfast 1 medium apple to lunch	¼ cup unsalted dry-roasted almonds to A.M. snack ½ cup cooked brown rice to dinner	2 slices of whole-wheat toast and 3 tbsp. almond butter at breakfast
To make it 2000 Kcal add:	¼ cup unsalted dry-roasted almonds to breakfast ¼ cup walnuts to A.M. snack 1 apple and a 1 oz. slice of whole-wheat baguette to lunch 5 dried figs to P.M. snack	1 slice whole-wheat toast with 1 ½ tbsp. almond butter and 1 medium apple to breakfast 1 Fig Bar (p.120) to A.M. snack 20 unsalted dry-roasted almonds to P.M. snack ½ cup cooked brown rice to dinner	2 slices whole-wheat toast and 3 tbsp. almond butter at breakfast ¼ cup unsalted dry-roasted almonds to A.M. snack 1 apple and a 1 oz. slice of whole-wheat baguette to lunch 1 Fruit and Nut Bar (p.120) to P.M. snack

Day 4	Day 5	Day 6	Day 7
Warm Quinoa with Berries (p.25)	Toast with Almond Butter (p.24)	Fruity Yogurt Parfait (p.20)	Peach and Berry Pancake (p.23)
Fig Bars (p.120)	1 medium plum 4 walnuts halves	10 unsalted dry-roasted almonds 1 medium pear	1 medium apple, sliced sprinkled with cinnamon
Turkey and Artichokes Mix (p.73)	Bean Hummus (p.52)	Cod and Corn Chowder (p.27)	Lentil Curry (p.56)
1 medium banana	2 clementines	Fruit and Nut Bar (p.120)	4 Tea Cookies Flavored (p.117)
Greek Lemon-Drop Soup (p.29)	Curried Pork Tenderloin (p.77)	Allspice Shrimps (p.83) Tasty Zucchini (p.116)	Rice and Beans Salad (p.47)
Kcal: 1211 Sodium: 612 mg Protein: 58 g Carbs: 84.5 g Fat: 49 g	Kcal: 1282 Sodium: 521 mg Protein: 53 g Carbs: 107 g Fat: 39 g	Kcal: 1313 Sodium: 774 mg Protein: 78 g Carbs: 99 g Fat: 35 g	Kcal: 1197 Sodium: 497 mg Protein: 55 g Carbs: 144 g Fat: 45 g
¼ cup unsalted dry-roasted almonds to breakfast 1 medium pear to lunch	¼ cup unsalted dry-roasted almonds to breakfast 1 medium apple for lunch	¼ cup unsalted dry-roasted almonds to A.M. snack ½ cup cooked brown rice to dinner	2 slices of whole-wheat toast and 3 tbsp. almond butter at breakfast 3 dried figs to A.M. snack
1 slice whole-wheat toast with 1 ½ tbsp. almond butter to breakfast ¼ cup walnuts to A.M. snack 1 pear to lunch ¼ cup unsalted dry-roasted almonds to P.M. snack	¼ cup unsalted dry-roasted almonds and 1 cup raspberries to breakfast ¼ cup walnuts to A.M. snack 1 apple and a 1 oz. slice of whole-wheat baguette to lunch 5 dried figs to P.M. snack	¼ cup unsalted dry-roasted almonds to breakfast ¼ cup walnuts to A.M. snack 1 apple and a 1 oz. slice of whole-wheat baguette to lunch 5 dried figs to P.M. snack	1 slice whole-wheat toast with 1 ½ tbsp. almond butter to breakfast ¼ cup walnuts to A.M. snack 1 pear to lunch ¼ cup unsalted dry-roasted almonds to P.M. snack

	Day 8	**Day 9**	**Day 10**
Breakfast (1 serving)	Blueberry Breakfast Quinoa (p.17)	Banana Almond Yogurt (p.16)	Healthy Low-Fat Granola (p.21)
Snack A.M.	1 medium pear	3 dried figs	10 unsalted dry-roasted almonds
Lunch (1 serving)	Chicken and Veggies (p.67)	Lentil Soup (p.32)	Curried Lentil Soup (p.28)
Snack P.M.	5 dried figs	1 5 oz. container nonfat plain Greek yogurt 1½ tbsp. chopped walnuts	1 medium apple
Dinner (1 serving)	Rosemary Salmon (p.89) Salad Greens with Pears (p.48)	Quinoa Bowl (p.59) Quinoa Burger (p.59)	Chicken and Dill Green Beans (p.66) Red, White and Blue Parfait (p.124)
Tot Nutritions	Kcal: 1174 Sodium: 486 mg Protein: 57 g Carbs: 91 g Fat: 30 g	Kcal: 1185 Sodium: 243 mg Protein: 50 g Carbs: 133 g Fat: 22 g	Kcal: 1263 Sodium: 809 mg Protein: 74 g Carbs: 108 g Fat: 43 g
To make it 1500 Kcal add:	¼ cup unsalted dry-roasted almonds to A.M. snack ½ cup cooked brown rice to dinner	¼ cup unsalted dry-roasted almonds for breakfast 1 small apple for lunch.	¼ cup unsalted dry-roasted almonds for breakfast 1 small apple to lunch
To make it 2000 Kcal add:	1 slice whole-wheat toast with 1½ tbsp. almond butter and 1 small apple to breakfast 1 oz. pita chips (p.113) and 3 tbsp. hummus to lunch 20 unsalted dry-roasted almonds to P.M. snack ½ cup cooked brown rice to dinner	¼ cup unsalted dry-roasted almonds to breakfast 1 apple and a 1 oz. slice whole-wheat baguette to lunch 1 pear to P.M. snack 2 cups mixed greens and ½ an avocado to dinner	¼ cup unsalted dry-roasted almonds to breakfast ¼ cup walnuts to A.M. snack 1 apple and a 1 oz. slice of whole-wheat baguette to lunch 5 dried figs to P.M. snack

Day 11	Day 12	Day 13	Day 14
Toast with Almond Butter (p.24)	Fruity Green Smoothie (p.19)	Healthy Start Yogurt Bowls (p.21)	Egg Burrito (p.18)
1 medium pear	1 medium banana	4 whole-grain crackers 1 medium apple	1 pear, sliced, topped with cinnamon
Chicken and Mustard Sauce (p.67)	Bow Ties and Beans (p.52)	Whole-Wheat Spaghetti Ragu (p.107)	Hummus with Carrot (p.112)
5 dried figs	¼ cup walnut halves 1 cup of low-fat yogurt	1 5 oz. container nonfat plain Greek yogurt	¾ cup raspberries ½ oz. chopped walnuts
Tuna Stuffed Zucchini Boats (p.92)	Salmon with Basil and Garlic (p.90) Potato Salad (p.47)	Vegan Chili (p.61) Low-Fat Creamed Spinach (p.98)	Grilled Salmon with Lemon (p.105) Chopped Greek Salad (p.42)
Kcal: 1227 Sodium: 609 mg Protein: 62 g Carbs: 90 g Fat: 55 g	Kcal: 1218 Sodium: 664 mg Protein: 48 g Carbs: 93.7 g Fat: 18.5 g	Kcal: 1230 Sodium: 968 mg Protein: 71 g Carbs: 149 g Fat: 23 g	Kcal: 1277 Sodium: 997 mg Protein: 65 g Carbs: 86 g Fat: 54 g
2 slices of whole-wheat toast and 3 tbsp. almond butter at breakfast	¼ cup walnut halves to breakfast 1 medium pear to lunch	2 slices of whole-wheat toast and 3 tbsp. almond butter at breakfast 3 dried figs to A.M. snack	¼ cup unsalted dry-roasted almonds to breakfast 1 small apple for lunch
2 slices whole-wheat toast and 3 tbsp. almond butter at breakfast ¼ cup unsalted dry-roasted almonds to A.M. snack 1 apple and a 1 oz. slice of whole-wheat baguette to lunch 1 serving Apple Lettuce Salad (p.39) to dinner	¼ cup walnut halves to breakfast 1 medium pear and a 1 oz. slice of whole-wheat baguette to lunch 2 cups mixed greens and ½ avocado to dinner	2 slices whole-wheat toast with 3 tbsp. almond butter at breakfast ¼ cup unsalted dry-roasted almonds to A.M. snack 1 medium banana to lunch 5 dried figs to P.M. snack	1 slice whole-wheat toast with 1½ tbsp. almond butter to breakfast ¼ cup walnuts to A.M. snack 1 pear to lunch ¼ cup unsalted dry-roasted almonds to P.M. snack

	Day 15	**Day 16**	**Day 17**
Breakfast (1 serving)	Apple-Cinnamon Baked Oatmeal (p.15)	Healthy French Toast (p.20)	Chocolate Smoothie (p.18)
Snack A.M.	6 oz. light yogurt, nonfat 1½ oz. almonds	1 medium banana	6 oz. strawberries
Lunch (1 serving)	Minty Chickpea Tabbouleh (p.57)	Cream of Wild Rice Hot Dish (p.28) Apple-Fennel Slaw (p.39)	Sweet Potato Balls (p.60)
Snack P.M.	1 medium pear, sliced topped with cinnamon	Fruit and Nut Bar (p.122)	5 dried figs
Dinner (1 serving)	Pasta with Grilled Chicken (p.73)	Basil Halibut (p.83)	Turkey Soup (p.36)
Tot Nutritions	Kcal: 1333 Sodium: 528 mg Protein: 41 g Carbs: 134 g Fat: 22 g	Kcal: 1212 Sodium: 802 mg Protein: 64 g Carbs: 90.5 g Fat: 60 g	Kcal: 1289 Sodium: 307 mg Protein: 87 g Carbs: 79 g Fat: 46 g
To make it 1500 Kcal add:	¼ cup unsalted dry-roasted almonds to breakfast 1 medium banana to lunch	¼ cup walnut halves to breakfast 1 medium pear to lunch	¼ cup unsalted dry-roasted almonds for breakfast 1 medium apple for lunch
To make it 2000 Kcal add:	¼ cup unsalted dry-roasted almonds to breakfast ¼ cup walnuts to A.M. snack 1 banana and a 1 oz. slice of whole-wheat baguette to lunch	¼ cup walnut halves to breakfast 1 medium pear to lunch 2 cups mixed greens and ½ avocado to dinner	¼ cup unsalted dry-roasted almonds and 1 cup raspberries to breakfast ¼ cup walnuts to A.M. snack 1 apple and a 1 oz. slice of whole-wheat baguette to lunch

Day 18	Day 19	Day 20	Day 21
Mediterranean Scramble (p.22)	Veggie Omelet (p.24)	Apples and Cinnamon Oatmeal (p.15)	Whole Grain Pancakes (p.25)
1 medium pear	6 oz. blueberries 10 almonds	4 oz. light yogurt, nonfat 1 oz. almonds	1 medium apple
Dash Diet Apple Sauce French Toast – 2 servings (p.104)	Chicken Fajitas (p.104)	Rice and Beans Salad (p.47)	Mint Meatballs Spinach Sauté (p.79)
1 cup grapes	Fig Bars (p.122)	½ cup walnut halves	1 cup raspberries
Tofu Stroganoff (p.61) Spinach Berry Salad (p.49)	Black Bean Cakes (p.108) English Cucumber Salad (p.44)	Tomato Halibut Fillets (p.91)	Baby Beet and Orange Salad (p.40) Grilled Salmon with Lemon (p.105)
Kcal: 1256 Sodium: 1019 mg Protein: 58 g Carbs: 98 g Fat: 61 g	Kcal: 1195 Sodium: 1041 mg Protein: 62.5 g Carbs: 87 g Fat: 49 g	Kcal: 1150 Sodium: 455 mg Protein: 90 g Carbs: 109 g Fat: 32 g	Kcal: 1139 Sodium: 697 mg Protein: 49 g Carbs: 105 g Fat: 35 g
¼ cup unsalted dry-roasted almonds to breakfast 1 small apple to lunch	¼ cup unsalted dry-roasted almonds to breakfast 1 medium banana to lunch.	¼ cup unsalted dry-roasted almonds to breakfast 1 small apple to lunch	¼ cup unsalted dry-roasted almonds to A.M. snack ½ cup cooked brown rice to dinner
¼ cup unsalted dry-roasted almonds and 1 cup raspberries to breakfast ¼ cup walnuts to A.M. snack 1 small apple to lunch 5 dried figs to P.M. snack	¼ cup unsalted dry-roasted almonds to breakfast 1 banana and a 1 oz. slice whole-wheat baguette to lunch 1 pear to P.M. snack	¼ cup unsalted dry-roasted almonds to breakfast ¼ cup walnuts to A.M. snack 1 medium apple to lunch 5 dried figs to P.M. snack	1 slice whole-wheat toast with 1½ tbsp. almond butter and 1 small apple to breakfast 20 unsalted dry-roasted almonds to P.M. snack ½ cup cooked brown rice to dinner

INGREDIENTS INDEX

A

almond butter; 2; 6; 7; 19; 43; 45; 47; 49

almond flour; 14; 15; 18; 19; 44; 404

almond milk; 2; 4; 8; 10; 12; 14; 15; 30; 33; 41; 45; 53; 74; 398

almonds; 7; 13; 19; 31; 53; 101; 104; 106; 145; 437; 457; 460; 470

apple; 1; 2; 3; 4; 14; 31; 33; 34; 62; 91; 101; 102; 103; 104; 105; 110; 113; 195; 214; 238; 267; 279; 280; 301; 314; 325; 334; 347; 349; 351; 359; 388; 402; 406; 409; 423; 459; 461; 472; 483; 485; 487

apple cider; 14; 34; 105; 195; 267; 301; 314; 325; 334; 347; 402

apple juice; 31; 91; 103; 105; 280; 351; 406; 472; 483; 487

applesauce; 53; 279; 400; 409; 472

apricots; 44; 355; 402; 420; 457; 460; 461; 470

artichoke; 38; 184; 190; 212; 252

arugula; 106; 113; 413

asparagus; 60; 120; 121; 220; 221; 350; 360; 371; 378; 379; 414

avocado; 15; 72; 146; 156; 170; 200; 209; 213; 217; 220; 225; 226; 234; 239; 245; 247; 249; 257; 265; 272; 283; 292; 297; 300; 301; 307; 311; 316; 322; 326; 327; 331; 332; 347; 361; 396; 397; 428; 432; 451

avocado oil; 15; 72; 156; 170; 200; 209; 217; 220; 225; 226; 234; 239; 245; 247; 249; 265; 272; 292; 297; 301; 307; 311; 316; 322; 326; 327; 331; 332; 347; 396

B

baking powder; 14; 36; 46; 53; 211; 425; 443; 450; 472; 490; 499

baking soda; 14; 44; 46; 450; 456; 462; 469; 472; 477; 490; 499

balsamic vinegar; 96; 106; 109; 110; 111; 113; 114; 122; 136; 138; 141; 142; 147; 206; 216; 217; 232; 233; 234; 247; 259; 272; 279; 283; 284; 378; 395; 463

banana; 6; 7; 8; 9; 14; 17; 25; 43; 49; 53; 101; 367; 445; 462; 478; 495; 498; 499

barley; 10; 75; 82; 259

basil; 11; 70; 72; 80; 93; 99; 118; 126; 130; 148; 149; 150; 151; 186; 214; 221; 225; 239; 251; 252; 255; 291; 332; 343; 374; 381; 394; 395; 396; 411; 412; 446; 451; 454

bay leaf; 56; 62; 64; 65; 73; 75; 83; 89; 124; 365

beans; 5; 20; 54; 61; 64; 69; 70; 75; 79; 80; 89; 93; 95; 96; 97; 109; 129; 133; 134; 139; 154; 167; 180; 194; 202; 203; 209; 224; 229; 251; 275; 352; 381; 386; 390; 416; 427; 453

beef; 55; 56; 73; 142; 249; 259; 260; 261; 262; 263; 264; 269; 273; 287; 405; 412

beets; 108; 110; 135; 391

bell pepper; 51; 115; 117; 126; 229; 261; 397

blackberries; 12; 52; 91; 464; 500

blue cheese; 102; 111; 142; 280

blueberries; 9; 12; 13; 14; 15; 16; 22; 23; 26; 44; 91; 141; 363; 463; 464; 487; 488; 500

bread; 30; 39; 48; 49; 133; 273; 302; 374; 375; 400; 444; 446; 450; 462; 499

broccoli; 50; 51; 79; 114; 156; 232; 254; 255; 262; 293; 354; 419

brown rice; 62; 134; 228; 250; 355; 361; 420; 437; 499

brown sugar; 3; 28; 46; 53; 103; 137; 216; 349; 440; 443; 445; 450; 456; 459; 461; 463; 469; 477; 480; 486; 491; 498

Brussels sprouts; 192; 356; 380

bulgur; 144; 180; 202

butter; 7; 15; 17; 41; 42; 49; 60; 70; 238; 357; 359; 366; 370; 376; 393; 405; 440; 456; 462; 469; 475; 486; 498

C

cabbage; 64; 89; 93; 107; 108; 229; 257; 353; 388; 429

canola oil; 59; 61; 82; 88; 92; 100; 103; 163; 165; 228; 230; 259; 264; 280; 282; 286; 287; 330; 355; 363; 383; 390; 413; 420; 422; 477

cardamom; 37; 172; 429; 445; 456; 465

carrot; 56; 57; 61; 63; 64; 65; 66; 70; 73; 75; 77; 80; 82; 88; 89; 90; 94; 95; 98; 100; 104; 105; 107; 113; 119; 124; 126; 132; 146; 157; 175; 204; 205; 207; 219; 243; 257; 259; 262; 272; 273; 276; 351; 369; 370; 389; 393; 412; 435; 447; 449; 450; 451; 452

cashews; 107; 173; 398

cauliflower; 85; 158; 159; 201; 227; 286; 358; 366; 374; 438

cayenne pepper; 94; 97; 102; 189

celery; 59; 60; 61; 62; 63; 64; 65; 66; 71; 73; 75; 77; 80; 88; 89; 90; 93; 96; 98; 104; 108; 109; 110; 112; 113; 116; 124; 125; 126; 132; 145; 202; 204; 215; 222; 228; 229; 256; 258; 259; 262; 294; 305; 359; 365; 398; 412; 417; 421; 435; 449

cheddar cheese; 20; 39; 50; 231; 270; 421; 423

cheese; 20; 23; 38; 39; 48; 50; 97; 110; 142; 154; 162; 186; 207; 218; 231; 252; 254; 262; 270; 293; 314; 316; 345; 372; 374; 375; 413; 421; 423; 426; 439; 444; 459; 468; 474; 485; 488; 492; 498

chicken; 59; 62; 64; 68; 70; 72; 74; 75; 77; 78; 80; 81; 83; 84; 89; 90; 92; 97; 98; 100; 114; 116; 124; 125; 130; 145; 182; 202; 207; 209; 212; 213; 214; 215; 218; 219; 220; 221; 222; 223; 224; 225; 226; 227; 228; 229; 230; 231; 232; 233; 234; 235; 236; 237; 238; 239; 241; 243; 244; 245; 247; 248; 250; 251; 256; 279; 281; 394; 395; 396; 397; 402; 421; 437

chickpea; 58; 67; 95; 151; 153; 160; 161; 164; 180; 188; 204; 324; 434; 435; 436

chili flakes; 162; 178; 179; 184; 185; 203; 204; 336

chili powder; 11; 55; 78; 97; 164; 181; 205; 207; 211; 222; 223; 246; 264; 265; 266; 326; 339; 407; 453

chilli flakes; 54; 78; 100; 178; 306; 311; 336; 345

chilli peppers; 87; 162; 386

chives; 123; 135; 217; 222; 234; 236; 249; 269; 296; 357; 394; 408

cider vinegar; 126; 129; 131; 135; 141

cilantro; 20; 54; 58; 67; 74; 95; 97; 99; 107; 117; 127; 128; 131; 138; 139; 146; 155; 160; 164; 185; 193; 203; 214; 223; 226; 230; 231; 235; 236; 239; 246; 255; 258; 265; 266; 272; 287; 298; 303; 307; 314; 334; 352; 361; 384; 386; 407; 408; 415; 416; 428; 429; 431; 432; 455

cinnamon; 1; 2; 3; 4; 6; 7; 8; 13; 14; 18; 22; 28; 30; 31; 33; 36; 46; 49; 53; 86; 91; 114; 140; 147; 172; 232; 238; 258; 346; 351; 362; 388; 400; 409; 424; 437; 440; 445; 450; 471; 477; 480; 483; 484; 485; 489; 493; 496

cloves; 20; 38; 50; 51; 61; 63; 65; 77; 81; 88; 89; 90; 92; 93; 96; 115; 124; 125; 135; 140; 221; 228; 229; 259; 261; 262; 273; 286; 287; 302; 350; 352; 358; 361; 362; 372; 377; 388; 392; 397; 402; 405; 409; 410; 411; 412; 424; 434; 436; 446; 450; 452; 485; 493

coconut; 14; 15; 18; 19; 31; 33; 40; 45; 46; 52; 63; 74; 101; 161; 162; 166; 167; 168; 173; 174; 178; 183; 189; 193; 196; 198; 203; 204; 205; 208; 226; 239; 240; 252; 255; 287; 303; 309; 336; 394; 398; 399; 404; 430; 452; 461; 468

coconut milk; 18; 40; 52; 63; 173; 174; 208; 226; 287; 430

coconut oil; 14; 18; 33; 46; 161; 162; 166; 167; 168; 174; 178; 183; 189; 193; 196; 198; 203; 204; 205; 309; 336

cod fillet; 290; 293; 296; 297; 298; 299; 300; 316; 322; 399

cooking spray; 2; 3; 29; 35; 36; 46; 97; 125; 186; 221; 231; 241; 243; 248; 251; 254; 258; 273; 279; 374; 382; 426; 427; 441; 443; 453; 462; 469; 475; 477; 480; 486; 492; 499

coriander; 151; 156; 164; 170; 174; 237; 258; 270; 303; 304; 313; 314; 347; 388

corn kernels; 59; 66; 117; 164; 330

cornmeal; 362; 376; 424; 425

cornstarch; 244; 267; 351; 466; 470

cranberries; 44; 363; 383; 457

cucumber; 58; 67; 111; 115; 119; 122; 123; 304; 377; 386; 410; 436; 439; 451

cumin; 66; 85; 95; 96; 97; 118; 123; 151; 174; 189; 228; 229; 235; 237; 258; 264; 266; 270; 315; 386; 388; 397; 431

curry powder; 62; 63; 141; 161; 171; 173; 174; 179; 267; 287; 305; 366

D

Dijon mustard; 103; 112; 122; 124; 132; 141; 277; 402; 405; 417

dill; 85; 90; 120; 121; 132; 133; 135; 144; 165; 181; 224; 306; 308; 315; 316; 337; 384; 399; 403; 426; 427; 442; 452; 455

E

egg; 11; 15; 19; 20; 21; 22; 29; 30; 36; 38; 39; 42; 44; 45; 46; 47; 50; 51; 68; 146; 156; 157; 159; 181; 186; 193; 198; 263; 273; 274; 400; 404; 425; 428; 443; 450; 456; 462; 469; 472; 474; 475; 477; 490; 493; 499

eggplant; 76; 166; 170; 171; 207; 373

F

fennel; 56; 61; 84; 105; 124; 136; 228; 233; 268; 272; 281; 282; 289; 300; 344

feta cheese; 29; 38; 76; 154; 186; 439

firm tofu; 169; 178; 179; 196; 197; 198; 200

flax seeds; 2; 18; 19; 26; 31; 156; 159; 175; 204; 450; 470; 472

flour; 18; 36; 42; 44; 46; 56; 57; 59; 60; 66; 98; 162; 183; 185; 197; 198; 208; 256; 261; 263; 264; 270; 331; 336; 364; 405; 425; 443; 450; 462; 469; 470; 472; 475; 477; 480; 490; 493; 499

G

garam masala; 160; 161; 173; 199

garbanzo; 95; 109; 129; 134; 167; 180; 427; 453

garlic; 11; 20; 38; 47; 50; 51; 58; 61; 62; 63; 64; 65; 66; 67; 69; 70; 72; 77; 80; 81; 82; 87; 88; 89; 90; 92; 93; 95; 96; 97; 107; 109; 115; 123; 124; 125; 130; 135; 151; 153; 154; 158; 160; 163; 169; 176; 177; 181; 183; 186; 191; 195; 210; 213; 214; 216; 221;222; 225; 228; 229; 233; 234; 237; 239; 240; 242; 243; 247; 248; 249; 250; 251; 252; 255; 259; 260; 261; 262; 268; 269; 270; 273; 274; 275; 286; 287; 291; 297; 298; 302; 308; 312; 315; 317; 318; 319; 332; 333; 334; 336; 350; 352; 353; 354; 358; 361; 364; 365; 368; 372; 377; 381; 386; 388; 390; 392; 394; 396; 397; 399; 403; 405; 406; 411; 412; 416; 418; 419; 427; 431; 435; 436; 438; 441; 446; 452; 453; 454

ginger; 22; 27; 46; 74; 95; 160; 170; 174; 235; 253; 287; 339; 362; 365; 377; 393; 395; 402; 409; 424; 433; 471; 484; 486; 493

grapes; 145; 367; 401; 473

Greek yogurt; 6; 26; 372; 397; 410; 478; 484

H

halibut; 291; 314; 341; 343

hazelnuts; 10; 350; 443

honey; 8; 10; 13; 48; 52; 113; 137; 141; 170; 172; 192; 208; 241; 370; 403; 433; 437; 450; 453; 460; 464; 470; 478; 479; 488; 493

I

ice cream; 465; 467; 495; 500

Italian seasoning; 157; 159; 163; 178; 182; 188; 190; 196; 227; 243; 262; 290; 441

J

jalapeno; 66; 128; 139; 160; 229; 230; 415; 428; 431; 458

K

kale; 34; 51; 61; 64; 89; 259; 271; 353; 418

kiwi; 26; 367; 489

kosher salt; 73; 117; 135; 238; 284; 287

L

lamb; 265; 266; 268; 271; 272; 286

leaf lettuce; 125; 137

leek; 55; 168; 245; 358; 438

lemon; 33; 36; 60; 67; 68; 71; 74; 84; 95; 102; 103; 104; 118; 120; 123; 126; 127; 138; 139; 144; 145; 153; 167; 170; 180; 187; 213; 214; 226; 244; 245; 250; 285; 289; 300; 302; 307; 310; 318; 319; 321; 322; 324; 329; 330; 335; 340; 346; 348; 350; 353; 354; 356; 367; 374; 378; 380; 384; 385; 386; 389; 397; 398; 401; 403; 407; 408; 409; 410; 415; 418; 419; 422; 426; 433; 434; 435; 436; 437; 444; 448; 450; 452; 455; 472; 473; 474; 475; 480; 484; 497

lentils; 63; 77; 78; 95; 124; 126; 127; 174; 175; 208; 392

lettuce; 103; 105; 109; 116; 121; 123; 125; 130; 131; 137; 233; 261; 264; 270; 393

lime; 58; 67; 71; 74; 117; 131; 139; 142; 148; 244; 246; 261; 320; 321; 335; 361; 367; 386; 428; 429; 431; 432; 458; 482; 497

M

mango; 37; 127; 128; 139; 230; 307; 430; 458

maple syrup; 14; 16; 31; 33; 111; 362; 424; 462

margarine; 55; 78; 290; 304; 313; 315; 318; 319; 328; 333; 339; 341; 348; 349; 358; 368; 389; 437; 438; 480

mayonnaise; 116; 132; 145; 219; 422; 449

milk; 1; 4; 5; 9; 13; 16; 17; 18; 22; 28; 36; 37; 42; 46; 57; 59; 60; 61; 62; 84; 85; 86; 90; 99; 150; 273; 286; 331; 359; 362; 368; 372; 376; 400; 424; 425; 466; 467; 474; 475; 476; 477; 481; 486

mint; 34; 71; 101; 123; 139; 180; 210; 274; 287; 320; 322; 351; 373; 410; 464; 476; 489; 496

mushrooms; 29; 56; 65; 82; 98; 130; 167; 181; 182; 183; 186; 200; 205; 218; 240; 243; 251; 259; 263; 268; 376; 378; 405; 406; 426

mustard; 35; 39; 51; 103; 112; 122; 124; 225; 228; 234; 277; 304; 323; 324; 333; 365; 380; 390; 396; 405; 417

N

nutmeg; 1; 3; 30; 33; 36; 46; 57; 85; 86; 88; 111; 140; 150; 166; 209; 228; 275; 320; 362; 388; 424; 433; 437; 445; 450; 471; 480; 481; 483; 485; 493

O

oatmeal; 1; 3; 4; 6; 8; 12; 16; 22; 33; 165; 189; 193; 211

oats; 1; 2; 3; 4; 6; 7; 8; 12; 16; 22; 28; 31; 33; 41; 43; 454; 460; 469; 470; 472; 480

onion; 20; 21; 29; 35; 38; 50; 51; 54; 56; 58; 59; 60; 61; 62; 63; 64; 65; 66; 67; 69; 70; 71; 73; 75; 76; 77; 78; 80; 81; 82; 84; 86; 87; 88; 89; 90; 92; 93; 94; 95; 96; 97; 98; 107; 108; 109; 111; 114; 115; 117; 118; 119; 120; 124; 125; 127; 128; 129; 130; 131; 132; 133; 134; 139; 141; 142; 148; 151; 155; 160; 163; 173; 175; 179; 183; 184; 185; 186; 188; 189; 198; 199; 200; 204; 206; 208; 211; 214; 215; 217; 219; 220; 223; 224; 226; 227; 228; 229; 230; 231; 232; 233; 234; 236; 237; 240; 243; 246; 249; 250; 251; 256; 258; 259; 260; 261; 262; 263; 265; 266; 267; 268; 269; 270; 271; 272; 274; 275; 276; 279; 281; 292; 293; 298; 299; 302; 306; 307; 310; 311; 325; 336; 337; 340; 342; 365; 369; 381; 383; 386; 388; 392; 393; 394; 397; 402; 404; 406; 411; 412; 415; 422; 426; 427; 428; 437; 439; 442; 447; 449; 458

orange; 25; 101; 108; 125; 129; 140; 149; 238; 247; 248; 277; 281; 282; 296; 355; 379; 383; 420; 433; 445; 459; 461; 468; 469; 471; 472; 478; 479; 483; 484; 493

orange juice; 25; 129; 247; 248; 296; 355; 379; 420; 433; 445; 459; 461; 469; 471; 478; 479; 483; 484

oregano; 21; 38; 89; 97; 115; 118; 126; 130; 221; 229; 234; 235; 243; 249; 270; 302; 342; 381; 382; 397; 411; 412

P

paprika; 21; 69; 71; 96; 179; 193; 198; 199; 201; 208; 220; 228; 235; 239; 241; 242; 246; 263; 265; 269; 270; 276; 280; 295; 326; 327; 340; 374; 398; 405; 429; 434; 436; 450

Parmesan; 64; 76; 99; 136; 203; 221; 251; 262; 364; 374; 407; 412

parsley; 21; 56; 57; 58; 59; 61; 65; 66; 67; 69; 73; 75; 76; 87; 100; 109; 118; 123; 124; 126; 133; 134; 135; 144; 151; 164; 167; 180; 191; 206; 244; 250; 256; 259; 282; 311; 328; 337; 350; 365; 368; 383; 385; 389; 404; 412; 427; 434; 436; 445; 458

peaches; 42; 106; 138; 217; 468; 480; 481; 496

peanut butter; 17; 41; 146; 287; 393

peanuts; 95; 146; 287; 457; 459

pear; 136; 147; 149; 483; 484; 489; 504

peas; 90; 92; 107; 146; 180; 184; 250; 286; 299; 334; 365; 393; 415; 437

pecans; 12; 13; 52; 141; 440

pine nuts; 210; 363; 407

pineapple; 101; 114; 119; 230; 232; 344; 367; 453; 468; 470; 472; 482

plum; 163; 297; 302; 465; 489

pork; 35; 258; 267; 269; 270; 274; 275; 276; 277; 278; 279; 280; 281; 282; 283; 284; 285; 370; 404; 405; 406; 407

potatoes; 54; 55; 56; 60; 79; 82; 83; 84; 91; 92; 94; 132; 155; 162; 166; 172; 176; 177; 185; 193; 205; 243; 246; 259; 357; 358; 368; 369; 382; 387; 409; 438; 442; 445; 447; 493

pumpkin; 31; 46; 85; 86; 87; 88; 192; 349; 443; 485; 486; 493

Q

quinoa; 13; 52; 156; 187; 188; 203; 205; 334; 393; 470; 499

R

raisins; 3; 7; 28; 105; 144; 147; 362; 424; 437; 440; 443; 450; 453

raspberries; 41; 42; 91; 463; 464; 476; 483; 495; 500

red wine; 56; 110; 115; 124; 125; 132; 133; 149; 259; 260; 388

rice; 61; 62; 68; 98; 119; 120; 134; 178; 181; 184; 187; 194; 215; 228; 242; 250; 287; 355; 361; 393; 420; 430; 437

rice vinegar; 134; 178; 287; 393

romaine; 116; 123; 130; 142; 146

rosemary; 64; 77; 122; 147; 155; 200; 216; 228; 240; 246; 247; 248; 256; 259; 279; 284; 285; 294; 323; 329; 382

S

saffron; 95; 184; 340; 355; 420

sage; 35; 88; 168; 259; 370

salad greens; 103; 110; 119; 121; 136; 145

salmon; 90; 138; 289; 303; 304; 306; 307; 310; 311; 329; 330; 331; 332; 333; 403

scallions; 116; 121; 135; 144; 235; 253; 268; 297; 330; 361; 363; 384; 423; 432; 451; 455

sesame oil; 107; 157; 181; 197; 208; 258; 298; 312; 334; 339; 340; 343; 393; 402; 434

sesame seeds; 44; 119; 197; 258; 301; 393; 435

shallot; 56; 72; 134; 149; 205; 225; 239; 247; 255; 335; 356; 384; 395; 396; 399

shrimp; 121; 139; 148; 288; 304; 321; 336; 340; 348; 386; 408; 431; 448

sirloin; 55; 73; 142; 261; 262; 273; 287

sour cream; 112; 263; 401; 417; 428; 449; 473; 491; 498

soy milk; 150; 161; 172; 175; 176; 177; 182; 183; 198; 199; 364; 467; 479; 493

soy sauce; 107; 192; 197; 287; 360; 377; 393; 414

spinach; 20; 21; 25; 29; 39; 79; 80; 81; 88; 107; 111; 113; 114; 138; 141; 161; 169; 186; 190; 197; 207; 212; 219; 232; 239; 274; 283; 341; 371; 372

squash; 85; 87; 88; 95; 113; 137; 168; 273; 302; 349; 383; 493

stevia; 7; 15; 18; 30; 41; 44; 398; 443

strawberries; 12; 23; 25; 26; 48; 91; 141; 142; 367; 463; 476; 478; 487; 488; 489; 491; 492

sugar; 28; 35; 36; 42; 57; 87; 105; 114; 119; 129; 131; 216; 232; 244; 360; 367; 369; 389; 400; 401; 402; 414; 430; 440; 447; 456; 461; 465; 466; 468; 469; 472; 473; 474; 475; 476; 480; 482; 484; 485; 489; 490; 492; 496; 498; 499

sunflower seeds; 8; 11; 19; 31; 34; 44; 45; 47; 76; 137; 452

T

tarragon; 135; 145; 215; 250

thyme; 56; 59; 62; 65; 73; 82; 83; 98; 112; 124; 183; 214; 259; 260; 310; 376; 383; 391; 392; 406; 417; 444

tilapia; 302; 312; 325; 326; 342

tomatoes; 11; 20; 39; 58; 62; 67; 69; 70; 72; 73; 75; 76; 77; 78; 79; 80; 87; 89; 93; 95; 96; 97; 99; 111; 115; 117; 120; 121; 123; 130; 135; 144; 149; 154; 160; 161; 162; 163; 164; 171; 177; 180; 187; 191; 196; 199; 202; 203; 204; 205; 207; 208; 209; 212; 214; 218; 220; 221; 223; 224; 227; 229; 231; 233; 234; 245; 250; 257; 259; 260; 262; 264; 265; 266; 270; 271; 272; 274; 275; 283; 292; 297; 301; 302; 307; 313; 336; 337; 342; 343; 353; 365; 375; 381; 386; 392; 411; 412; 415; 418; 436; 439; 446

tortillas; 219; 229; 231; 257; 261; 270; 397; 429

trout; 308; 328; 347

tuna; 133; 324; 327; 335; 344; 345; 346; 458

turkey; 35; 75; 77; 89; 93; 94; 200; 217; 240; 242; 246; 249; 252; 253; 254; 255; 256; 257; 454

turmeric; 85; 95; 158; 193; 201; 264; 346; 355; 420

V

vanilla; 3; 7; 9; 12; 14; 15; 28; 30; 31; 42; 53; 140; 401; 459; 462; 463; 465; 466; 467; 468; 471; 472; 473; 474; 476; 477; 479; 481; 484; 485; 488; 490; 492; 493; 494; 496; 498

vinegar; 76; 106; 110; 113; 114; 115; 119; 120; 122; 124; 125; 126; 129; 131; 132; 133; 135; 136; 149; 216; 232; 259; 260; 277; 279; 285; 287; 388; 390; 463; 477

W

walnuts; 3; 4; 13; 14; 44; 53; 110; 111; 136; 142; 189; 383; 401; 423; 443; 462; 469; 472; 473; 504

watermelon; 140; 148; 301; 307; 487; 497

white wine; 98; 120; 141; 215; 219; 256; 278; 280; 281

whole grain; 30; 48; 80; 120; 133; 150; 162; 177; 182; 183; 185; 218; 219; 221; 436

Y

yogurt; 6; 15; 17; 26; 37; 42; 104; 113; 116; 135; 140; 145; 165; 171; 179; 372; 399; 403; 410; 440; 464; 468; 471; 478; 484; 488; 490; 500

Z

zucchini; 36; 50; 71; 80; 89; 100; 118; 130; 154; 155; 165; 167; 191; 194; 206; 209; 210; 211; 243; 273; 302; 345; 371; 384; 411; 455

CONVERSION MEASURES

WEIGHTS

IMPERIAL	METRIC
½ oz.	15 g
¾ oz.	20 g
1 oz.	30 g
2 oz.	60 g
3 oz.	85 g

16 oz. = 1 pound = 435 g

1 oz. = 28.35 g | 1 g = 0.035 oz.

OVEN TEMPS

F	C
250	120
275	140
300	150
325	170
350	180
375	190
400	200

COMMON INGREDIENTS

CUP	IMPERIAL	METRIC
Flour	5 oz.	140 g
Almonds	4 oz.	110 g
Uncooked Rice	6½ oz.	190 g
Brown Sugar	6½ oz.	185 g
Raisins	7 oz.	200 g
Grated Cheese	4 oz.	115 g

LIQUIDS

CUPS	METRIC	PINT	QUART
¼	60 ml	-	-
½	125 ml	-	-
-	150 ml	¼	-
-	200 ml	-	-
1	250 ml	½	-
-	300 ml	-	-
-	400 ml	-	-
2	500 ml	-	-
-	950 ml	-	1

SPOONS

LIQUID		DRY	
¼ tsp.	1.25 ml	¼ tsp.	1.1 g
½ tsp.	2.5 ml	½ tsp.	2.3 g
1 tsp.	5 ml	1 tsp.	4.7 g
¼ tbsp.	3.75 ml	¼ tbsp.	3.5 g
½ tbsp.	7.5 ml	½ tbsp.	7.1 g
1 tbsp.	15 ml	1 tbsp.	14.3 g

Printed in Great Britain
by Amazon